MONUMENTS
AND MEN OF
ANCIENT ROME

TEMPLE OF VENUS GENETRIX,
FORUM OF JULIUS CÆSAR

MONUMENTS AND MEN OF ANCIENT ROME

BY

GRANT SHOWERMAN, Ph. D.

Professor of Classics in the University of Wisconsin
Author of "Eternal Rome," "Rome and the Romans," etc.

D. APPLETON·CENTURY COMPANY
INCORPORATED
NEW YORK   1935   LONDON

TO
JOHN PARKER SHOWERMAN
(JANUARY 9, 1908 — MARCH 25, 1933)
COMPANION THROUGH MANY LANDS
AND OVER MANY WATERS

PREFACE

TO BECOME better acquainted with the Romans of today, we have only to accept the aid of them "that do business in great waters," or, in Horace's phrase, "to make trial of the airy void on wings not given to mortal man." To be on intimate terms with the ancient Romans, we must somehow transport ourselves not only five thousand miles over sea and land, but also two thousand years back over the paths of time.

To accomplish these far transfers, we have many conveyances. We have our histories. We have always as a lamp unto our feet and a light unto our path the word of the Latin classics. We have the monuments, the inscriptions, the sculpture and paintings, and the more minute and more commonplace antiquities of the Roman people. Among the sculptures, we have the almost living reality of their unexcelled portraiture in marble. Our Roman forefathers in culture have left behind them a cloud of witnesses.

Yet we need not only knowledge, but the personalization and humanization of our knowledge. In this need we are not left without resource: for human witness, the ages have preserved us the memories of great and representative men of Rome. We may know almost as intimately as if they were living still the idealist Cicero, the magnanimous but cynical Cæsar, the grave and calculating but human Augustus, the sensitive-souled Virgil, the observant and philosophic Horace, not to mention all who are to move across our pages.

To become acquainted with these men and other personalities like them who towered above their times, to know their appearance and bearing, their accomplishments, their careers, their mode of life, the attitudes of mind and soul that underlie their judgments and actions, is to meet so many interpreters. The acts in which we see them engage, the real and living qualities we feel in them bring us into immediate relation with their times and with the unknown millions who made up the vast Empire of Rome. Whatever the faults and failures of the great Roman figures we know best, whatever the distance between their ideals and their achievements, they nobly represent the virtues of intelligence, courage, loyalty to purpose, and endurance. Their lives and the words they have left us are a protest as well as a witness against the base and the ignoble. Their very vices as men of action, if we are to charge against them the selfishness and arrogance, the violence, the hardness and cruelty, of an age of great movement and dangerous living, were not unmingled with the engaging qualities of men in the mass.

Our study shall be of Monuments and Men, but of monuments as a background to men. Inasmuch as in old and established countries like Italy landscape may be a witness more unchanged than crumbling temple or aqueduct, we shall interpret the monuments liberally as including also scene. We shall see the Roman in the physical setting of city and country, against the background of his native landscape and the monuments of street and marketplace among which he went about the business and pleasure of his eventful life. Nothing so brings to life the ancient authors, nothing so makes dynamic the content of their works, as viewing with them the scenes their eyes once looked upon and their feet once trod, and reading the words they wrote on the spot on which or concerning which they wrote them.

GRANT SHOWERMAN

ACKNOWLEDGMENTS

M Y CORDIAL thanks are due to Dr. Marion E. Blake, Dr. Dorothy M. Schullian, Dr. May A. Allen, Miss Lulu Grosh, George W. Hodgkins and Henry C. Atyes for generous permission to use their original photographs; to Secretary Riccardo Davico of the American Academy in Rome for aid in assembling commercial photographs; and to Secretary Roscoe Guernsey of the New York office for procuring the photograph of the Academy. Dr. Mary Johnston and Dr. G. A. Harrer have placed me under deep obligation by reading and criticizing my manuscript for substance and doctrine but without responsibility for errors which inevitably remain undetected in a work involving the use of much detail. My daughter, Anita Showerman Noer, has competently and devotedly come to my aid in time of great need by assisting with the proof, annotations, and index. All these have been my associates, and most of them my students, during periods of my connection with the School of Classical Studies, American Academy in Rome, as Fellow, Visiting Student, Annual Professor, and Director of the Summer Session, periods extending from 1898 to 1932.

I express my thanks also to Longmans, Green and Company and to the Yale University Press for permission to quote from my *Horace and His Influence* and *Eternal Rome,* respectively, and to the Macmillan Company for allowing me the use of certain of my photographs which have already appeared in *Rome and the Romans.* I have appreciated further the kindness of Franz Cumont, of the French Academy, and the always helpful members of Casa Girardet, in their attentive keeping me informed from Rome of the rapidly moving archæological events of the past three years.

Finally, it is a pleasure to avail myself of the translations in the Loeb Classical Library, especially those of Professors John

C. Rolfe and Walter Miller. With such renderings at hand, one would hardly be justified in translating anew.

Most of the obligations here expressed in general will be found in detail in the annotations and list of illustrations.

G. S.

CONTENTS

ILLUSTRATIONS

xiii

ILLUSTRATIONS XV

ILLUSTRATIONS

xix

MAPS AND PLANS

MONUMENTS
AND MEN OF
ANCIENT ROME

The RUINS of ANCIENT ITALY

0   50   100   150
Scale of Miles

. I .

THE RUINS OF ANCIENT ITALY

SALVE, *Saturnia tellus!*—"Hail, Saturnian land!" In saluting thus the land of his birth, Virgil reverenced Italy as the ancient of days, with beginnings in the hoary times of Saturn, the "Sower" god, forerunner of Jupiter. The Italy about the poet, Roman Italy, was only the latest phase of the Italian land.

Italy abounds in relics not only of ancient Rome but of remote pre-Roman times. First of all, a great deal of material has been found in the graves of the Neolithic or Late Stone Age, when earth burial was universal throughout the peninsula. The Neolithic inhabitants came probably from the south, arriving in Italy by way of Sicily and also by way of Spain, the Rhône valley, and the Alps. Their civilization was invaded from the north, considerably earlier than 1000 B.C., by the Bronze Age people, who brought the practice of cremation with them over the Alps from central and eastern Europe. Succeeding the Bronze Age immigrants came the Iron Age people from the same source and with the same custom, in waves of invasion which lasted until about 900 B.C.

The Bronze and Iron Age races spread over large parts of northern and central Italy, conquering and blending with the earlier Stone Age race. Their civilization, like that of the Stone Age, is known from the contents of many graves and even more abundantly. The space occupied in the soil of Italy and in its museums by these graves, and by the pottery, implements, and ornaments discovered in them, is always a surprise to those who have thought only of Roman Italy. Near Giubiasco, at the head of Lago Maggiore, for example, where the valley of the Ticino leads down from the St. Gotthard Pass and the Lake of Lucerne, and the valley of the Moesa leads down from the Splügen Pass and the Lake Constance region, over twelve hundred graves have been examined, all in the space of a mile or two, and these are only

1

part of a chain of cemeteries. At Terni, in central Italy seventy-one miles north of Rome, a score of cremation burials and over two hundred earth-burial graves have been studied, and other graves in hundreds were destroyed when the steel works were built. On the slopes of the Alban Mount, on the Esquiline in Rome, and even at the head of the Roman Forum, similar graves have been found by scores.

The next migration into Italy occurred about 800 B.C., when successive waves of adventurers from somewhere in the East, probably Lydia, began taking possession of the west coast of central Italy, spread over the inland region now known as Tuscany, conquering its Iron Age inhabitants, and became the Etruscan people, who for a time were the dominant force in the affairs of Rome. The hills of Tuscany contain many of their cemeteries, whose tombs are large chambers in the rock, decorated with brilliant paintings and once furnished with vases, armor, and beautiful jewelry. The Etruscan museums at Florence, Tarquinia, and Rome are filled with splendid exhibits of the contents of these tombs, which are known in greatest number at Cerveteri, Tarquinia, Veii, and Chiusi.

Beginning not long before 700 B.C. came the Greek migrations to Sicily and south Italy which made those regions Magna Græcia, the seat of a culture second in both extent and quality only to that of Greece in the East. Unlike the Etruscans and the earlier peoples of the Iron, Bronze, and Late Stone ages, the Greeks in the south left behind them not only tombs richly furnished with the objects of beauty and usefulness they loved, but monumental temples and theaters above ground whose remains are still to be seen. The temples of ancient Pæstum, on the west coast fifty-eight miles south of Naples, of Metapontum, twenty-seven miles west of Tarentum, and of Syracuse, Selinunte, Agrigento, and Segesta in Sicily, and the theaters at Taormina and Syracuse, are among Europe's most famous monuments, and the museums at Palermo, Syracuse, and Naples are great treasure-houses of Greek sculpture, vases, coins, and gems.

The founding of Rome, dated by the ancients at 753 B.C., took place at a time when the Etruscans were establishing themselves

ETRUSCAN TOMBS AT CERVETERI

TEMPLE AT METAPONTO

ARCH AT AOSTA

TEMPLE-TOMB OF THE GORDIANS

not far to the north, and about the time when the Greeks began their westward colonizing movement. After three centuries and a half of growth by alliance, assimilation, and conquest to the south and east of the Tiber, the siege of Veii and its fall in 396 B.C. brought all Etruria, once the mistress of Rome, under Roman authority. The defeat of the Latin allies in 338 B.C., the end of the Samnite wars in 290, and the fall of Tarentum in 272 were the successive stages by which the Roman State came into control of Italy as far north as a line running west to east at about the latitude of Ariminum, the modern Rimini, a line roughly coincident with the southern limit of the Ligurian mountains not far north of Pisa, Florence, and the Arno, and with the river Rubicon, a small stream near Ariminum.

The portion of Italy between the Rubicon and Arno valleys and the Alps continued legally outside of Roman territory, although long practically under Roman administration, until in 89 B.C. it was formally erected into the province of Cisalpine Gaul, with the two chief divisions of Transpadana, beyond the Po, and Cispadana, to its south. Its southern boundary was the Rubicon. In 42 B.C. the province became a regular part of the Roman State, and all Italy south of the Alps was for the first time a unit. Octavian, the future Augustus Cæsar, who caused the change, also divided Italy into eleven regions, or administrative districts: Venetia, Gallia, Liguria, Umbria, Etruria, Latium, Picenum, Samnium, Apulia, Lucania, Bruttium.

The complete Romanization of Italy was thus a process of some seven hundred years. During the process every part of the peninsula, except perhaps the nearest lands in Latium originally allied to Rome, had been first the subject of Rome and then her ally, and finally had become an integral part of the Roman State. As conquered or annexed territory, it had been under the civil and military authority of a prætor or consul, if before Sulla's time, or, if after, usually under a proprætor or proconsul, whose word in all matters was law for the year of his tenure, but whose general policy, after the claim to tribute, conscription, and obedience to the Roman law was satisfied, was to leave to the subject people in local and private affairs whatever liberties were possible. As an

integral part of the State, it had enjoyed the protection of Rome
and in many cases the rights of Roman citizenship in full or part.
After the enrichment of the State by the Macedonian conquest
in 168 B.C., it had been exempt from the tribute or land tax levied
on all other Roman territory. With the revolt of the Italian allies
in 90-89 B.C., the number of communities possessing full citizenship and also those receiving the Latin rights, which meant all
citizen rights except the vote, had greatly increased.

The granting of the full franchise in Italy increased in liberality until in Caracalla's time it became universal for free men.
The exemption from the land tax continued until the time of
Diocletian, A.D. 284-306, when the mother land of Rome was
levelled for the first time in upward of five centuries to the provincial rank, and was compelled with the rest of the Roman world
to render unto Cæsar. Italy thus reached the provincial status as
a unit from Alps to sea at a time when other Roman lands had
existed for centuries in provincial form.

Italy today is the richest of all the provinces in reminders of
the life of the ancient Roman State. In the North, Aosta with
its giant arch and amphitheater walls, Turin with its Palatine
Gate and palace ruins, Verona with its wonderfully preserved
amphitheater and gate and its Piazza delle Erbe perpetuating the
outlines of the ancient forum, Aquileia with its choice and well-
ordered museum collections—are places full of interest for traveller and scholar. Padua has its amphitheater fragments, Ravenna
its Tomb of Theodoric, Rimini its great bridge, Ancona its Arch
of Trajan.

The larger cities on the grand route through inland Italy, from
Milan through Piacenza, Parma, Reggio, Modena, and Bologna,
though always living and thriving centers in a fertile plain and
therefore prone to consume their ancient selves, are by no means
devoid of the archæological interest. In central Italy, Fiesole has
its theater, Perugia its walls and gate, Narni its monster arches
picturesquely bridging the river, Sulmona its Ovid relics, Tivoli
its villas, Tusculum its theater and massive concrete ruins, Anzio
its dock and villa remains, Terracina its temple, forum, and cliff
dressed down to give passage to the Appian Way.

In the Naples region, Capua and Pozzuoli have their amphitheaters, Cumae its acropolis and grot, Baia its terraces and reservoir, Capri its imperial palace remains, Benevento its wonderful Arch of Trajan. In south Italy, the Greek ruins are not unmingled with Roman.

And these are only the monuments most visible and best known. There is probably not a town of size or importance which does not possess its municipal or national collection of antiquities and art, or its monuments in the open, like the arch at Fano or the bridge at Rimini. When the civil government lacks a museum or collection, it is quite likely that the Church or some noble family will be found supplying it. The humblest villages are rarely without some ancient monuments, and roadside and field, especially in the neighborhood of Rome, are dotted with the ruins of tomb, villa, aqueduct, bridge, and shrine. Not to mention the Appian Way and its tomb remains, on the less known Via Praenestina not far out from Rome one comes upon a temple-tomb which probably belonged to the villa of the Gordians, emperors A.D. 238-244. A few miles farther on is the Ponte di Nona, one of the grandest of surviving Roman bridges, 238 feet long and 52 feet high. Such is the abundance of ancient monuments in what was once the home land of the Roman Empire.

And yet, with all these, we have made no mention of the wonders of Rome itself, or of Herculaneum now coming again to light, or of the never-ending riches of Pompeii, or of Ostia, which during the past forty years has constantly grown in importance.

Nor are even these all that Italy has preserved from the days of the Roman Empire. The monuments we have mentioned are only the actual and tangible remains of Roman Italy. Not to comment here on the many features of the Italian land that remain the same—its landscape of mountain, plain, and river, its plant and animal life—the language that strikes upon the traveller's ear or meets his eye is the language of ancient Rome, sometimes even unchanged, and always little disguised to one who knows the Latin tongue. Parma and Roma of the Cæsars are still Parma and Roma; Placentia and Mutina have become Piacenza and Modena; Forum Julii has become Friuli and Forlì. Forum Sempronii is Fossombrone, Augusta is Aosta. The *ilex* is the *elce,* the *cupressus* is the *cipresso,* the *bos* is the *bove,* the *exercitus* is the *esercito.* Julius Cæsar is Giulio Cesare, Hannibal and Scipio still exist as Annibale and Scipione, Cicero and Vergilius and Horatius as Cicerone, Virgilio, and Orazio.

ROMAN RUINS IN FAR LANDS

THE mere mention of Rome, Pompeii, and Ostia is enough to demonstrate the importance of Italy in the study of Roman remains. The Italian peninsula, however, was only a part of the empire ruled by Rome, and for several centuries preceding the fall of the Western Empire was in reality a province like other provinces. If we set apart Pompeii, Ostia, and the capital, the remains of Roman times in Italy are hardly of greater importance than those to be seen in France or Spain or Africa. To realize the number and significance of the monuments outside Italy, let us pass in brief review the various parts of the Empire.

The Roman Empire in the first decades of the second century of the Christian era, when Trajan completed the drawing of its outlines practically as they were to remain for the five centuries up to the Arab conquest of the East, was not greatly different in extent from the Roman territory of Augustan times. From the Atlantic where its billows fixed the western boundary of Spain, to where the Arabian and Syrian desert and the Euphrates fixed with less precision the eastern border, the Empire measured some 3,000 miles. From the Solway and the Tyne, beyond which Roman prudence declined to contest the ground with the wild races of Scotland, to the long line of outposts that fringed the Great Desert in Africa, it measured about 2,000 miles. It comprised two million and a half square miles of land, more than two-thirds the size of the United States, and supported about one hundred million inhabitants, the half of those who live today in the same area. The Mediterranean was a giant Roman lake.

A traveller would best appreciate these far spaces of ancient Roman dominion by following from country to country the line that divided Roman civilization from barbarous lands. To remind himself that the ruins of Rome are of concern to him, he might

7

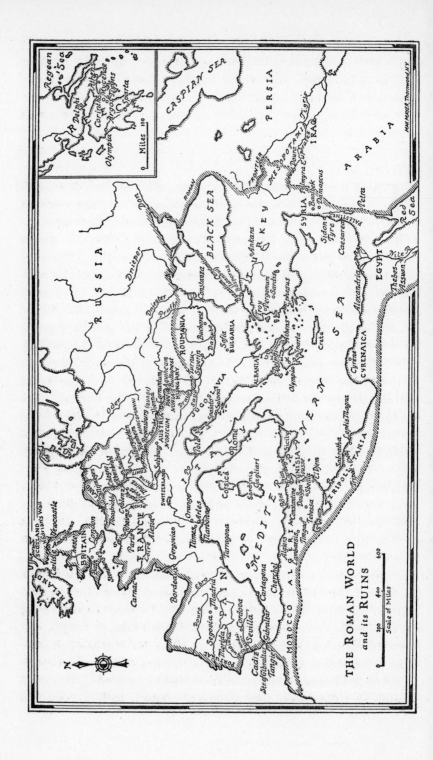

THE ROMAN WORLD
and its RUINS

begin with our ancestral England, which was occupied by Romans four hundred years, and whose language today contains nearly three words of Latin origin in five. He would then pass to the Low Countries, follow the Rhine through Germany, trace across country into Austria the wall and palisade of the *limes,* the fortified limit or threshold which extended three hundred and forty-five miles between the upper Rhine below Coblenz and the upper Danube near Regensburg, sail the Danube to Vienna and from Vienna into Hungary at Budapest, traverse Roumania to Constanza on the Black Sea, and continue to Constantinople. From Constantinople, before crossing the Bosporus, he might make a grand tour of Bulgaria, Jugoslavia, and Greece. He would then enter Asia Minor, travel the Black Sea coast of the Turkish Republic until he came to the Armenian border, turn south until he came to the valleys of the upper Tigris and Euphrates, follow the windings of the Tigris some distance south, and strike out on the line of outposts, not until the present decade definitely explored, across Mesopotamia and along the Syrian Desert through the ruins of Palmyra and through Damascus to Arabia and the Red Sea. He would make an excursion up the Nile Valley at least as far as the island of Philae, six hundred and eighty miles from Cairo. By sea and rail and motor he would travel the long thin fringe of Africa, some 2,500 miles, visiting Cyrenaica, Tripolitania, Tunisia, Algeria, and Morocco, until he arrived at Tangier, where he would cross the Straits of Gibraltar and continue his journey by traversing the Spanish peninsula, not omitting Portugal, the ancient Lusitania. He would complete his long journey by crossing France to Belgium, one of Cæsar's three parts of Gaul and the home of its bravest.

In England, the ancient province of Britannia, the chief ruin of Roman interest is the Great Wall of Hadrian, the middle section of which, about half its length, is preserved in surprising completeness. The wall, once seventy-four miles in length, extended from Carlisle to Newcastle. Other ruins, of smaller dimensions and less impressive character, have been unearthed in many places in town and country. They represent city walls, fortresses on the sea and inland, villa properties, baths, roads. In the city of Bath, the waters are still used as in Roman times, and ancient piping and pool arrangements may still be seen. More minute remnants, in the shape of coins, inscriptions, weapons, implements, and utensils of various kinds, are preserved in great numbers in museums and collections.

In the Low Countries there are almost no monumental ruins from Roman times. In 56 B.C., after his defeat of the Veneti at Auray, Julius Cæsar marched four hundred miles north into the lands of the Menapii and the Morini, well into what is now Holland, before returning to winter quarters in Gaul. When the Romans gained a permanent foothold in these regions, it was among the great waterways of the Rhine, Meuse, Waal, and Scheldt, and to their south in what is now Belgian territory. Most of the cities of Holland and Belgium, such as Utrecht, Ghent, Namur, and Brussels, go back for their founding only to the seventh century. Nijmegen, on the Waal seventy miles east of Rotterdam, is ancient Noviomagus, but few towns are like it in claiming Roman origin. Not very important collections of Roman antiquities, as at Namur and Brussels, are about all that is visible from Roman times.

The Dutch and Belgian territory was part of the Roman province of Lower Germany, Germania Inferior. As one advances up the Rhine and into Germania Superior, he may see in Cologne the remnants of Roman fortifications. At Trier, or Trèves, on the Moselle he may see the colossal Porta Nigra, a towered gate in three stories over a hundred feet long and nearly as high, the ruined Roman palace, and the great amphitheater, besides parts of the baths and the Moselle bridge. Outside of Mainz stand the imposing ruins of an aqueduct, the cemetery occupies the place of the Roman burial ground, and the museum contains an excellent exhibit of Roman antiquities. The most interesting of all reminders of Rome, however, is the long line of the German *limes,* which begins fifteen miles west of Coblenz at Rheinbrohl, and is traceable by means of occasional fragments in its whole length to Hienheim on the Danube west of Regensburg. At Wilburgstetten, forty miles southwest of Nuremberg, several hundred feet of the wall, a yard wide and once eight feet high, are an

ROMAN CAMP-CITY OF AMBOGLANNA IN ENGLAND

THE SCIPIO SARCOPHAGUS IMITATED IN BUCHAREST

ROMAN AQUEDUCT IN CONSTANTINOPLE

A ROMAN RUIN IN SOFIA

impressive sight. Another interesting point on the *limes* is the celebrated fortress of the Saalburg, forty miles north of Frankfort-on-the-Main, the largest known station of the one hundred that strengthened the long wall of defence.

The Roman sites in Austria are of exceeding interest. Near Salzburg, the great salt mines whose galleries in several stories penetrate the mountain more than half a mile were operated by the Romans. At Halstatt also are the remnants of the Roman settlement whose men worked the salt deposits nearly two thousand feet above the town and lake which had been worked by their prehistoric predecessors of many centuries before. The Hoher Markt neighborhood in the older part of Vienna lies on the site of the Roman city-camp of Vindobona, where the Emperor Marcus Aurelius is thought to have spent his last hours, and the Roman Museum of Vienna contains most interesting relics discovered in the city only. Most fascinating of all is the site of Carnuntum at Petronell, twenty-seven miles east of Vienna. Here are to be seen the lonely ruins of an ancient tomb or other structure, forty feet high, called the Heidentor, the monumental remains of two great amphitheaters, one of them for the garrison and situated near the camp, of which the outlines are clear, and a multitude of tombstones, inscriptions, and minor finds preserved in the Museum Carnuntinum and the private collection of Count Traun.

The ancient province represented by Austrian soil was Noricum. To the east was Pannonia, in which Aquincum, on the Danube a few miles north of Budapest, was the legionary headquarters. A well preserved amphitheater, plentiful remains of the town, and a museum containing the results of its excavation make Aquincum an important site. Opposite Pannonia and Noricum, and beyond the Danube, were the lands of the Marcomanni and Quadi, roughly equivalent to Czechoslovakia.

By following the Danube south and east, or by crossing Transylvania and the Carpathians, the traveller reaches Bucharest, capital of Roumania, the Dacia of Emperor Trajan's conquest, made a Roman province A.D. 106. The remains of a great bridge on the Danube at Turnu-Severin, the Carol Park museum in Bucharest with its many reliefs from the great round monument sixty feet high, perhaps a mausoleum, perhaps a victory memorial, at Adamklissi, southeast toward the Black Sea, and the museum collections in Constanza, are the chief Roman relics in Roumania, which still retains also the Roman tongue.

At the southern end of the nine miles of the Bosporus, we are at one of the world's most beautiful and most historic spots. Founded seven centuries before the Christian era as Byzantium, it became a Greek city when the Persians were thrown back by the Greeks in 490-78 B.C., was made the capital of the Roman Empire A.D. 330 as the City of Constantine, remained at the head of the Eastern Empire as Constantinople until its downfall before the Turks A.D. 1453, and has since that time, excepting the international period of 1918-23, been Turkish. Istanbul is now its official name. Besides important museum relics and the Great Mosque which was once the Church of Holy Wisdom, erected by the Roman Emperor Justinian, A.D. 527-565, there are left from earlier Roman times the two obelisks and the Serpent Column belonging to Constantine's hippodrome, a great circus which was also the meeting place for many exciting public events, the monster underground reservoir of a thousand and one pillars, also of Constantine, the great column which once bore a statue of the Emperor and marks the location of his forum, and extensive remains of an aqueduct of the Emperor Valens. At Ankara, ancient Ancyra, the capital of the Turkish Republic, three hundred and sixty miles east of Istanbul, is the Monumentum Ancyranum, the temple of Augustus and Rome on whose walls is inscribed in Latin and Greek the famous *Res Gestae* of Augustus, the Emperor's account of the achievements of his administration.

Bulgaria, covering the territory of ancient Thrace, has extensive museum exhibits in the capital at Sofia, but few monumental remains. Jugoslavia is rich in Roman ruins only in Dalmatia, which fronts Italy from the east side of the Adriatic and has always until its recent assignment to Jugoslavia shared intimately in the life of Italy. The ruins of Diocletian's palace at Spalato and the amphitheater at Pola are in the grand style. Spalato is built almost entirely of material from the great palace, and is largely comprised within its limits. Salona, a few miles away, has a ruined theater, amphitheater, and other remains.

Inasmuch as Greece became Roman territory with the fall of Corinth in 146 B.C., and remained so for centuries, it is not surprising to find in Olympia, Delphi, Eleusis, and even in Athens, the signs of Roman occupation. In Athens, the Arch of Hadrian, bearing on its faces the inscriptions, "This is the City of Theseus," and "This is the City of Hadrian," indicates extensive transformations by that Roman Emperor. Similar changes no doubt took place in many Greek cities.

In Asia Minor, besides the Monumentum Ancyranum, may be mentioned the site of Troy, whose ruins are in part the late Roman form of the city; Pergamum, which in 133 B.C. was bequeathed by King Attalus to Rome; and other cities, like Sardis and Ephesus, which in their public buildings give evidence of Roman occupation.

On the Euphrates, the most important site at present is Doura, a recently excavated outpost of Roman trade and defence illustrating both Christian and pagan culture on the eastern border. To the south, also in Syria, are the mighty ruins of Palmyra, which flourished as a great caravan center for the trade between Mediterranean regions and Mesopotamian lands. Damascus, Tyre, and Cæsarea also are not without Roman interests. Sixteen miles from Damascus is Baalbek, with some of the world's most gigantic ruins in the shape of propylæa and temple from the second century of the Christian era. Still farther south is Petra, the rock town in Arabia which was another important trade city.

With this, we are at the Red Sea, the Isthmus of Suez, and Egypt, where Alexandria interests the Latin student with its so-called Pompey's Pillar, a late Roman monument eighty-eight feet high, its catacombs, displaying Egyptian, Greek, and Roman character, and its museum of Græco-Roman antiquities, containing many relics of Roman sculpture, painting, inscriptions, and architecture, with lesser objects. Cairo and the ruins of its ancient predecessor, Memphis, have almost nothing to offer of Roman character, and Egypt in general south of Alexandria gives little evidence of the centuries of Roman control which began formally in 30 B.C. with its annexation by Augustus. That the Nile valley was a travelled region is shown not only by chance mention in Roman literature but by the travellers' inscriptions left on the Memnon statues at Thebes from the time of Nero onward. On the island of Philae, near Assuan and the great modern dam, the pharaohs in relief on one of the colonnades and on the Temple of Isis are portraits of Augustus and Tiberius, and the near-by Gateway of Hadrian shows the figures of Hadrian, Marcus Aurelius, and Lucius Verus. The famous Kiosk portrays Trajan bringing sacrifices to Isis and Horus. Egypt passed from the control of the Eastern or Byzantine Empire A.D. 640, when the forces of Caliph Omar appeared in the Delta, two years subsequent to the fall of Jerusalem before Mohammedan arms, eighteen years after the beginning of the Mohammedan calendar, and eight years after the death of Mohammed.

The ruins along the narrow northern coast of Africa from Alexandria to Tangier and the Straits of Gibraltar are among the most imposing of the Roman world. Cyrene, in Roman hands from 96 B.C., was the capital of the ancient Cyrenaica, now Italian territory. It was essentially a Greek city and region, but the Roman occupation left behind many ruins, which are visited from the modern capital Benghazi. In Tripolitania, an Italian possession since 1912, there are three great Roman sites, Leptis Magna, Tripoli, or ancient Oea, and Sabratha. Sabratha and Leptis display some of the greatest ruins of Roman times. Leptis Magna, native town of Septimius Severus, has gigantic baths, temples, porticoes, a basilica, market places, and docks. At Sabratha are an amphitheater, a theater, temples, baths, porticoes, and markets, besides monuments of the early Christian era. Ancient Oea, largely consumed by Tripoli, which covers the ancient site, survives in the Arch of Marcus Aurelius and numerous museum relics. Reservoirs, villa remains, and presses for oil and wine testify to Roman enterprise in the once flourishing country districts. In Tunisia, a French protectorate since 1881, there are the vast ruins of Roman Carthage, comprising theater, amphitheater, temples, aqueduct, reservoirs, baths, cemeteries, harbor, and villas. To the east and south of Carthage are Sousse, ancient Hadrumetum, with its famous collection of mosaics, among them Virgil writing the *Æneid;* Sbeitla, ancient Sufetula, with temples, triumphal arch, and aqueduct; and El Djem, with a great amphitheater. To the west are Dougga, ancient Thugga, with theater, temples, arches, and tombs; and Utica, which gave its name to Cato Uticensis after his defeat by Cæsar, with aqueduct, reservoir, baths, theater, and amphitheater. In Algeria, French since 1831, are Tebessa, ancient Theveste; Bône, once the Roman Bona; Constantine, the ancient Cirta, home of Fronto, the tutor of Marcus Aurelius; and Lambæsis and Timgad, the famous camp-cities on guard near the Sahara. In Morocco, Cherchell, the ancient Cæsarea, sixty miles west of Algiers, was the capital of eastern Mauretania, and Tangier the capital of western Mauretania. The sites in Algeria and Morocco, like those farther east, exhibit monumental ruins.

These are only the chief of the greater African sites. With sites of lesser extent, and with isolated ruins, they form a total which makes the north coast of Africa a richer field for the Roman archæologist than any other part of the Empire save Italy.

The most impressive ruins in the Spanish peninsula are the mighty aqueducts at Tarragona and Segovia, the amphitheater at Italica, near Seville, the aqueduct, theater, and great bridge at Merida, near the borders of Portugal, and the ancient columns in the mosque at Cordova which once were parts of Roman buildings. On these sites and on others are less monumental remains of temple, wall, circus, baths, forum, and other characteristic Roman structures.

In France, the Rhône Valley is the district of most interest. This formed the richer part of Gallia Narbonensis, whose familiar designation, Provincia, "the Province," survives in French Provence. In it are Orange, ancient Arausio, and its triumphal arch and theater with restored seats and stage still in use; Arles, ancient Arelate, with amphitheater, theater, town walls, Constantinian palace, and cemetery relics; Nîmes, with the temple called Maison Carrée, an amphitheater, and the Gate of Augustus. Ancient Narbo, which gave its name to Gallia Narbonensis, is now Narbonne. Other parts of France afford fewer large ruins, but in many far separate places the traveller meets with reminders, in the names of places if not in material remains, that he is on Roman soil. In Bordeaux, ancient Burdigala, are huge fragments of an amphitheater. Rheims, ancient city of the Remi, has a triumphal arch. Autun, ancient Augustodunum, has two fine Roman city gates, a lofty tomb monument, and the foundations of an amphitheater. Near Clermont-Ferrand are the remnants of Gergovia, scene of Cæsar's repulses by Vercingetorix and his Gauls. Alise-Sainte Reine preserves the name and remains of Alesia, where Vercingetorix was besieged and compelled to surrender, and the Cæsar campaigns in Gaul are traceable throughout by names and monuments. Paris itself, once Lutetia, has not entirely blotted out the ancient city, which occupied the space of the Cité, comprising the Isle and contiguous parts. Museums throughout France contain fine collections of Roman antiquities.

If we mention Sardinia, with its amphitheater and tombs in Cagliari, and Sicily, whose antiquities from Roman times are overshadowed by its Greek monuments, and dismiss other islands of the Mediterranean, most of which exhibit marks of the Roman presence, we shall have completed our rough survey of the archæology of the Roman Empire. It remains to comment on its monuments as a whole.

In the first place, we may note the universality of Roman remains. There is no part of the Empire, however short the period in which it was ruled from the Tiber, or however old and established and different from the Roman its culture, that was not affected by contact with Rome. If it has preserved none of the larger monuments, the signs of the Roman presence will be found in the smaller but equally significant museum antiquities.

It is to be noted also that the lack of visible monuments, great or small, is not necessarily evidence of slight contact. There are many districts in which no systematic exploration or excavation has taken place, and in which such antiquities as are known are the result of chance discovery. This is true especially of the far Balkan neighborhood and the more distant parts of the East, where until recently the explorer was likely to be met with distrust, or even hostility. Even in the most sympathetic and convenient surroundings, there are enterprises which cannot be carried out because of lack of funds, and no doubt many monuments await discovery.

In the third place, if we make the probably truthful supposition that the more distant northern provinces of Europe, such as the Low Countries and the provinces from the head of the Danube to the Black Sea, were less rich in the characteristic large buildings of the Romans, we may draw the conclusion that, in the far away provinces of extended agricultural and pastoral areas and severe cold, Roman civilization took a less intimate and tenacious hold than in the regions nearer the Mediterranean which were more like Italy in produce and climate, and more easily accessible. The rigor of the northern winter and the solitudes of wide plains devoted to pasturage and grain were less attractive to the Roman colonist than the genial heat of more thickly settled Italy and the Gallic and Spanish and African provinces, where the olive and vine and the fruits and gardens shared the landscape with grain and cattle husbandry. The traveller who leaves Italy today and journeys through the limitless flat plains of the Danube in Hungary and Roumania, with their little villages of little houses, or through the remote valleys of Balkans and Alps, or over the watery grass levels of the Low Countries, is impressed by the smallness and simplicity of their habitations, and, in all but the larger towns, of their civic buildings. In antiquity the towns themselves were fewer and less substantial and the villages even more slight and simple. The Mediterranean lands were of longer standing, and their villages and cities had been established for centuries when Roman occupation stimulated, enlarged, and enriched them.

Again, we may note with interest how the major archæological sites are near the water—on the Rhine at Cologne, Bonn, and Mainz; on the Moselle at Trèves; at Carnuntum and Aquincum on the Danube; in Constanza and the neighborhood on the Black Sea; at Byzantium on the Bosporus; at Alexandria on the Nile; at the African sites along the coast; at Cadiz and Cartagena and Tarragona on the Spanish coast; at Marseilles and in the Rhône valley; on the Meuse and Rhine in Holland; at London on the

Thames; at the forts along the Saxon Shore. The causes of this are to be seen in both the defensive and the commercial value of the waterway. The Rhine and Danube were important both as trade routes and as barriers against the invader. The Rhône and Mediterranean waters and the Black Sea were the great carriers, supplemented by forty to fifty thousand miles of good roads, which also are marked by archæological sites.

In the fifth place, there is to be noted in Italy and the provinces nearest the Mediterranean a remarkable uniformity both in buildings and material. In the excavation of almost any site representing even the smallest city, the archæologist expects to find market place, basilica, temples, shops, pavements, walls, gates, mill and bakery, houses of rich and poor, and, beyond the gate, tombs and villas and roadbeds. According to the size, wealth, and public spirit of the city, will be its equipment in amusement and luxury. A town of no very great size may have its theater and portico, amphitheater, baths, aqueduct and water works, and even circus. The library is not unknown. Roads, bridges, and walls of defense are usual features. Temples and important civic buildings are likely to be at least in part of marble, even if imported, and brick and concrete are always present in large quantities. The pavement of street and road are according to the material available near by.

In the sixth place, the period represented by the chief ruins is nearly always the Empire rather than the Republic, and is usually the later first century or the second. The time from Trajan to Septimius Severus might be called the period of affluence, though earlier emperors are not without their witness, and though in the fourth century Constantine and his successors were not infrequent builders. Christian as well as pagan buildings are found.

To realize how natural was this uniformity under the Roman Empire, we have but to think of a French or Italian city in Africa today, with the invariable public square, market, commissary's offices, post office, bank, theater, café, tobacco-salt-and-postage-stamp shop; or, the American town with its main street, station, post office, hotel, tavern, cinema, etc.

Finally, something may be said regarding what might be called

BASILICA AT LEPTIS MAGNA

AMPHITHEATER AT CARTHAGE

BRIDGE AT MERIDA, ANCIENT EMERITA, IN SPAIN

THE DANUBE NEAR CARNUNTUM

the archæology of language. The Roman Empire covered or touched a multitude of peoples whose speech was not its own, and it is of exceeding interest to contemplate the result. In Italy the various non-Latin tribes were not long in dropping their native idiom and adopting the language of Rome, though their speech varied from the Latin much as Venetian, Piedmontese, and Neapolitan vary from standard Italian today. In Sardinia and Sicily, with their Punic and Greek as well as native basis, the divergence was greater. But peoples more distant and unrelated in blood also took over the Latin tongue. The Latin of Spain was probably the most loyal of the daughter tongues, and Spanish today, in spite of its Arabic intermingling, is hardly less Latin than Italian itself. The Latin of Farther Spain and of the Gauls is the Portuguese and French of today. From Gibraltar to the Rhine, the Latin displaced all the native tongues except the Basque on the Spanish and French border, the Breton in France, and the Teutonic in parts of Belgium. In Britain it withdrew in the fifth century with the Roman forces, to enter again with the Norman French six hundred years later and make English an Anglo-Latin tongue. Along the upper Rhine and along the Danube the native idiom was not permanently displaced, except in Dacia, where the Latin of Trajan's soldier colonists somehow survived the inundations of the Slavs and the contact with Teuton, Hungarian, Greek, and Turk, to become the Roumanian of today, a manifestly Latin tongue with contributions from its neighbors. In the Greek lands of the Byzantine Empire, Latin made its way only as a second administration language. The Greeks of the mainland, of the islands, of the Asian and east African coasts, retained their idiom through Roman and even through Mohammedan and Turkish times. The rest of Africa, after the Roman and Byzantine periods, was lost to the Latin tongue and Roman civilization in the seventh century when the Mohammedan conquerors overran it, to be restored with the advent of the French and Spanish in the nineteenth century and the Italians in the twentieth.

The remains of the ancient Roman tongue thus do not always coincide with the material remains of the Empire. Roman ruins are found in many lands whose languages are of other origin. Yet even in the linguistic field we meet with interesting surprises. In German Köln and French Cologne it is easy to see Latin Colonia, and in Bonn Latin Bona; but German Coblenz seems to have nothing to do with Latin until we are told that it is Confluentes, from the flowing together of Moselle and Rhine; French Autun is an effective disguise of Augustodunum. English Chester does not easily betray Castra, the camp, and Nijmegen and Maastricht look entirely Dutch to those who have not learned to see in them Noviomagus and Mosae Trajectus, the Ford of the Meuse.

We may conclude this survey of the Roman monuments in the homeland of Italy and in the provinces with the reflection that for their preservation and care, and in many cases their discovery and excavation, we are indebted to the science of archæology. The remains of ancient times have not always been so well understood, and have never been so highly valued and so well guarded, as they are today.

ARCHÆOLOGY AND THE ROMAN MONUMENTS

WE have seen that in most countries of Europe, and in all countries of Africa and Asia that border on the Mediterranean, notably in the lands about ancient Carthage and in Tripolitania, and even in far-away Palmyra and the towns on the Euphrates, Roman ruins are likely at any turn to dominate the landscape. There are scores of theaters and amphitheaters and bathing establishments in places where they are not expected by the unarchæological traveller. The amphitheater at El Djem, a day's journey southeast of Carthage, the world's fifth in dimensions, is so colossal that at first one fails to notice the town built beside and out of it. The Roman triumphal and honorary arches number hundreds, and the inscribed tomb and other private personal memorials are myriad. Christian as well as pagan history is illuminated. At Carthage, where in the amphitheater stands the reminder of the martyrdom of Saints Perpetua and Felicitas, we are surrounded by memories of Augustine as pagan student and Christian bishop, though the greater fascination of the Punic city will always be the story of the queen, of all too human clay, who perished pitifully and before her time, and the flames of whose funeral pile on the high hill of her capital struck upon the eyes of the recreant lover already far on the Romeward paths of the sea.

But thus far we have only surveyed the monuments of the ancient Roman world. Let us now pay some attention to the character of recent and current archæological enterprise.

In Italy, the Antiquities and Fine Arts form a department in the Ministry of Public Instruction. The kingdom is districted, each district has its inspector, and everything in the process from initiation to publication, exhibition, and interpretation is admirably provided for. Wherever Italian authority reaches today, the study of ancient times is sure to follow. Cyrene, won back from the Turk in 1911, has yielded one of the most valuable prizes of recent times in the Venus now in the National Museum at Rome. The statue was suddenly exposed to the light on December 1, 1913, by a torrential rain which started the crumbling of the bank in which it lay buried. The Italians have established a museum in Rhodes, and have undertaken an archæological survey of the whole Dodecanese. These are only scattered examples of Italy's interest in antiquities.

Roman archæology has two great centers in Italy: Rome itself, whose yield of interest and substance has been continuous, though uneven, since the early Renaissance aroused Italian pride and intelligence; and Pompeii, which after a hundred and fifty years of periodic digging is still nearly half unexcavated. To these, Ostia, fifteen miles from Rome near the coast, is making itself a good third.

After Giuseppe Fiorelli, who from 1860 to 1875 contributed so remarkably to the technique of excavation, administration, and preservation that all Pompeii bears the imprint of his former presence, the great name in the study of Pompeii is that of August Mau, the German scholar who devoted to it the last thirty years of his life, and whose work, translated by Francis W. Kelsey as *Pompeii, Its Life and Art,* has done more to make the city known than any other book. Its most active students in recent years are its administrator, Superintendent Matteo della Corte, who has published numerous authoritative studies of it in Italian and a guide in English called *Pompeii, the New Excavations,* and Director Amedeo Maiuri of the Naples Museum, whose many publications include a beautiful book on the Villa of Mysteries. As long ago as 1891 more than five hundred books and pamphlets on Pompeii were known. At the past and present rate, the completion of the excavation, now less than two-thirds accomplished, would require upward of another century.

Current activity at Pompeii has to do principally with a single locality and project, namely, the prolongation of the discovered portion of the Strada dell' Abbondanza, or Abundance Street, in the direction of the amphitheater, to which it now gives access, thus doing away with the former inconvenience of making a detour along the highway in order to reach the entrance. The essential principle of excavation today is the scrupulous preservation of the remains of the ancient city in their original place and condition.

This is not a policy unheard of before. The museum in the ruins had long contained casts of Pompeian bodies, made by pouring plaster into the cavities left as they wasted away in their gradually caking envelope of ashes. It had contained also reproductions of doors and other objects, possible because of the imprints surviving on ashes after the wood had disappeared. These objects, however, were not in their original position, and their treatment was only occasional.

The active beginnings of the new policy may be associated with the House of the Vettii and the House of the Amorini Dorati, where the roofs were restored, the ornamental sculptures re-erected, the flowers and shrubs identified and replanted, the fountains again set to playing, all as they had been during the life of their possessors. The new excavations, however, are marked by a much more ingenious and a much more thorough application of the policy. The houses of Abundance Street, which leads out of the east side of the town, are not like those of other streets of excavated Pompeii, stripped of their best furnishings and sculptures, denuded of their most brilliant paintings, and with peristyles and gardens bare and lifeless, so that for an acquaintance with movable detail a visit to the Naples Museum is necessary, but retain as far as possible utensils, furniture, ornament, fountains, and shrubbery as they were when overtaken by the eruption of A.D. 79. One enters a street at present some sixty rods long and thirty feet wide, paved with blocks of basalt between high stone or earthen sidewalks, and bordered on both sides by houses and shops for the most part two stories high. The brightness of the Italian sun on street and wall, the dark shadows, the ruddy election notices, the frequent pictures and patches of tinting on the façades, produce a brilliant and colorful effect. The doors of restaurant and shop are open, the wares in some instances are on the counter or in the case, the vestibules of rich men's houses invite with vistas of spacious cool interiors, the rooms and gardens within are gay with lively pictures and plashing fountains. It requires only a slight effort of the imagination to people this new section of the Strada dell' Abbondanza with the buyers and sellers and dwellers of eighteen hundred and fifty-six years ago. The mode of operation in Herculaneum has been similar, and has accomplished reproductions quite as wonderful.

The city of Rome as an archæological site differs from Pompeii and Ostia in having been a capital instead of a provincial town, in having always continued to be a capital and dwelt in, instead of being overwhelmed by sudden calamity or overtaken by slower but equally complete destruction, and in being today a growing city in need of space and continually under necessity of choosing between utility and the sentiment for art and antiquity instead of being consecrated to archæology. None the less, there is in Rome a general separateness between the areas of the modern and the ancient which has made of ancient Rome almost as distinct a site as Pompeii. Forum and Palatine are set apart and barred against encroachment, and much of the southern part of the city adjacent to them is quite as safe from invasion.

The story of Roman excavation contains many great names. The official leadership during the past century has included Visconti, Canina, Fea, Rosa, Fiorelli, Lanciani, the Christian archæologists De Rossi and Marucchi, and Giacomo Boni. No classicist visiting Rome for the first quarter of the twentieth century has failed to become acquainted with the name of Boni. A picturesque blend of architect, archæologist, and poet, living by himself on the Palatine near where it overlooks the Forum, both of which were under his charge upward of thirty years, he had so grown to be a part of the trees, flowers, and ruins in the midst of which he dwelt that on his death in July, 1925, there was but one thought as to the fit place for his last repose, and he was laid away near his villino on the Palatine at the foot of his favorite palm.

But the scholars just mentioned are Italian only, and only the appointees of the Italian State. To appreciate fully the brilliance of Roman archæology, one should be told of many other Italian scholars, of the many scholars of prominence from other coun-

THE TOMB OF GIACOMO BONI

RUINS IN OSTIA

A STREET IN POMPEII

HOUSE OF THE VETTII IN POMPEII

tries, and of the learned institutions established by them in Rome. These archæological bodies include the British School, long associated with the names of Thomas Ashby and Eugenie Sellers Strong, both of whom have lectured in our American cities; the American Academy; the French and German and Dutch and Swedish Institutes of Archæology; and the recently founded Roumanian School. One should be acquainted also with the great numbers of articles, periodicals, monographs, and larger works, representing everything from the severely special to the no less necessary work of the scholarly stylist.

Of the wonders wrought by Italian archæologists of this generation, we shall speak at greater length in other chapters. Let the remainder of this chapter be devoted to the participation of American scholars in Roman archæology.

Among the foremost names indicating our interest must stand that of Professor Kelsey. Francis Willey Kelsey, for more than forty years teacher of classics, editor, author, archæologist, enthusiastic patron of music, letters, and the arts, died on May 14, 1927, at the age of sixty-nine. Already at the age of 27 interested in archæology, he visited the German excavations at Pergamum in Asia Minor. Eight years later, in 1893, he made a study of Carthage. In 1899, he published his translation of August Mau's *Pompeii, Its Life and Art.* From 1907 to 1912 he was president of the Archæological Institute of America, for which during the previous twenty-five years he had many times gone on the lecture circuit. Not to mention every important act in his career, in 1919 he took charge of the first University of Michigan Expedition to the Near East, and until his death was identified with the individual and coöperative undertakings of all the University of Michigan expeditions. In March to May, 1925, in company with the enthusiastic Byron de Prorok and with a large staff including the geologist Henry S. Washington as scientific adviser, Père Delattre of the White Fathers as interpreter of Christian antiquities, Père Chabot as interpreter of Punic discoveries, a petrographer, an engineer, and others, he directed a preliminary campaign at Carthage. Their principal achievement was the excavation of the temple area of the goddess Tanit, near the sea and the commercial harbor, and the unearthing of over 1,100 urns, of which Professor Kelsey says, in *Art and Archæology*, February, 1926: "To judge from the contents of the three dozen selected urns examined by us . . . we are warranted in believing that most of them contain the charred bones and ashes of young children. . . . In these charred bones of infants do we find evidence that the Carthaginians were guilty of the horrible practice—with which they were charged by Greek and Roman writers—of 'passing children through the fire' to their gods?" "If the excavations are continued," says the last sentence of this report, "we may reasonably expect that future discoveries will throw light upon many things that are now obscure."

Other instances of American scholarship taking the field in Roman archæology are the exploratory excavations of the American Academy in Rome at Hadrian's Villa and Horace's Farm, the excavations at Minturnae by the University of Pennsylvania, and the individual work of Arthur L. Frothingham on the Arch of Constantine, Tenney Frank on Republican buildings, Esther Boise Van Deman in her authoritative studies of building material and methods and in her monumental work on the aqueducts, and Marion Blake's unique work on mosaic pavements.

Here, though it is going beyond the formal border of the Roman Empire, must be mentioned also the excavations at Doura, a last outpost of Rome on the Euphrates about a hundred and forty miles east of Palmyra and twice that distance from the Mediterranean coast. The work at Doura, initiated by British explorers after the World War and first actively prosecuted by Franz Cumont, the famous authority on Mithras and the Oriental religions, in a two years' campaign whose results were published in 1926, was taken over in 1927 by Yale University in collaboration with the Rockefeller Foundation and the French Academy of Inscriptions. Michael Rostovtzeff of Yale, international authority on ancient history, and Franz Cumont of the French Academy are in charge of the scientific-historical side of the work, with Clark Hopkins of Yale directing the excavations. The importance of Doura lies in its contacts with Palmyra, Syria, and the Hellenistic and Roman Empires on the one hand and Arabia and Parthia on the other.

The work of Cumont, Rostovtzeff, and Hopkins at Doura, with Rostovtzeff's studies of Petra, Jerash, Palmyra, and the caravan trade, forms a welcome contribution to the archæology of the eastern border of the Roman Empire, the most recent and most remarkable advancement of our acquaintance with which is due to the air explorations of Father Poidebard on the Syrian frontier. Stimulated by the chance archæological observations of aviators in the World War, and profiting by their technical experience, Father Poidebard first prepared himself by several years of experimentation during which he developed a remarkable technique of air photography, and then in 1929-32 systematically explored from the air the zone or network of military and caravan roads, with their forts, barracks, caravanserais, wells, conduits, reservoirs, watch towers, and other accessories, which constituted the Roman *limes* along the ridges and streams bordering the Syrian desert and Upper Mesopotamia—a zone 600 miles long and 60 to 120 miles deep reaching from the northern end of Arabia at Bostra, 90 miles from the Mediterranean, by way of Damascus and Palmyra to Soura and Circesium on the Euphrates, and thence up the valley of the Khabur to Nisibis and to the Tigris, whence the line continued upstream to the Armenian border and the Black Sea.

The title "Father of Archæology in America" belongs with good right to Charles Eliot Norton. Mr. Norton was born in 1827, and died in 1908. He was not himself an archæologist, but a broadly and solidly educated man, an author, a traveller, and the friend of distinguished writers and scholars. He numbered among his friends Clough, Morris, Burne-Jones, Ruskin, Carlyle, Longfellow, Lowell, Holmes, Parkman. He entered Harvard at 14, graduated at 19 with the class of 1846, and at the age of about 23, in the employ of the East India Company, made a voyage to India, returning by way of Egypt and Italy, and afterward going into business. In 1855-57 he visited Europe, spending the winter months principally in Rome. The result of this was the volume called *Travel and Study in Italy*, published in 1860, and Dante's *Vita Nuova* in English. Mr. Norton had been a contributor to the first number of the *Atlantic Monthly* in 1857, and wrote also for the

North American Review, becoming later Mr. Lowell's assistant
on that periodical. In the autumn and winter evenings of 1865
and 1866, in company with Lowell, he listened to Longfellow's
confidential reading of his Dante translation. In 1868 he went
again to Europe, where he remained for five years, the first part
of the time in Italy and the remainder in Germany and England,
where he became acquainted with Carlyle and Mrs. Gaskell. In
1875 he was made Professor of the Fine Arts at Harvard, a chair
which he occupied until 1897.

Great, however, as was Mr. Norton's contribution to American
culture in the translation of Dante, in his occupation of the first
chair of the Fine Arts at Harvard, and in his other written work,
it is hardly to be doubted that his greatest service to American
intellectual life will prove to have been his founding, in 1879, of
the Archæological Institute of America, an organization which
soon had branches in every state possessing a scholastic or cultural
center. This was the consequence of his visit to Egypt and Italy
in 1851, of the sojourns of 1855-57 and 1868 in Italy, and of a
naturally catholic taste in art and intellect. Mr. Norton had the
vision of a more enlightened teaching of the classics and art in
America that should result from the stimulation of American
scholars by participation in the archæological enterprises of European scholarship.

The Archæological Institute of America has founded and aided
directly and indirectly in the support of five schools active in the
archæological field. A word about each will show the range of
its interest.

In 1882, as a result of the Institute's committee action of 1881,
the American School of Classical Studies in Athens was established.
It occupies quarters of its own on the slope of Mount Lycabettus
next to the home of the British School, and has recently dedicated a beautiful new building containing the Gennadios library,
the gift of a prominent Greek gentleman of that name. It has
to its credit fifty-three years of distinction in excavation, research, and cultural mediation between antiquity and modern
times and between Greece of today and America, enjoys the
entire confidence of the Greek ruling classes, and, besides the

THE AMERICAN ACADEMY IN ROME

CEÇERE STUDIO IN THE AMERICAN ACADEMY

A SUMMER SESSION OF THE AMERICAN SCHOOL

excavation of Corinth, is now active in the excavation of ancient Athens itself. In 1895 occurred the opening of the American School of Classical Studies in Rome, which in 1913 united with the American Academy in Rome. In 1900 the American School of Oriental Research in Jerusalem was founded. In 1907 came the founding of the School of American Archæology, with head-quarters and museum in historic Santa Fe and branch in San Diego. Fifth and latest to be founded was the American School of Prehistoric Research, primarily a summer school prosecuting its work in the cave-culture sites of Spain, France, and elsewhere from June 25 to September 25. In 1923 its enrollment was fifteen, it visited forty-four museums and seventy-seven prehistoric sites, and heard lectures from forty-two foreign specialists.

It will be appropriate to close this chapter on the archæology of classical lands with the words of Charles Eliot Norton himself, to whom the American and Canadian public is indebted not only for the Archæological Institute and the five schools which have been its creation, but for its service in providing the platform for the past fifty years with lecturers bringing from the study and from the actual field the latest and most living messages of antiquity in every phase. After speaking of the temptations of scholarship to exalt "the discovery of the trifling into an end by itself, and to take pleasure in the mere accumulation of... matters of fact, which, till ordered in their relation to some general truth, are nothing better than fragments in a heap of rubbish," the founder of the Institute and the source of a great liberalizing influence in American scholarship thus defines the humanistic scholar: "The true scholar is he who, avoiding useless specialism on the one hand, and loose inexactness on the other, never mistaking the roots of knowledge for its fruits, or straying from the highway of learning into its by-paths, however attractively they may open before him, holds steadily to the main objects of all study, the acquisition of a fuller acquaintance with life in its higher ranges, of a juster appreciation of the ways and works of man, and of man's relation to that inconceivable universe in the vast and mysterious order of which he finds himself an infinitesimally small part."

HOW ANCIENT ROME WAS BURIED

A GREAT modern Rome, with as great a fume and din of big business as that of which Horace complained, now covers the site of ancient Rome, with giant fragments of the ancient city still rising out of the midst of the modern. To appreciate more fully the character of the ancient capital, we should know something of the city's fortunes in the long centuries between its decline and the rise of the Rome of modern times. What happened to the Rome of the Cæsars when the Cæsars were no more?

The first surprise of the visitor to modern Rome is the great number, the great variety, and the great massiveness of the remains of ancient Rome that rise above ground. Their enormous size especially is something of which the photographs have given him no conception. His next surprise is the discovery that the modern city is at an average of twenty to thirty feet above the level of the city of Cicero's and Cæsar's time.

When these marvels have grown familiar, still another wonder is the discovery that, mighty as are the larger ruins, and numerous as are the smaller, they all together form but a fraction of the ancient city. The towering ruins of the Colosseum are only a remnant; all but one third of the gigantic building has disappeared. The colossal masses of the Palatine are only the ground floors and basements of the imperial palaces. The hugest buildings in the Forum, and most of the others, do not rise above their foundations. Millions of cubic yards of coarser masonry, and all but fragments of the vast wealth of marbles brought from the ends of the earth, have vanished utterly. If it were not for the immensity of some of the very fragments, we should not know of "the grandeur that was Rome."

Roma quanta fuit, ipsa ruina docet—
How great was Rome, her very ruin shows.

The questions that naturally follow this surprise are two. How was the city so utterly ruined, and how was it so deeply buried? Both questions will find answer in a brief account of the long history of the city's physical downfall.

In the first place, it must be remembered that Rome is not a Pompeii or a Herculaneum. These two cities were overwhelmed in the full tide of life; their people hardly had time to escape before the ash and pumice fragments falling in heavy showers from the sky enveloped them completely. Pompeii lay beneath twenty feet of pumice and loose ash, Herculaneum beneath forty to eighty feet of mingled ash and water which rolled or fell upon the city in muddy torrents and soon solidified into a mass which today requires pick and drill for its removal. Herculaneum was practically sealed. Pompeii was for a time burrowed into and plundered; but the rains and the decay of the years soon caused it to settle into itself, and for a thousand years and more the gardens were growing in the level fields above its forgotten ruins. But the city of Rome was not buried in this way and so preserved. Rome has always been a city with people dwelling in it.

In the second place, it should be remembered that ancient Rome passed through a long period of shrinkage in population and decay in buildings. The city was probably at its greatest in Hadrian's time. There were monumental buildings erected as late as Constantine, but active growth, whether in men or buildings, had long since ceased. The use of materials from buildings already old and crumbling began as early as A.D. 203. The Portico of Octavius, restored that year by Septimius Severus, contains parts of buildings erected in the time of Titus, a hundred and twenty-three years before. The upper story of the Colosseum was repaired in the same way from either old or damaged buildings. By A.D. 476, the usual date of the Western Empire's end, when the city had been entered and pillaged by Goths and Vandals, and the population had greatly fallen off, we must think of many great public buildings and monuments in a state of neglect and ruin, and a larger number of palaces and apartment houses and tenements in whole or in part abandoned. As the population decreased, and desertion and decay progressed in buildings public and private, the dismantling of old buildings when new were needed became a matter of course. Many a building, especially in the half-deserted and sometime popular living districts, crumbled into a heap of brick and mortar. When in A.D. 537 the aqueducts were destroyed by the Gothic Vitiges, the natural tendency for the city to shrink toward the center received a greater impulse, and the population gravitated into the Campus Martius near to the Tiber, which now became the chief source of the water supply, to remain so for upward of a thousand years.

But there were other causes of destruction than the natural decay thus described. There were fires; the greater amount of timber used in antiquity made conflagrations both more frequent and more disastrous than they are today in Mediterranean cities. No doubt many buildings wrecked by fire in the later centuries were never replaced. Again, there were the floods of the Tiber. These may not have caused directly the downfall of buildings, but they weakened the foundations and prepared them for ruin. Thirty floods are recorded for the first five Christian centuries, and those recorded were of course not all that occurred. Besides fire and flood, there were earthquakes to hasten the fall of structures already beginning to crumble. The very sweep of the winds and the beating of the rains, year in and year out through the cloudy Roman winters, were not without effect.

Still further, there was the actual destruction by the hand of man. The dismantling of unused buildings, public and private, in the erection of other structures, has already been mentioned. The practice became so common that the later emperors were obliged to legislate against the abuse. Majorian, on July 10, 458, determined "to remedy the detestable process which has long been going on, whereby the face of the venerable city is disfigured. . . . For it is too plain that the public edifices, in which all the adornment of the city consists, are being everywhere pulled to pieces at the suggestion of the city officials, on the pretense that the stones are wanted for the public works." The Emperor Theodosius stationed night watches to prevent the stealing of statuary.

Besides these peaceful spoliations, there was the violence of war. The taking of the city by Alaric in A.D. 410 was accompanied by fires and mutilation of the monuments. The defence of the Mausoleum of Hadrian against the Goths in 537 involved the sacrifice of its ornamental sculptures, which were torn from its terraces and balustrades to hurl upon the assailants below. And to these spoliations of war and peace must be added the building activities of the early Christians, who either purchased, received as gifts, or appropriated without objection, many an ancient temple or other pagan edifice. The many Constantinian churches, such as Saint-Lawrence-Outside-the-Walls, were beautified, if not wholly constructed, from the older buildings. One needs but to look at the ancient columns in these oldest churches in Rome to realize what their erection meant to the buildings of the pagan city.

The same causes of destruction continued in the dark centuries. The whole former Roman world was in disorder, decay, and ruin. What Pope Gregory the Great, 590-604, said in a sermon was literally true of the neighborhood of Rome: "Cities are destroyed, fortresses levelled to the ground; farms laid waste; the earth reduced to a desert. No husbandman is left in the fields, scarcely a dweller remains in the towns, and still the remnant of mankind is daily stricken." There was no more building in Rome in the ordinary sense. The remnants of the nobility adapted the old-time palaces to their needs, restoring or repairing them from the ruins of other buildings. The poor lived on in their miserable tenements until the crumbling walls were no longer safe, and then found shelter in the nooks and corners of circus, theater, temple, portico, and palace, now sinking with the weight of centuries. If stone or timber or metal was needed, they were found in the remains of the ancient city. If lime was wanted, the marble architraves and statues of ancient temples were broken in pieces and taken to the kiln. Unused and decaying buildings no doubt were wrecked and sold by their owners to those in the building business. Visitors wonder at the dark spots that cover like a pox the walls of the Colosseum and the temple of Antoninus at the east end of the Forum. They are the little pits dug by the mediæval Romans in

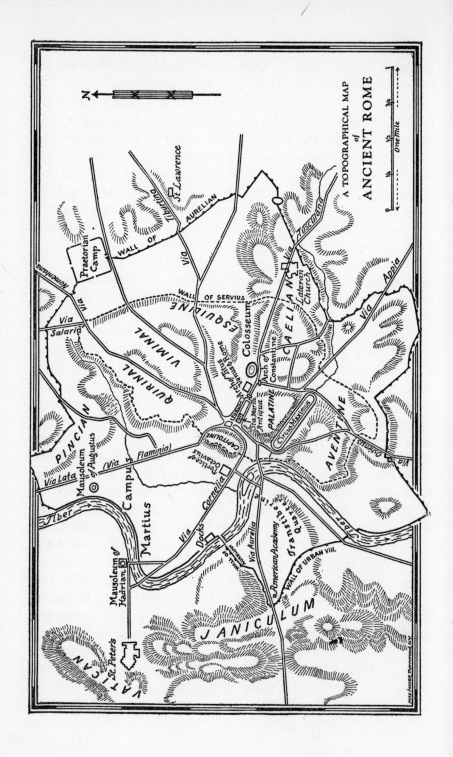

A TOPOGRAPHICAL MAP
of
ANCIENT ROME

One Mile

the search for the metal clamps by which instead of by mortar the ancient building blocks were firmly held in place.

In the later dark centuries, the rise of the barons and their feudal quarrels hastened this destruction. Many a monument, like the arches of Severus, Titus, and Constantine, was utilized as a stronghold, and many a watch tower and fortress, both in the city and in the lonely Campagna towns, was reared in the midst of or with the material of ancient buildings. The ancient quarries and clay pits and brickyards were no longer used. The vast city that once contained a million inhabitants and now was shrunk to a fifty thousand or fewer, slowly and quietly consumed itself.

In the latter part of the eleventh century, the age of the great adventures of the Normans in England and elsewhere, there occurred the famous quarrel between Pope Gregory the Seventh and the German Emperor Henry the Fourth. The Pope, besieged in the Mausoleum of Hadrian, already known for centuries as the Castello Sant' Angelo, called to his aid the Norman adventurer, Robert Guiscard, then in the south of Italy. On the 28th of May, 1084, Robert broke through the gates, rescued the Pope, and for several days burned and plundered the city. The fires completed the ruin of many areas. The concentration of the population in the Campus Martius was greater than ever now, and the outer parts of the city were left to themselves. The Aventine and Cælian became with the Palatine one great deserted area. Now for the first time the Forum was wholly abandoned, later to become known as the Campo Vaccino, the "Cattle Field," perhaps because it was a pasture, perhaps because it was a place for cattle fairs. The building of towers and strongholds was more active than ever; it was the age of the rise of the great families whose petty wars kept city and Campagna in disorder. The Colonna made the Mausoleum of Augustus one of their fortresses. The Colosseum was contested by the Frangipane, who controlled the Cælian and the Palatine Hills, and by the Anibaldi, who were supreme in the Lateran quarter. The Orsini reared a gigantic defense out of the ruins of Pompey's Theater. Rome between the eleventh and thirteenth centuries bristled with towers, and all were made of ancient material.

To make the ruin general, in these same centuries the city began again to grow. The dawn of the Renaissance had not long to wait. The twelfth century, the great building era in France and the North, was a great building century in Rome also. It is from about 1120 to 1200 that the present form of the most charming of the mediæval churches dates, with their floors in exquisite pattern of ancient colored marbles, their interior colonnades of ancient origin, their choirs and pulpits dainty with the carvings and mosaics of the Cosmati craftsmen, and their loveliest of cloisters. Much of the building consisted in restoration, but there were also new churches and palaces, and the restoration of the old was on a large scale. Every ancient marble building or monument of size was a manner of quarry, and in or near it was a kiln for burning its marbles into lime, or a stone-cutter's shop for cutting them into slabs and mosaic for the altars and pavements of churches. Ancient honorary and sepulchral inscriptions, together with those of the time, went into the composition of many a wall and floor. The famous Church of the Aracœli, once the Temple of Juno on the Capitoline, and visited by every traveller today, is approached by a broad and lofty stairway of a hundred and twenty-four steps taken from various marble monuments in 1348. Its pavement is all of marble slabs, tomb inscriptions, and mosaics in many colors; its altars and pulpits are rich with Cosmati work in ancient material; its pillars are the columns of ancient temples. Outside of Rome as well, churches in Italy, in Sardinia, and even in other lands, might have ornaments or other features consisting of Roman marble.

But we have so far taken no account of the burial of the city. How came it that the Forum was buried by thirty feet of soil and débris, and that even in the highest parts of Rome there is almost as thick a layer hiding from view the ancient levels? The answer is easy: the city buried itself. Ancient Rome was a city of palaces and tenements sixty and seventy feet in height, the greater part of them built of brick and mortar and concrete and stucco. When the centuries of decay had weakened them, and they had sunk in crumbling heaps of brick and tiles and crushed rock and stucco, and men had ceased to delve into them for the substantial

THE TIBER

ARCH OF JANUS QUADRIFRONS AND SAN GIORGIO IN VELABRO

THE SENATE HOUSE AND COLUMN OF PHOCAS

parts of their material, the winds and rains of the winter and the hot suns of summer levelled what was left into the stratum of dusty débris that mantles everywhere today the ground level of ancient times. From the buildings of Constantine about A.D. 315 to the times of Raphael and Michelangelo twelve centuries later, the great city, before and after its monuments and habitations settled into themselves, was the chief resource of the builder.

Let us look upon the city in the darkest days before the dawn of the Renaissance, the days when Petrarch was present in it and waiting to be crowned, and Cola di Rienzo was dreaming among the monuments that inspired in him the ambition to recover its lost glories. To quote from *Eternal Rome:*

The whole southern part of the city was deserted. The Palatine was a mass of grass-grown débris. The Forum was a pasture under whose sod were hidden dismantled foundations and quarries of broken blocks and mutilated columns and statues. Hills were rounded and valleys filled.

In the middle of the century, the western half of the great shell of the Colosseum had come crashing to the ground, and a mountain of travertine blocks lay at the base of the gigantic remains. Column, façade, and wall throughout the city were pitted and scarred by the tools of the searcher after the coveted clamps of metal hidden in their joints. On the crumbling foundations of concrete, stripped of their marble and useless now, shrubbery and grass were growing, and ivy mantled the great walls of bath and circus, and the marble pillars that still stood; while here and there from amid the desolate ruins of the civilization whose origin and character were an enigma to the generation that walked among its remnants, rose convent, monastery, and church, with bell-towers of brick and marble and colored stones, and rugged feudal strongholds dotting the crests and slopes of the hills.

There were waste areas even in the more densely peopled quarters, and vacant, tumble-down dwellings with staring windows stood side by side with the habitations of the noble. Eleven of the 424 churches were in ruins, 44 were without clergy, and the rest but poorly provided. The gable of the Lateran had fallen in an earthquake, and the upper half of the Torre delle Milizie. The Church of the Twelve Apostles was overthrown, Saint Paul's lay a heap of ruins, Saint Peter's stood abandoned.

When the Renaissance arrived and Rome began the more active growth from the huddled city in the Campus Martius and about St. Peter's which in the end resulted in the great capital of today, there arrived also the beginnings of respect for the ancient monuments. The use of the great buildings like the Colosseum as quarries for the churches and palaces now rising in greater numbers continued, but not without protest. With the increase of knowledge and of pride in the ruins as an ancient heritage, and especially with development of the method and spirit of science, the Romans and Italians, and the world in general, have grown so conscientious in the treatment of antiquity that every stone of ancient Rome today is little less than sacred.

V

HOW ROME WAS EXCAVATED

THE excavation of ancient Rome in the sense of mere digging began as soon as any part of the city had settled into heaps of ruin. Whoever had need of building material secured or assumed the right to delve for what he required.

When the great churches and palaces of the Renaissance began to rise, the richest supplies of marble and travertine were in the heart of the city where the monumental public buildings had stood, and where what the earlier centuries had left lay buried in thirty feet of ancient materials in dissolution. In the middle of the ninth century the little Church of Santa Maria Antiqua, at the base of the Palatine where it touches the Forum, was abandoned because the palace walls above it threatened to fall. Not long afterward they did fall, and buried the church and its surroundings with a huge mass which hid them until the first year of the twentieth century. By the twelfth century, the Forum was so filled with fallen buildings that no formal passage through it was possible. It was in the Forum and along the Sacred Way to the east that the builders of the fourteenth century found much of their material.

Digging only for material, however, is not the kind of excavation we wish to discuss. Excavation in the archæological sense is exploration by digging with the purpose of advancing our knowledge of antiquity or of adding to our possession in its material remains for purposes not wholly utilitarian. A generation ago the British explorer David Hogarth defined archæology as "the science of the treatment of the material remains of the human past." Excavation today is scientific digging for a scholarly purpose.

The rise of excavation in the scientific spirit, like the destruction of ancient monuments on a large scale for building purposes, dates from the fourteenth century. The two were not unconnected; no doubt the interest in antiquity was stimulated by the sight of the ancient material that was being dug up and sacrificed to utilitarian needs. It was in this century that material for the Lateran Church was taken from the Senate House, the Temple of Antoninus and Faustina, and the Temple of the Sacred City. In the fifteenth century, the Atrium of the Vestals and the Temple of Venus and Rome were among those to be despoiled. In 1499, an act was passed giving the rights to one-third the material recovered between the three columns of Castor and Pollux and a certain point east of them. In 1509, marbles were taken from the Temple of Vespasian and near the Arch of Severus at the west end of the Forum and from before the Temple of Antoninus and Faustina. In 1540, the Company of the Builders of Saint Peter's received the right to search the Forum. This resulted in the taking away of the staircase to the Temple of Antoninus and Faustina, many fine fragments of the columns, frieze, and cornice of the Temple of Castor and Pollux, and of the Regia and the temples of Vesta and Julius Cæsar. The years 1540-60 were especially destructive of the Forum monuments. Most of the material came from underground, and after its excavation the pits were filled again and the surface levelled, to remain undisturbed until the reëxcavations of three centuries later.

The earliest recorded interest in the remains of ancient Rome for their own sake is that of Cola di Rienzo, the enthusiast who in 1347 attempted to restore the Republic of Rome. "The whole day long he contemplated the old blocks of marble. There was no one who could read the old epitaphs as he could. He understood how to read all the old inscriptions and to explain rightly all the marble figures." Nicholas Signorili, Secretary of the Roman Senate, about 1425 wrote a work called *De Excellentiis Urbis Romae,* "On the Excellencies of the City of Rome." About 1445, Flavio Biondo wrote the first treatise on the monuments of Rome and their locations, entitled *Roma Instaurata,* "Rome Restored." The Palatine, which from the fourteenth century on was the Farnese Gardens, was the scene of careful excavation in some parts in 1535 and again in 1750.

The excavations up to 1800, however, whether in purpose or

FROM THE ARCH OF CONSTANTINE TO THE CAPITOLINE

THE THEATER OF MARCELLUS

BASILICA JULIA AND TEMPLE OF CASTOR

RUINS AND DEMOLITION NEAR THE THEATER OF
MARCELLUS

in method, were not in the strict sense scientific. The chief motive was the discovery of statuary or other objects to grace the numerous public and private collections inspired by Renaissance enthusiasm for antiquity, and the method, judged by present standards, was far from thoroughgoing. It was with the awakening of spirit everywhere at the turn of the nineteenth century that excavation began to concern itself with the discovery, identification, and preservation of the monuments strictly and only for the sake of adding to knowledge.

The Swedish ambassador to Rome, Friedenheim, the first scientific excavator of the Forum, in 1788, and the German Winckelmann, the first scientific student of ancient sculpture, whose anniversary is still an event in the archæological circle at Rome, were the leaders. From their times up to the present, there has been a long succession of famous names in the history of excavation in Rome. Carlo Fea was active from 1801 to 1815 in the Napoleonic period, excavating about the Arch of Severus, the Basilica Julia, and the Temple of Castor and Pollux, resetting the ruins of the Temple of Vespasian, and removing many of the modern buildings that covered parts of the Forum. After an interval of ten years, Nibby, Bunsen, and the architect Canina were for ten years the most prominent excavators and publishers of books on the ruins. Another interval of ten years was followed by five years of scattering effort, begun during the short-lived Roman Republic of 1848-49, after which nothing was done until the taking of Rome in 1870 and the transfer of government to the new capital in 1871.

Up to this time, the Forum had been excavated only in separate spots. Pietro Rosa, the new commissioner, 1870-78, and his successors, Giuseppe Fiorelli, excavator also of Pompeii, and Rodolfo Lanciani, from 1878 to 1885, completed for the time the laying bare of the Forum. Finally, after thirteen years of inactivity, work was resumed in 1898 under Giacomo Boni, superintendent of the Forum and Palatine up to his death in 1925, during whose administration the Forum area was extended by the excavation of the Basilica Æmilia, the temples of Julius Cæsar and Vesta, and the buildings under Santa Maria Liberatrice, a church which was expropriated and demolished in 1900. Most of the operations of the whole hundred years were the reëxcavation, for a much different purpose, of monuments and areas despoiled by the builders of centuries ago.

This brief account of Forum excavations for the six hundred years from Cola di Rienzo to the present time, like that of the excavations at Herculaneum and Pompeii, is really an epitome of modern archæology. Whether in Rome, which ranks as first in "the science of the treatment of the material remains of the human past," or in Ostia or Pompeii, or in Africa or England or Egypt, there has been the same advance from private to public control, from selfish to scientific interest, from haphazard to expert method.

VI

ANCIENT MONUMENTS AND MODERN MEN

WE have seen that the excavation of today is scientific digging with a scholarly purpose. The statement does not mean that this chief and essential purpose may not find itself associated with other aims. In Italy today two such secondary aims are allied with scholarly endeavor. The one is economic; the other, political. It may be said at once that neither the one nor the other, nor both together, interfere with or threaten the supremacy of the scholarly purpose.

Italy is a much travelled land and has always derived a revenue from the entertainment of strangers within her gates. Attracted by her art, her history, her religion, her scenery, her climate, her mode of living, and her humanity as the home of an inspired and ingenious people, for centuries the world of travel has converged on Italy as upon a goal of pilgrimage. Whatever increases her wealth in historical or æsthetic interest will swell the stream of travel and its contribution to the well-being of the land. The monuments of ancient Rome are always of historical, and frequently of æsthetic, value, and their care is therefore the part of good management. The argument may not be necessary in a land whose attractiveness it is hardly possible to enhance, but one may imagine it used with effect before the practically minded guardians of state finance.

The political argument may be quite as effective. During the past twelve years it has exercised an even stronger appeal.

It is quite true that prior to the Fascist régime the people of Italy appreciated their ancient heritage, and in their care of the monuments were actuated by profound sentiment for the past. Yet the pride of the citizen as he saw the stranger visiting the ruins of Forum and Palatine was not without the bitter reflection that the world as it contemplated the wonders of ancient Rome was insultingly careless of, if not quite unconscious of, the fact that modern Rome was the descendant of ancient Rome, and herself not unworthy of notice. To the foreigner, the glories of the ancient Romans were the bright background against which the achievements of the Rome of today appeared in dull unworthiness, if indeed they were not entirely obscured. The visitor from beyond the Alps or the sea went back home to America or England, or to almost equally Shakespearean Germany, repeating with arrogant self-satisfaction,

O what a fall was there, my countrymen!

In so far as the world's esteem of present-day Italian character was concerned, ancient Rome was almost a liability.

All this the new régime has changed. The ancient monuments and ancient Roman character are not regarded now by either citizen or stranger as of a remote and separate world. The Italian of today has been awakened to the proud consciousness that he and his State are one with the ancient Roman State, that there is no gap between Augustan Rome and the Rome of today save that of time. The ruins of Rome, wherever found, are the monuments of *his* past, of the times when *his* ancestors conquered and ruled the nations and stood for the cause of the world's advancement.

When Benito Mussolini, outraged by the civic stagnation of Italy after the war, founded in 1919 the patriot organization which by November, 1921, had attained to such importance as to meet in congress at Rome and form itself into a great national party, he called the unit of his organization a *fascio*—a "bunch," or "bundle." The movement became known as *fascismo*, its individual member as a *fascista*, its collective members as *fascisti*. To cultivated Italians whose thoughts went back to ancient Rome, these terms inevitably brought to mind the *fasces* of the Roman consul, the bundle of rods tied together about an axe and borne by his attendants, the lictors, as the symbol of his authority. It was not long before the ancient consular symbol became also the modern fascist symbol.

FASCISTI ON PARADE

THE PIAVE, VICTORY STREAM, AT BELLUNO

TEMPLE OF ANTONINUS COLUMNS AND FORUM

The rods and axe were not a symbol unknown or unused before the Fascist régime. They are to be seen on many a monument or document of nineteenth century Italy, and appear with entire innocence even on the American dime. What the Fascisti did was to recognize their appropriateness and to make them the official symbol of the forceful and authoritative new State. They made the symbol conspicuous everywhere, on uniforms and insignia, on legal documents and public notices, on monuments, on airplanes and ships, on the locomotives of the State railway system. The term *fascismo*, which originally suggested the *fascio* and the "bundle" system of patriots, suggests now the Roman *fasces* and instant obedience to the absolute and inflexible authority of the State. The greatness of ancient Rome and the duty of proving worthy of it are thus kept alive in the minds of the two million members of the Fascist party and of the citizenry in general.

The ever present and emphatic reminder of descent from ancient Rome and of the obligation it entails has put new life into many observances which hitherto were little more than idle forms. The name of ancient Rome's first naval hero, Duilius, on a battleship as *Duilio*, or of *Roma* and *Augusto* on the great transatlantic liners, is now more than a gracious historical allusion. Such reminders as the assembling of the fleet at Ostia, ancient port of Rome, or the reference to the Mediterranean as *Mare Nostrum*, "Our Sea," or the name of Libya given to the new African possessions of Tripolitania and Cyrenaica, or the numberless allusions to the ancient imperial sway of Rome throughout the Mediterranean and her mission with the ancient backward races, have been so quickened as to become inspirational. The disappointment at the award of Dalmatia to Jugoslavia after the World War was the greater because ancient Rome had conquered the region beyond the Adriatic and bestowed upon it what culture it had long before the descent of the Slavs in the seventh century after Christ. The tenacity of the Italian hold on Tripoli is all the greater because in subduing the African lands in the Eastern Mediterranean and teaching the desert to blossom as the rose the modern government in Rome is doing step by step what the ancient Roman government did eighteen centuries ago. The

name Via dell' Impero, "Avenue of the Empire," given to the
newly created thoroughfare between the Capitol and the Colosseum, is a challenge to modern Rome as well as a reminiscence
of ancient Rome. Even the pronouncement that in sixty years
Italy and Rome will be predominant in the Mediterranean world
seems to indicate the dwelling of the modern Roman mind on
ancient Roman patience and constancy to purpose: the inevitable
Roman Empire was not built in a day; the inevitable Italian
Empire must likewise have its time.

Thus it is that the care of Rome's heritage in the shape of the
ancient monuments also has taken on a new and vigorous inspiration. The scholars, artists, and educators who determine the
character of the Department of Public Instruction find it less
difficult than formerly to win support for archæological undertakings. Government is not only willing but anxious to prosecute
enterprises which by revealing the grandeur that was Rome will
stimulate the Italian citizen to greater pride and keep ever
before him the obligation to prove worthy of his ancient Roman
heritage.

We can best realize the spirit and action of Government in
Italy the past thirteen years by reviewing the archæological enterprises it has carried through. These projects have not been confined to Rome, or even to Italy, but represent also the far parts
of the ancient empire of Rome. Some of them were already under
way before the World War.

Even before the occupation of Tripoli in September, 1911, an
Italian archæological mission had made explorations in Libya.
These activities were continued with greater vigor after its conquest from Turkey and permanent occupation in 1912, but the
difficulties of pacifying the native tribes in the vast areas, together
with the uncertainties caused by the World War, and afterward
by the halting policy of the socialist Government in Rome, prevented the carrying out of any single great enterprise.

The prompt announcement of the Mussolini Government's
determination to reconquer the territory lost during the World
War and to establish Italian authority over all Libya enabled the
governors at Tripoli and Cyrene now to base their action on

settled policy. The hitherto more or less random and incomplete explorations and excavations were replaced by steady effort in greater enterprises, chief among which was the recovery of the great ruins of Leptis Magna and Sabratha from the sands to the east and west of the city of Tripoli. The clearance of gigantic remains of these cities, together with the disengagement and restoration of the Arch of Marcus Aurelius in Tripoli, and various minor enterprises elsewhere in Libya, justified Guido Calza's announcement of "the conquest of a monumental zone which not only equals, but is perhaps superior to, any other in northern Africa," and his declaration that "Latin civilization has returned, throwing light upon the past and continuing the glorious traditions of Rome."

Guido Calza, for many years superintendent of the excavations at Ostia, wrote thus in 1925 in an article entitled "Sabratha and Leptis Magna, the Glories of Roman Tripolitania." The spirit of Italian effort in the recovery and preservation of Roman monuments is well expressed in the same essay.

A city twice as large as Pompeii or Ostia, built for the most part of stone and marble, which did not have time to grow old or to wear out, and which neither time nor man could disfigure or sack, represents an *unicum* in Roman archæology. It alone may illustrate the pomp of an Empire, the generosity of an Emperor who was never forgetful of his far-away fatherland. Destiny has ordained that we Italians should bring to light this, the most brilliant gem, perhaps, which Rome has left in all Latin Africa, so rich in cities and memorials of the great central Power. All civilization will recognize and acclaim, in the monumental character of this colony, the august image of the common fatherland: *Roma communis patria.* But we must not forget that Leptis Magna represents, above all else, the heroism and sacrifice of the soldiers of Italy, for by making our tenure of it secure, they have enabled us to be the instruments of its resurrection, a glory to the Italian Government and to Italian archæology.

With these illustrations of Italian energy in the remote areas of the Mediterranean world, let us pass to the review of recent archæological activities in Italy. Outside of Rome, we shall notice important operations at Ostia, Pompeii, Herculaneum, Cumae, Pæstum, and Nemi. In the capital, we shall witness one of the century's greatest displays of vigor in the study of the monuments of Rome's past.

At Ostia the quickening of operations already long in process has resulted in the clearing out and restoration of the Roman theater, the prolongation of the excavated portion of the main street, the laying bare of the forum with the remains of its temple to Augustus and Rome, and the excavation of basilica, baths, meeting places of guilds, and other structures in the center of the city. These operations have been illuminated by studies of the ruins and the numerous inscriptions already known or recently published, which have helped to establish the character of Ostia as a busy seaport, somewhat hindered by the silting of the Tiber, whose not very wealthy population in the first and second centuries after Christ, the period of its prosperity, numbered some hundred thousand persons, largely of the working classes and including many of non-Latin blood. The installation in 1925 of the electric tram service from Rome to the resort of Ostia-by-the-Sea has made the excavations at Ostia a much visited site.

At Pompeii the steady and deliberate progress of the new excavations in the Strada dell' Abbondanza has been maintained. The character of the work there we have already described in our account of current archæological activities. An especially interesting detail in these excavations was the House of the Ephebus, so named because in it came to light, on May 25 and 26, 1925, the most important bronze statue discovered in the city for over fifty years. The figure of the Ephebus, or Greek Youth, was immediately recognized as a lamp-bearer, such as Lucretius in his poem *On Nature* (II, 24-26) describes as one of the luxuries that do not comfort the soul in travail: "The gilded images of youths through the halls, holding in their right hands the flame-bearing lamps, that lights may be supplied the feast by night." The statue was not in its original position, but had been covered by a coarse cloth and was probably in the process of attempted transfer to safety when the house was overwhelmed.

In the same house was discovered the painting of the pump called *cochlea,* or snail shell. Obscurely described by Vitruvius,

ARCH OF MARCUS AURELIUS IN TRIPOLI

TEMPLE OF AUGUSTUS IN OSTIA

THE NEW EXCAVATIONS IN HERCULANEUM

the snail-shell pump is made utterly clear by the wall painting, in which a pygmy slave operates the mechanism, shaped like a cylinder, by treading it as he steadies himself by clinging to a horizontal bar. The pump is the Archimedean screw, still to be seen in operation along the Nile, but revolved by two men using hands instead of feet. So neat a demonstration of an author's meaning as this painting affords for Vitruvius does not often occur.

In an orchard to the north of Pompeii an even more fascinating enterprise was brought to completion. This was the excavation of the Villa of Mysteries, the home of the mystic cult of Bacchus, on whose walls is painted, life size and in warm colors, a succession of scenes representing initiation into the cult. The establishment contained a great wine press and a kitchen, and was on a large scale. Nothing so important to the study of the mystery religions had ever been discovered.

Herculaneum, ten miles from Pompeii and five miles from Naples, lies forty to one hundred feet under the town of Resina. Like Pompeii, it has its old and its new excavations. The theater, discovered in 1719 eighty-five feet below the modern street, by a prince who was boring a well for the village of Resina, is the principal feature of the old excavation. At the bottom of the broad stairway leading to its chilly depths are corridors, stage, actors' rooms, and well preserved parts of the outside arcades of red painted stucco columns and pilasters. Other features of the older discoveries are to be seen in the open air—the royal excavations of fifty to a hundred years ago, reached by descending somewhat the slope where lay the ancient city, which ended suddenly at the sea. To the right of them, as one looks back from the seashore, are the new excavations, the enterprise of the Mussolini régime. Proclaimed on April 9, 1927, and begun on May 15, their plan of action included four points: (1) to make a single unified area of present and past excavations; (2) to acquire and demolish modern houses at the upper edge of the excavations and thus liberate the ancient baths; (3) to continue in that direction until the more important edifices along the main streets were uncovered; (4) to systemize the disposal of ash and soil removed from the buried city by terracing the near-by shore and making it into gardens. The erupted matter from Vesuvius has always made good soil.

The general appearance and the general procedure in the most recent diggings at Herculaneum are the same as in those at Pompeii. Wall decoration is made safe in its position; mosaics are carefully treated and protected; trees and plants are reset; fountains are fed with new waters; chambers are skilfully set in order with beds, furniture, clothes presses, and ornaments as they were left by their owners; stairways are restored to use, and even the charred planking of the folding doors is enclosed in glass and made to swing as of old. There are, however, some differences. Porticoes are more numerous than in Pompeii; houses with the gynæconitis, or women's part, suggest more emphatically the Greek tradition of the town; and because of the papyrus and bronze finds of the nineteenth century there is a livelier expectation of treasures in manuscripts and art.

Other differences are less pleasant for the excavator. Herculaneum was probably drowned in rolling waves of mingled stones and ashes and running water which reached the city as a dense and boiling or even incandescent mud, the cooling of which left an envelope of indurated matter so solid that the pneumatic drill is used to supplement the pick. This density, with a depth ranging from twice to five times that of the stratum over Pompeii, has heretofore been almost prohibitive of excavation. The very tunnels of bygone exploration are also a serious hindrance to the methods of today, threatening as they do the collapse of roof and wall and floor before their foundations can be reached and made firm.

Visitors of the past five years have found the approach to the ruins of Herculaneum a welcome change from the former narrow, sordid, and ugly streets of Resina. A dignified portal in masonry with iron chancel, flanked by the ticket window and custodian's offices, leads to an avenue 1,200 feet long and 25 feet wide between the laurel and oleander that thrive so magnificently in Italy; and before the walker as he descends the avenue are the emerging ruins of Herculaneum and the bright expanse of the Gulf of Naples.

To the west of Naples is the Virgil country. The center of interest here has been the wonders of Cumae, where from 1925 on the Grot of the Sibyl was explored and excavated, to become in 1930 one of the most inspiring monuments of the Virgil Bimillennium. This great memorial to the Sixth Book of the *Æneid*, together with the setting in order of the famous "Tomb of Virgil" in Naples, will better be described in the chapter on Virgil in Italy.

Another enterprise of the past decade in the south was the exploration at Pæstum, a site well known for its three great Greek temples. The excavations here began in 1929, and in 1931 Director Maiuri wrote of this enterprise:

In less than two years Pæstum is in a fair way to rank with Pompeii, Herculaneum, and Ostia as one of the great archæological undertakings of our time. For among all the complex monuments of Greek Italy, there was no excavation of a town to give us a more complete idea of a Greek city planned on Italian soil, of its public and private buildings, and of its ultimate history, when Italic folk replaced Greeks and were in turn replaced by Romans. Pæstum should soon fill this gap, and its excavations will rank among the most ample and complete presentations of the civilization of ancient Italy.

With these passing notices of archæological enterprise in the Naples region, let us return to the neighborhood of Rome and complete our survey of the discoveries of the past decade outside the capital by making acquaintance with one of this generation's most spirited and fascinating projects. The scene of this is the Lake of Nemi, familiar to travellers as one of the two crater lakes with which the dark-forested Alban Hills are bejewelled— the Lake of Nemi, resort of the Cæsars, three hundred feet below the crater rim, untouched and unruffled by any breeze; Nemi the *Speculum Dianae*, "Diana's Looking-glass"; Nemi, under whose waters, on the shelving side of the lake bottom near the modern village and the ruined shrine of Diana, were known to be lying two ancient ships.

Four times—in 1430, in 1535, in 1827, in 1895—has the peace of these famous boats or barges been disturbed by unsuccessful attempts to raise them from their muddy resting place fifty feet below the water level. The precious pieces of bronze ornament then salvaged were regarded as only samples of the treasures awaiting an entirely successful attempt at recovery.

Corrado Ricci, Professor of Fine Arts and counsellor of the Government, recognizing that further attempts to raise the deeply imbedded and decayed hulls would result in their continued and total destruction, in 1924 pronounced in favor of draining the lake as the only possible method. Two years afterward, acting on Ricci's advice, the Government, with the promise of money from four Roman firms and of pumping apparatus from a business house in Milan, announced its program. On October 21, 1928, the Premier himself inaugurated the work by starting the four pumps to sending daily through the ancient tunnel outlet 120,000 cubic meters of water.

The Italian press in January, 1929, reported that the level of the Lake of Nemi had been considerably lowered, and that an ancient stone border, or sort of quay, had come into view near one of the ships. At the rate of 2.6 inches per day, the original expectation was that in something like three months the tantalizing objects would be far enough disclosed to view to make their nature known—perhaps as houseboats or villas moored at the bank; or as unwieldy yachts; or even as appurtenances of the cult of Diana. Perhaps their builder would be known; would they prove the work of Caligula, or of Julius, or of Tiberius? The dimensions of the ships had been fixed by divers as 233 by 80½ feet and 210 by 60½ feet. The figures would now be verified, and some plan be devised for their conservation as material and their preservation as specimens. One sample of their wood had already been examined by the United States Forest Products Laboratory at Madison, Wisconsin, and declared spruce.

The prosecution of the Nemi enterprise was attended by doubts. The volume of water was enormous, the winter rains of Italy are copious, and Nemi might prove to be fed by abundant springs and impossible to drain. The undertaking went forward, however, and the calculations of archæologist and engineer proved correct so far as the lowering of the water level and the emergence of the ships were concerned. In early spring the prow of one boat

THE NEW EXCAVATIONS IN POMPEII

THE FIRST SHIP AT LAKE NEMI

THE SECOND SHIP AT LAKE NEMI

appeared, and by summer the greater part of it was visible. By August, 1929, about three fourths of the first ship was clear of the water. At the point where it rested, about halfway along the north side of the lake between Genzano and the town of Nemi, the usual precipitously steep bank of the lake gives way to a lower and almost flat shore at the edge of which the lake bottom consists of a broad shelf of mud some thirty feet deep. In this ooze, deeply imbedded and under many feet of water, the ship had rested through the ages, perhaps after a century or so during which it lay at anchor previous to foundering. Its timbers all rotted apart from their fastenings, it was spread out flat on the shelf of mud. Where the shelf comes to an end and the deeper water begins, the forward fifty-five feet of the ship was broken off, and lay sharply inclining toward the lake bottom. The second ship was at that time still some distance under water, further from the shore, and was expected soon to become visible.

The expectation of the public that a richly furnished ship, houseboat, or barge would be recovered, with a great wealth of treasure, was not realized. What came to light was a miserable, flattened out, scow-like wreck, and its furnishings and treasure, compared with what newspaper speculation had encouraged the world to hope for, were scant indeed.

The cause of the bare and disappointing condition of the craft was not difficult to imagine. It had lain at its moorings in antiquity until no longer of interest or value to its owners, and then, abandoned, had in the course of time been despoiled of everything attractive or useful, until finally it rotted, or was scuttled, and sank to its long repose in the mud.

There was nevertheless much to temper the world's disappointment. Specimen timbers, beautiful pieces of bronze ornament, bits of mosaic flooring, the great anchor, and fragments of mechanism including a surprisingly modern example of ball-bearings, with many minute objects of importance, were recovered, and were placed in a temporary building, to be kept on exhibition until a museum could be erected in a pleasant, garden-like spot about six hundred feet from the shore. It was planned to lay out a causeway from the ship to the museum, to refasten, reshape, and strengthen the wreck sufficiently to admit of its removal, and to rehabilitate and preserve it as the only surviving specimen of the ancient Roman ship, the symbol of Rome's one time dominion over European waters. The plan has been executed, and included the second ship also.

. VII .

THE EMPERORS WALK AGAIN

OUR survey of archæological enterprise in Italy and Italian lands has made vivid the inspirational effect of their ancient past upon the Romans of today. We shall appreciate even more thoroughly the appeal of the ancient monuments to modern men if we enter the city of Rome.

In Rome itself the archæological activities of the present Government have been so numerous and so extensive as to make the neighborhood of the Capitoline Hill, the Forum, and the Colosseum, to one who has not seen the city since 1931, all but unrecognizable.

The transformation began in 1924 with the clearing of the Forum of Augustus. The execution of this large enterprise was complete in its main lines after two years of active effort. Two years more were utilized in making secure the walls and floors and in setting in order such movable remains as architectural and sculptural fragments. Today, in addition to the mighty walls of the enclosure seen hitherto from the outside in only three fourths of their height, we may see the full hundred feet from within. In addition to the five columns hitherto visible from the street, there is to be seen the whole foundation of the giant temple of Augustus to Mars, with column fragments, the altar foundation, the ruined flight of steps, and the pedestals on them for statues now lost. In addition to the specimen of the forum pavement thirty feet from the street level, variegated by colored ancient marbles, there is visible the greater part of the area next the temple and in the large adjoining portico, with the colossal and lovely architectural fragments of an age which built both solidly and with refinement now being suggestively restored to their ancient places. There is the great stairway leading from the Forum to the higher street outside and so up the Quirinal. There is the great base near it, with the colossal bit of anatomy indicating the forty-foot statue once upon it. There are the floors of the convent which once occupied the Forum, covered with bits of sculpture, architecture, and inscriptions, all in process of ordering and study. There are the fifteenth-century rooms of the Knights of Rhodes, who lodged in these precincts, and their tasteful portals, windows, and mantels. Not least, there are the tens of thousands of marble chunks, lying as they were left hundreds of years ago, architrave and column and statue systematically broken up in preparation for the lime-burners who for some reason this time did not use their material—an impressive object-lesson in the fate of the city whose master found it brick and left it marble. With the massiveness of its members and with its towering walls, in the Forum of Augustus we have another monument in the Colosseum class to bring home to us the size and splendor of the ancient imperial capital.

The disengagement of the Forum of Augustus was not an enterprise by itself; it was but one important detail in one of the most comprehensive archæological programs of modern times. This program, advanced in 1911 by Corrado Ricci, Professor of Fine Arts, proposed nothing less than the purchase, disengagement, and excavation of all the Imperial Fora. There were five of these, laid out successively by Julius Cæsar, Augustus, Vespasian, Nerva, and Trajan. Those of Augustus and Trajan had long since been excavated in part; the other three were visible only in scant fragments. The clearing of all of them, and their union with the already excavated Great Forum into a great archæological area, was to result in an impressive monumental record of Roman history from earliest times down through the Republic and the first two centuries of the Empire. Corrado Ricci's plan, which he made and published only after minute examination of the whole area and all the modern buildings resting upon it, was accompanied by a demonstration of the comparatively little expense necessary for the purchase of the old properties covering the fora, and of the comparative ease of excavation and disengagement; but finance was difficult, the Turkish War and the World War intervened, the post-war years were chaos, and it was not

STATUE OF NERVA AND FORUM OF AUGUSTUS

STATUE AND MARKET OF TRAJAN

STATUE AND FORUM OF AUGUSTUS

until the second year of the new régime, eleven years after the scheme was published, that its execution began.

The Forum of Trajan, adjoining the Forum of Augustus on the west, was the next object of attack. Of this most magnificent of all the Imperial Fora, there was already visible the sunken area excavated by the French during their occupation of Rome more than a hundred years ago. The reërected column fragments of the Basilica and the Column of Trajan towering over them were known to everybody who had visited Rome. Between these monuments and the Forum of Augustus, the demolition and removal of the crowded tenement houses was sure to bring to light one of the great hemicycles of the Forum of Trajan, and either confirm or correct the conclusions already drawn regarding its outline.

Not only was the purpose of extending the knowledge of the area fulfilled, but there were unexpected results of great importance. Operations were begun at the southern slope of the Quirinal where it descends to the Forum of Trajan and touches it on the north side. Here, there had long been visible walls and doors of a building apparently for business purposes, to be seen by those who, whether for archæological or gastronomical gratification, penetrated to the diminutive old garden of the Ristorante Paolo Emilio and looked over its parapet down some thirty feet at a curving pavement fronted by these ruins, of which the face only was exposed, the building itself being hidden in and under the masses of modern construction that began here to mount the hill. The few who discovered the place remembered with exquisite pleasure the garden, scarcely large enough for forty guests, with its cheerful colored lamps among laurel, oleander, and ivy, and its monumental silence and calm under the stars—a deep well among the tall tenement houses, beyond which, unheard and unseen, though not far away, was the noisy turmoil of the city.

Before these few visible ruins, then supposed to belong in some way to a hemicycle of Trajan's Forum, could be understood, vast operations were necessary. The garden had to be excavated, and this revealed part of the area built upon by Trajan. The tall modern tenements had to be demolished. Beyond, to the north, there was the vast hulk of a soldiers' barracks, formerly the Con-

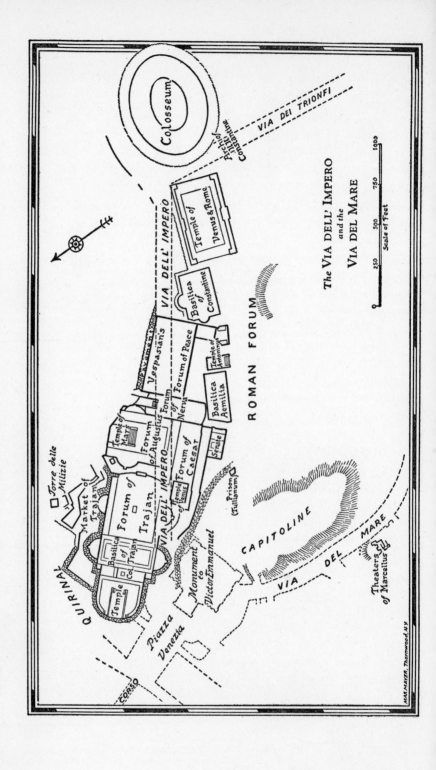

The VIA DELL' IMPERO
and the
VIA DEL MARE

Scale of Feet
0   250   500   750   1000

Colosseum

VIA DEI TRIONFI

Arch of Constantine

Temple of Venus & Rome

VIA DELL' IMPERO

Basilica of Constantine

Temple of Antoninus

ROMAN FORUM

Pavement

Forum of Vespasian's

Forum of Peace

Forum of Nerva

Basilica Aemilia

Temple of Mars

Forum of Augustus

Forum of Caesar

Senate

Temple of Venus

Prison (Tullianum)

Torre delle Milizie

Market of Trajan

Forum of Trajan

VIA DELL' IMPERO

Basilica of Col. Trajan

CAPITOLINE

QUIRINAL

Temple

Monument to Victor Emmanuel

VIA   DEL   MARE

Piazza Venezia

Theaters of Marcellus

CORSO

MAX MAYER, Thornwood, N.Y.

vent of Santa Caterina, and the School of the Principessa Jolanda, flanking the mediæval and long unused street known as Via Biberatica, which led from the Forum of Augustus over the end of the Quirinal to where the Via Nazionale now descends. In and under these buildings and this street, it was known both from the above-mentioned ruins and from Renaissance drawings of ample structures rising here previous to the barracks, and previous also to the Convent of Santa Caterina in which the barracks lodged, that important discoveries were likely to be made.

On April 21, 1926, the birthday of Rome, formal announcement of the project was made. Its prosecution was directed by the commission that had in charge also the disengagement of the Forum of Augustus which had begun on the birthday of Rome two years before. The president of this commission was Corrado Ricci, and its membership included Rodolfo Lanciani. The operations thus inaugurated yielded some of the great surprises of this generation.

The first surprise was that the curved pavement and façade so long known in the restaurant garden were not a part of Trajan's Forum, but that the paved street was a thoroughfare at the outside of that area, and separated it from a gigantic business block or section of which the brick façade representing the curved row of shops was the first part. The next surprise was to find that this business complex was a titanic pile climbing the end of the Quirinal Hill in a succession of curving terraces, all fronted by curving rows of business places, including one great covered hall, bazaar, or gallery in two stories. There have been distinguished seven of these tiers or terraces, rising in recession until the last tier, on a level with the summit of the famous Column of Trajan, commanded a marvellous prospect over the Forum.

Nothing like this in illumination of the commercial life of imperial Rome had ever come to light. Here, in the two hundred or more shops of this emporium in the grand style at the heart of ancient Rome, were once exposed the silks and rugs, the purples and the fine linen, the jewels and the perfumes, the rare spices and the fine wines of Roman times—the wares of an Empire come from every distant part, especially from

> Where the gorgeous East with richest hand
> Showers on her kings barbaric pearl and gold,

to its capital city. Here the fashions were displayed and set. Hither, in their sedans and with their trains of slaves, came the wealthy élite for their shopping, with the greater multitudes of the middle class. These terraced streets, these glittering shops, the great covered bazaar, and the monumental stairways mounting from curved story to story, alive and alight in the golden mornings of ancient Rome, were the swarming, sounding hive of the commercial commonwealth.

If we ask who it was that built thus in the grand style for the big business of Rome, and in what circumstances, the best answer will be that the Emperor Trajan was the builder, and that the lofty pile sustains a relation with the Forum of the Optimus Princeps. Bordering on and overhanging as it does the Forum, equalling in height the Column erected, as its inscription records, to declare the height of the hilly terrain which had to be removed for the achievement of the Forum enterprise, the market was planned and executed anterior to the Forum as a compensation to business for the area lost to it by the construction of the largest of the Imperial Fora.

Together with the work on the great Market of Trajan went the disengagement of the adjacent hemicycles and the giant fragments of the Forum. These operations and the setting in order of the Forum of Augustus called for the expenditure of much time and money, and there were still to think of the fora of Julius Cæsar, Vespasian, and Nerva, before Corrado Ricci's plan, the creation of the monumental promenade or zone connecting the Piazza Venezia and the Forum Romanum, could be realized. Italy is not a rich country—except in monuments and men—and has never found it possible, without painful sacrifice, to maintain the ideal attitude toward its art and antiquities. Yet the archæological program was not only not contracted, but was expanded.

The two thousandth anniversary of Virgil's birth, which was to occur in 1930, was a stimulus to the already lively ambition of the Government. The dark recesses of the Mausoleum of Augustus were explored, and the burial chambers identified and set in

THE FORUM OF AUGUSTUS

THE MARKET OF TRAJAN

VIA DEL MARE AND THE CAPITOLINE HILL

order; the "Tomb of Virgil" in Naples was disengaged and made accessible in tasteful surroundings; the Grot of the Sibyl at Cumae was cleared, and a beautiful avenue of oleanders planted to form the ideal approach; and in addition to these undertakings the much greater enterprise of clearing the Capitoline Hill was begun.

The disengagement of the Capitoline soon grew into a major undertaking. The decaying habitations of recent centuries that skirted the base of the famous hill were demolished and removed. The Theater of Marcellus, at last cleared of the miserable shops long lodged in its dark arcades, was now excavated to its foundations, strengthened by masonry, and set apart as one more of the capital's most impressive monuments. The old Piazza Montanara and its almost mediæval surroundings disappeared and gave way to airy freedom. Broad avenues on three sides and the Forum on the fourth, with spacious landscape gardens along the slopes that flank the thoroughfares, have set the hill apart as a sightly monument of the city's great historic periods. The colossal monument to Victor Emmanuel II of Savoy and Sardinia, first king of United Italy, forming its façade to the north, and embracing within its precincts the Tomb of the Unknown Soldier and the Altar of the Nation, has taken a surer place as the heart of Rome and Italy. The Church of the Aracœli loftily flanking it at the head of the magnificent staircase of marble already ancient six hundred years ago when it was taken from the ruins of the Forum, has been a part of the Roman's religious experience from the time it succeeded the temple to pagan Juno through all the Christian centuries. The Palace of the Conservators, the Capitoline Museum, and the Palace of the Senator, centering about the square in which the philosophic Emperor sits his famous horse from generation to generation, make the old Piazza del Campidoglio the peer of San Marco in Venice and the Signoria and Duomo in Florence. The foundations of Jupiter Optimus Maximus, the rugged remainder of the Tabularium, the primeval wall fragments of earliest Rome, and the wealth of museum antiquities, are memorials of the time when the hill was the visible center and head of the Roman world.

Among the beautiful results of the isolation of the Capitoline is the avenue in the grand style now skirting the west side of the Capitoline. It has been given the name of Via del Mare, the Road to the Sea. Originating in Piazza Venezia, it passes the Victor Emmanuel Monument, the great stairway of the Aracœli and the broad approach to the Piazza del Campidoglio, runs between the Theater of Marcellus and the garden slopes of the hill, and continues through the gardens and temple areas of Bocca della Verità along the Tiber and past the Aventine until it leaves the city at Porta San Paolo and becomes the magnificent special highway to Ostia Excavations and Ostia-by-the-Sea.

Ambitious as was the segregation of the Capitoline and the inauguration of the Via del Mare, there remained an enterprise of even greater magnitude. This comprised the wrecking and removal of the still remaining solid blocks of houses in the old quarter between the fora of Trajan and Augustus and the Capitoline Hill and Great Forum, the clearing of the Forum of Julius Cæsar and the Clivus Argentarius, the completion of excavation in Trajan's Forum, and the cutting of a great avenue straight from Piazza Venezia to the Colosseum, there to connect with the thoroughfare running south from the Arch of Constantine, between the Palatine and the Cælian, through the great gardens of the Archæological Promenade, with the Baths of Caracalla on the right, out of the Porta San Sebastiano, and away to the Alban Mount, recently made accessible by an automobile road to the summit. The newly created thoroughfare between Piazza Venezia and the Colosseum was to be called Via dell' Impero, Empire Avenue. From the Arch of Constantine it was to be Via dei Trionfi, Avenue of Triumphs, and in its total length the Via del Monte, the Road to the Mount.

The execution of this vast scheme was to be completed by the 28th of October, 1932, the date marking the end of the first decade of the Fascist régime. When operations were begun in the autumn of 1931, it was unbelievable that so gigantic an enterprise could be completed in the space of one year. The projected avenue was a full half mile long. Its bordering blocks of old tenements had to be razed and the huge mountains of débris removed, and not only wreckage but a vast ridge of native soil between the Basilica of Constantine and the Colosseum had to be excavated and carried away by tram. The Basilica and other monuments had to be repaired and strengthened, the fora of Julius Cæsar, Nerva, and Vespasian had to be explored, the environment where the avenue left Piazza Venezia and the Victor Emmanuel Monument had to be made æsthetically fit, and the avenue in its whole course had to be embellished with gardens.

The colossal undertaking was carried out with spirit and precision. All through the autumn and winter the wreckers, excavators, engineers, architects, archæologists, mechanics, and builders were steadily at work. On April 21, 1932, the birthday of Rome, the Forum of Julius Cæsar was opened to the public. What had hitherto been visible only in a few stone arches in the walls of an alley, was now brought to light in a third or more of its extent as a monumental enclosure bordered and occupied by shops and other business places and containing the great Temple of Venus Genetrix, ancestress and guardian deity of the Julian line. Because the great Via dell' Impero crossed the Forum of Julius, not all its area could be freed, and for the same reason parts of the fora of Augustus, Trajan, Nerva, and Vespasian remain for the present unexposed, though not unexplored.

The Via dell' Impero was formally declared open, according to plan, on the 28th of October. A great procession in the manner of a Roman triumph trod the new pavement from Colosseum to Capitol. At the head of the cavalcade rode Premier Mussolini, between his Head of the Militia and the Minister of War.

Thus, after more than twenty years, was realized the dream of excavating and setting in order the fora of the emperors. The visitor to Rome today, as he walks the length of Empire Avenue, may look from the balustrade upon some portion of the pavements, temples, basilicas, and porticoes of the five imperial fora which, with Hadrian's colossal Temple of Venus and Rome, the Great Forum, and the towering temples and palaces rising on the adjacent Capitoline and Palatine, made the center of Rome in the second century of the Christian era an architectural scene of a brilliance and richness unrivalled before or since in any city of the world. And as he looks, before him in the precincts once the objects of their special care stand the statues of the imperial builders—Julius, Augustus, Vespasian, Nerva, Trajan—their commanding presences lending reality to what remains of the grandeur that was Rome.

Nor did the activities of the Government cease with the achievement of this colossal undertaking. The year 1933 saw the completion of its details, and 1934 was marked by operations in the Circus Maximus whose termination was celebrated on October 28, the twelfth anniversary of the Fascist rise to power. On the 22d, Premier Mussolini had delivered the first strokes of the pick in the projected demolition of the hundred or more rotten tenements clustered about and against the Mausoleum of Augustus. The disengagement of the famous tomb and its inauguration as a distinguished national monument form one of the chief projects for 1935, which has already seen the tasteful and impressive reordering of the colossal remnants of Hadrian's Temple of Venus and Rome.

VIA DELL' IMPERO IN PROCESS, AUGUST, 1932

VIA DELL' IMPERO, NOVEMBER, 1932

VIA DELL' IMPERO, WITH FORA OF JULIUS AND AUGUSTUS

ARCH OF CONSTANTINE AND VIA DEI TRIONFI

. VIII .

THE STUDY OF ANCIENT ROME

THERE are two bodies of knowledge that enter into an acquaintance with ancient Rome. One is the knowledge of its material character; that is, of its monuments and their location. This is usually known as the science of Topography and Monuments. The other is the knowledge of Roman Life; that is, the use to which the buildings were put, the appearance, actions, and character of the people who used them, and their collective as well as individual actions and character. These two bodies of knowledge should not as they are acquired remain separate in our minds, but should blend into an appreciation such as that we have of our own times in our own city or country.

Our purpose in this chapter shall be to account for the existence of these two bodies of knowledge. How have we come to know so much about Rome and the Romans?

Our knowledge of the material side of Rome is gained from two classes of evidence. There are the sources contemporary with the ancient city, and there is the witness contributed by later times.

First among the ancient sources are naturally the monuments themselves. We know of Rome and Pompeii in their material aspect because we have actually found them. We know that people perished in Pompeii, and we know of the Roman Forum, and of temple, basilica, and tomb, because we have them before our eyes. Some of the monuments, like the arches of Titus and Severus in Rome, tell us plainly themselves with their inscriptions what they are; others, like the arch called Constantine's, tell us obscurely; still others, like the temples and palaces on the Palatine, tell us only of their class.

Inscriptions form a second source. Besides those which are actually a part of the buildings they identify, there are many which are separate from them. The inscription on an altar or pedestal may identify the statue of the deity or public man once standing on it; the marking on a milestone may identify the Appian Way; the brick stamp, a private house. The great inscription of Augustus at Ancyra, recording among his many achievements the Emperor's restoration of eighty-two temples in Rome, gives many a hint as to where the temples stood.

Thirdly, there are multitudes of coins which bear the design, or even the verbal mention, of temples, arches, bridges, roads, or other construction done by emperors and public men. A coin of Vespasian makes it clear that the Colosseum had a fourth story, though it is thought to have been of wood. Another coin shows that the Temple of Jupiter Optimus Maximus was of the Corinthian order.

Fourthly, the sculptures tell not only of themselves, but frequently of other monuments. A relief on the Arch of Constantine displays the Rostra on a state occasion. The reliefs on the famous Balustrades in the Forum are a picture of the Forum and its buildings in the time of Trajan. The tomb relief of the Haterii in the Lateran Museum proves that a shrine to the Great Mother once existed at the north border of the Palatine.

Fifthly, the ancient mosaics, paintings, and stucco designs are sometimes helpful. Pompeii contains many illustrations of this; among them, the painting which shows the Pompeians and the people of Nuceria rioting in the amphitheater. In Rome, examples are rarer; but the paintings in the tombs of Viale Manzoni are thought to show the Tiber and parts of the city, and those in the House of Livia tell something of window and balcony in the private house.

Sixthly, the marble map of the city called the Capitoline Plan, or *Forma Urbis Romae*, must be mentioned. This was a design of the city on the scale of about 1 to 250, with the top representing south instead of north, incised in marble affixed to a wall which fronted on Vespasian's Forum of Peace, and containing the great public buildings of the city with their names. In the ruin of the city, the Plan went down in hundreds of fragments and was buried. In May and June, 1562, the greater part of them were found, and became the possession of the Farnese family. About ten years afterward ninety-two of the largest were reproduced in drawings, a first edition of the Plan was published in 1673, and in 1742 the fragments were placed on the walls of the main stairway in the Capitoline Museum. Other fragments were discovered in 1867, and at several other times up to 1901—some behind the Farnese Palace, some in a house wall, nearly two hundred in the Tiber embankment, several hundreds at the base of the original wall, and some four hundred in the Great Forum. There are now about two thousand fragments, most of them very small, and most of

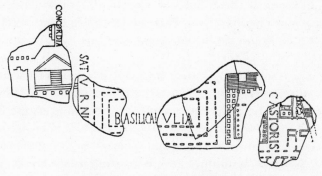

FRAGMENTS OF THE MARBLE PLAN

Numbers 2 and 3 represent B[asilica I]ulia. Number 2 shows that the Temple of Saturn was on the left of the Basilica, numbers 3 and 4 that the Temple of Castor and Pollux was at its right. Number 1 represents the Temple of Concordia.

the larger ones unidentified. They have been fitted together, so far as possible, like a great picture puzzle, and are now to be seen on the north wall of the garden of the Palazzo dei Conservatori on the Capitoline, a reproduction in the original dimensions.

The Marble Plan has been of great service in the study of topography and monuments. One irregular fragment, for example, displays parts of the lines of two buildings with a street between them, and shows on one the letters VRNI, and on the other, B. A second fragment also shows parts of two buildings with a street between them, with VLI and part of A on one of them. As the lines of the two fragments correspond, the B and VLIA are to be read as B[ASILICA I]VLIA, and the VRNI as [SAT]VRNI; the whole thus helping to identify the south side of the Forum as containing the Temple of Saturn, the Basilica Julia, and the Temple of Castor and Pollux. The steps of the last are drawn with an altar in their midst.

Seventhly, there are the ancient writers. They range from 200 B.C. to A.D. 400, and from poet and essayist to antiquarian and guide-book author. The poem and essay, and literature in general, tell us of specific buildings only by accident. Horace, for example, saunters on the Sacred Way and at ten o'clock comes to the Temple of Vesta; Cicero tells us his house is on the Palatine, and, by reference to the Temple of Salus as Atticus' neighbor, that his friend's house is at the end of the Quirinal; Propertius describes the Temple of Apollo on the Palatine; Pliny in a letter refers to his residence on the Esquiline; Ovid takes us walking with him from the Forum up the Sacred Way and conducts us to the Palatine. Of the less literary, Varro, the erudite friend of Cicero, has much about the Regions of the city in his treatise *On the Latin Tongue*; Pliny the Elder is evidence on walls and gates; Festus, author of a lexicon called *On the Signification of Words,* contains odd bits of information on Forum, Palatine, and other names denoting places or buildings; and there are the famous *Regionary Catalogues.*

These last documents are the *Curiosum,* or *Notable Things of the Fourteen Regions of the City of Rome*, dating about A.D. 357, and the *Notitia,* or *What to Know in Rome,* written within twenty-three years before the *Curiosum,* which is a revision of it; both being from a common original of A.D. 312-315. They contain, in not altogether clear order, the number and name of each region or ward of the city, the names of its noteworthy buildings, and statistics as to the number of stores, baths, street fountains, bakeries, bridges, basilicas, libraries, obelisks, etc., in some cases with their names. Many buildings and monuments recorded in these documents are no longer to be found. The *Curiosum* and *Notitia* are sometimes referred to as the *Constantinian Catalogues.*

If we pass now to later sources, we find certain mediæval documents of great interest. Foremost among them is the *Einsiedeln*

SUSPENDED FLOOR OF THE FLAVIAN PALACE

AN INSCRIPTION IN THE HOUSE OF THE VESTALS

TEMPLE AREA NEAR THE ARGENTINE THEATER

AN AUGUSTAN AND A LATER INSCRIPTION

Itinerary, a work compiled by a monk of the eighth century and preserved in the monastery of Einsiedeln in Switzerland, containing the names of monuments along eleven different routes through the city, with the first known collection of Latin inscriptions. Some of the inscriptions are no longer to be seen, and some are more complete in the *Itinerary* than they are at present. The ruins of the Temple of Vespasian at the west end of the Forum, for example, show now only ESTITVER; but when the *Itinerary* was written enough of the frieze remained to show a great deal more:

DIVO VESPASIANO AVGVSTO S.P.Q.R.

IMPP. CAESS. SEVERVS ET ANTONINVS PII FELICES
AVGG. RESTITVER[VNT]

To the Divine Vespasian Augustus, the Senate
and Roman People [Erected]

The Emperors, Cæsars Severus and Antoninus, Devoted, Fortunate,
August, Restored

This shows not only that the temple front was in a more complete state in the eighth century, but also that it was a temple to Vespasian and that it was restored by Septimius Severus and his son more than a century after its erection by the Senate and Roman people.

A century before the *Einsiedeln Itinerary*, or about 648-52, there had been written a work entitled *On the Number of Gates and the Saints of Rome*, compiled from an earlier work. The gates are those of the Wall of Aurelian, whose towers and other parts are enumerated, and the description appears also at the end of the *Itinerary* manuscript. It is later given by William of Malmesbury, 1126, in his book on the English kings.

In the twelfth century, Benjamin of Tudela, a Jewish visitor from Spain, wrote of the city and its wonders, not without marvellous tales to account for what he saw. In the same century, about 1150, a description of the city called *Mirabilia Romae, The Marvels of Rome*, was compiled by an unknown writer. It contains lists of the monuments by classes, a number of legends, and an account of monuments seen in a promenade from Saint Peter's into the city and back. The legends are entitled: "The Vision of the Emperor Octavian and the Answer of the Sibyl"; "The Marble Horse"; "The Horse Called Constantine's"; "Why the Pantheon Was Built"; "Why Octavian Was Called Augustus and Why the Church of Saint Peter Is Called 'In Chains'." Much from previous guide-books entered into the first part of this work. The *Graphia Aureae Urbis Romae, A Description of the Golden City of Rome,* is a later form of *The Marvels.* Francis Morgan Nichols's quaint translation of these mediæval works in *The Marvels of Rome,* London, 1889, is a charming book, as will be seen from a few specimens.

The first is from Benjamin of Tudela. "Rome," it begins, "is divided into two parts by the river of Tiber, the one part being on one side, the other part on the other. In the first is a right great temple, that is called Saint Peter's of Rome; and there also is the palace of the great Julius Cæsar; and there, moreover, are full many buildings and works, the like whereunto are not in the world. And around the part of Rome wherein men dwell, are spread out twenty and four miles of ruins." The "palace of the great Julius Cæsar" here mentioned was probably the ruin of Caligula's Circus near the old Saint Peter's, a ruin which disappeared at the building of the present church.

Another is from one of the legends. "In the times of the Consuls and Senators," we are told, "the Prefect Agrippa, with four legions of soldiers, subjugated to the Roman Senate the Suevians, Saxons, and other western nations. Upon whose return the bell of the image of the kingdom of the Persians, that was in the Capitol, rang. For in the temple of Jupiter and Moneta in the Capitol was an image of every kingdom of the world, with a bell about his neck, and as soon as the bell sounded, they knew that the country was rebellious. The priest therefore that was on watch in his week, hearing the sound of the bell, shewed the same to the Senators."

In the *Graphia,* this is how the story of Rome's founding begins: "After the sons of Noah built the Tower of Confusion, Noah with his sons entered into a ship, as Hescodius writeth, and came unto Italy. And not far from the place where now is Rome, he founded a city of his own name; wherein he brought his travail and his life to an end."

The Renaissance sources are naturally much more numerous, though farther removed from antiquity and often less direct. Cola di Rienzo's collection of inscriptions, given in Signorili's *Excellencies of Rome,* has already been mentioned, and also Flavio Biondo's *Rome Restored.* When Poggio Bracciolini wrote his *Description of the Ruins of the City of Rome,* about 1430, the now bare and unattractive ruins of the baths of Caracalla and Diocletian still had their pillars and coatings of marble. Pomponius Lætus, in the same century, a professor in the University of Rome, was moved to tears as he contemplated the ruins of the ancient city. Pius the Second, Æneas Sylvius, 1458-64, noted everything ancient as he travelled. Scholars and literary men of the time wrote in Latin, were enamored of antiquity, and left much in their works to illuminate for a later day the state of Rome in the Renaissance. "Cast the eye over the other hills of the city," writes Poggio in his work *On the Variableness of Fortune;* "you will see them all empty of buildings and filled with ruins and vineyards." Pomponius Lætus had a vineyard on the Quirinal and a cottage and garden on the Esquiline.

Besides the scholars and literati of the Renaissance, there were many architects and artists whose drawings and paintings are frequently of great service as evidence of some monument later fallen into further ruin or wholly disappeared. Marten van Heemskerck, a Dutch visitor who lived 1498-1574, left many sketches preserving for us the appearance of the Forum monuments and others. The Forum in 1575 may be seen in the engraving of Étienne Dupérac. Piranesi, 1720-78, made free-spirited engravings of many famous ruins. The architects who made drawings of the ruins include Sangallo, Brunelleschi, Palladio, and Peruzzi, whose drawings of the Mausoleum of Augustus are in the Uffizi Gallery at Florence.

Such are the sources with which the scholar of today works in his efforts to reconstruct for us the ancient city of Rome. The results of his labors are seen in an extensive literature in many languages. In English, they are best exemplified in the American

Samuel Ball Platner's *Topography and Monuments of Ancient Rome,* published in 1904 and revised in 1911, and in *A Topographical Dictionary of Ancient Rome,* 1929, another work by Professor Platner, not finished at his death in 1921, and completed and revised by the late Thomas Ashby, the foremost British authority on Ancient Rome, author of *The Roman Campagna in Classical Times* and many monographs on Roman subjects.

Thus far we have considered the study of material Rome—the discovery, identification, description, and care of buildings. It remains to say something of the sources of our knowledge of Roman history and Roman life.

Our modern histories of Rome, and our systematic treatises on Roman life, are written in greatest part from literary sources. For the Republic, which has been most written of, there are Livy, Cæsar, Cicero, and Nepos among the Latin writers, and, among the Greek, Polybius, Dionysius of Halicarnassus, Diodorus Siculus, Plutarch, and Appian of Alexandria; for the Empire, Tacitus and the Plinys, Suetonius, the biographer of the first century of emperors, Spartianus and later biographers, Ammianus Marcellinus, and the Christian Fathers. The data for the various topics of Roman life are extracted from the same authors, and from Catullus, Lucretius, Virgil, Ovid, Martial, Petronius, Seneca, Juvenal, and Apuleius. The writers who give us the greatest sense of familiarity with actual living among the Romans are Horace in his satires and epistles, Cicero and Pliny in their letters, Martial and Juvenal in epigram and satire, Suetonius in biography, and Petronius and Apuleius in the novel.

These authors, and others in less degree, were in former times almost exclusively the sources for Roman history and Roman life. As archæology developed, however, the literary sources were more and more supplemented. Every building excavated added to the reality of life, and many added to the facts of history. The coins and inscriptions incidental to the main discoveries con- tributed the face and the record of many an important citi- zen. The thousands of small objects—pottery, kitchen utensils, hairpins, jewelry, safety pins, razors, weapons, bits of clothes and shoes, lamps, fragments of food, surgical instruments, styluses—suggested the hands that once had held them, and the consciousnesses that guided the hands. Paintings and sculptures in relief and in the round made clearer not only the ancient feeling for art, but contributed many a living scene: the sacrifice at the altar, the mystic dance in honor of Bacchus, the shepherdess and fisherman, the emperor addressing his troops and staff, the dog at the house door, the warship in action, the poet reciting his verses, the actor rehearsing the scene, the soldier marching to war and engaging in all its operations, the girl at her mother's side, little boys at play, the bride and groom at the wedding, the orator haranguing the people, vintagers gathering grapes and pressing out the wine, the shoemaker at his bench.

The result of this use of archæology has been a greater reality in the more recent works on Rome, of which the greatest are Michael Rostovtzeff's monumental *Rome* and *The Social and Economic History of the Roman Empire.* The history of the Roman world is no longer the unappealing account of battles and politics, prefaced by the formal repetition of the legends of the Greek immigration and the Seven Kings, but the narrative of a people going about the affairs of life in the same environment and with the same movements and the same feelings as those of modern times.

. IX .

THE CICERO COUNTRY

THE moment the reader of Virgil and Horace sets foot on Italian shores or descends from the Alps into Italian fields, he begins to recognize the trees, the plants, the animals, the mountains and streams and valleys and plains, that so appealed to him in Virgilian line and Horatian stanza. In spite of their stately artificialities, the *Eclogues* and the *Georgics* are warm with the realities of Italy; and to look through Horace's eyes is to glimpse a thousand sunny scenes in country and town. Virgil and Horace are poets, and poets who felt the charm of their native land.

Cicero does not permeate the Italian landscape as the poets do. Born in the country, Cicero still was a man of the town. He was an orator, not a poet, a man who associated much with men and little with nature. His presence in Italy is felt most not in the landscape, but among the ruins of Rome and in the haunts of men.

The first place of Ciceronian interest to one who enters Italy from the Alps is the neighborhood of Florence. On a hill three miles north of the city lies Fiesole, ancient Fæsulae, the place where Manlius and the followers of Catiline awaited the arrival of their leader from Rome; *in faucibus Etruriae,* Cicero describes it, "in the passes of Etruria," meaning that it was a commanding position on the great route leading to Cisalpine Gaul. There are still to be seen at Fiesole the remains of an Etruscan wall and a Roman theater and baths. To enhance the interest of a visit to them, at the foot of the beautiful hill on which the town is situated lies the monastery in which, five hundred years ago, lived Fra Angelico of Fiesole.

Twenty-one miles to the northwest of Florence is Pistoia, the ancient Pistoria, near which the battle was fought in which Cati-

THE MULVIAN BRIDGE

TEMPLE OF JUPITER STATOR

THE ARPINO COUNTRY

THE LIRIS AND THE CITADEL OF SORA

line lost his cause and his life. "Catiline himself," writes Sallust, "was found far in advance of his men, among the dead bodies of the enemy. He was not quite breathless, and still expressed in his countenance the fierceness of spirit which he had shown during his life."

Catiline left Rome by the Via Aurelia, which led from the Æmilian Bridge past San Crisogono up and over the Janiculum near the American Academy, beyond which the highway still bears the name of Via Aurelia Antica. The road reached the sea about twenty miles west of Rome, thence following the coast on the way to Genoa, Marseilles, and the Rhône. Catiline may have followed it to Pisa and then turned eastward up the Arno valley, thus travelling the line of the Rome-Pisa and Pisa-Florence railway divisions of today.

In Rome, the center of Ciceronian interest is the Roman Forum. About three hundred yards from its east end, where the Sacred Way leading out of it is joined by the Clivus Palatinus descending from the Palatine, are the foundations of the Temple of Jupiter Stator, in which Cicero delivered the *First Oration against Catiline*.

Do you feel no fear as you see the guarding of the Palatine by night, no fear as you see the watches throughout the city, as you see the terror of the people and the banding together of all good citizens, as you see this strongly defended place of holding the Senate, as you see the looks on the countenances of those present?

This was on November 8, 63 B.C. On the 9th, from the Rostra in front of the Senate House, at the northwest corner of the Forum, the *Second Oration* was delivered, announcing to the people that Catiline had left the city, and inviting his friends to follow:

One thing I will concede them even yet: let them go forth, let them set out, lest they allow Catiline to pine in misery for lack of them. I will show them the road he took; he left by the Via Aurelia. If they are willing to hurry, they will overtake him by evening.

There are no clearly identifiable remains of the Rostra from which this oration was delivered. It was the platform from which

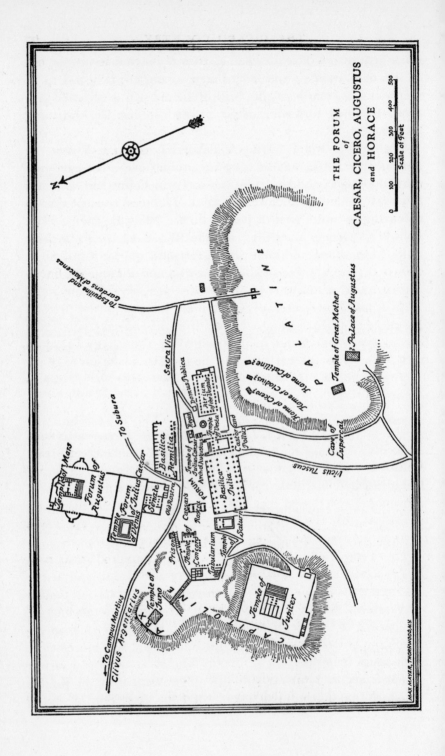

THE FORUM
of
CAESAR, CICERO, AUGUSTUS
and HORACE

Scale of Feet
0   100   200   300   400   500

MAX MAYER, THORNWOOD, N.Y.

To Esquiline and
Gardens of Maecenas

Sacra Via

Temple of Great Mother

Palace of Augustus

P A L A T I N E

Home of Catiline?

Home of Clodius?

Home of Cicero?

Cave of
Lupercal

Vicus Tuscus

Domus Publica

Atrium
Vestae

Temple
of the
Vestals

Temple of
Julius Caesar

Arch of Augustus

Castor and
Pollux

Basilica
Aemilia

Temple of
Julius Caesar

Basilica
Julia

Senate

Rostra

To Subura

Forum
of Augustus

Forum
of Julius Caesar

Temple
of Venus

Temple of Mars

Caesar's
Rostra

Prison

Temple of
Concord

Tabularium

Temple of
Saturn

C A P I T O L I N E

Temple of
Jupiter

Temple of
Juno

Clivus Argentarius

To Campus Martius

many generations of orators had addressed the Roman people, but in less than twenty years from Cicero's consulship it was to be removed and rebuilt at the head of the Forum a hundred feet away. This new Rostra was about 75 feet long, 30 feet wide, and 10 feet high.

The *Third Oration* also was delivered from the Rostra, on December 3. In the middle of the preceding night, the envoys of the Allobroges, with the conspirator Titus Volturcius, who was conducting them with incriminating dispatches in their possession to Catiline's camp, were captured at the Mulvian Bridge. The Pons Mulvius spanned the Tiber on the Via Flaminia about three miles to the north of Rome, and large parts of it are still to be seen in the modern Ponte Milvio, long known as Ponte Molle.

Cicero tells of the part played by his men, who without delay

undertook the matter, and at fall of evening secretly went out to the Mulvian Bridge, and there stationed themselves in two parties in the nearest farm buildings, so that the Tiber and bridge were between them. . . . At about three o'clock in the morning, as the envoys of the Allobroges with a large party, and with Volturcius in their company, were already beginning to advance over the Mulvian Bridge, a rush upon them was made.

At a meeting of the Senate called by Cicero as soon afterward as possible in the Temple of Concord, the dispatches were read, Volturcius turned State's evidence, and Lentulus, Cethegus, Gabinius, and Statilius, confronted by these testimonies, were proven guilty. It was at the close of the session, which lasted most of the day, that Cicero appeared on the Rostra and in the *Third Oration* informed the people of what had happened.

The Temple of Concord was less than a hundred yards west of the Rostra, at the northwest corner of the Forum and at the base of the Capitoline Hill. It was three hundred years old, though once rebuilt, having been erected in 367 B.C. to commemorate the passing of the Licinian Laws and the temporary concord between the orders. Owing to the surroundings, it was much wider than usual in proportion to depth. The great mass of concrete which served as foundation is still to be seen, with the marble threshold and a few fragments of the floor. A section of one of the world's most magnificent cornices, preserved in the Tabularium near by, belongs to it, and also a capital in the Berlin Museum.

On December 5, the next day but one, at a meeting of the Senate in which Cicero, Consul-elect Silanus, Cæsar, and Cato were the chief speakers, the four conspirators already named, with a fifth named Ceparius, were voted deserving of death.

Cicero's speech was the *Fourth Oration:*

I see that up to the present moment there are two opinions: one, that of Decimus Silanus, who moves that the men guilty of this attempt to destroy the State be punished by death; the other, that of Gaius Cæsar, who is not for applying the death penalty, but one which includes all the severities of all other punishments. Now, conscript fathers, I see where my interest lies. If you act according to Gaius Cæsar's recommendation, inasmuch as he has always stood in public matters for what is regarded as the people's interest, perhaps with him as advocate and sponsor of our vote I shall have less reason to fear the attacks of the people; but if you act according to the other recommendation, I shall probably be involved in greater difficulty. But, even so, let any regard for my safety yield to the welfare of the State.

The speech of Cato in favor of the death penalty decided the vote. The five conspirators were executed the same evening by strangling in the Tullianum, the rock chamber which since its establishment by Ancus Martius, the fourth king, had served as dungeon for those condemned to death. It was just across the street that ascended the Capitoline to the north of the Temple of Concord, and consisted of an upper and a lower chamber, the latter having been perhaps a spring house in origin.

Sallust describes the scene in his *Catiline:*

There is a place in the prison which is called the Tullian dungeon, and which, after a slight ascent to the left, is sunk about twelve feet under ground. Walls secure it on every side, and over it is a vaulted roof connected with stone arches; but its appearance is disgusting and horrible, by reason of the filth, darkness, and stench. When Lentulus had been let down into this place, certain men to whom orders had been given strangled him with a cord. Thus this patrician, who was of the illustrious family of the Cornelii, and who had filled the office of consul at Rome, met with an end suited to his character and conduct. On Cethegus, Statilius, Gabinius, and Ceparius punishment was inflicted in a similar manner.

The Tullianum today, with the building of which it is a part, is one of the examples of stratified history so often found in Rome. The dungeon itself, the death cell not only of the Catilinarians but of Vercingetorix, Jugurtha, and others of less fame, is in the living rock. The chamber above it was built perhaps about 100 B.C. The two continued to be used as places of detention at least up to A.D. 368, when the prison was mentioned by the historian Ammianus Marcellinus. At some unknown date they became the Church of Saints Peter and Paul in Prison, and the lower chamber contains the stone post to which the Apostles are said to have been chained, with an inscription recording their baptism of the jailors Processus and Martinianus and forty-seven others into the Christian faith with the waters of the spring in the pavement. Above this church there was erected, in the sixteenth century, the Oratory of the Crucifix, and above the Oratory not much later was built the Church of Saint Joseph of the Woodworkers, altered in 1598 to its present form. There are thus preserved here four strata of pagan and Christian history.

When the execution had taken place, the event was announced by Cicero in person at the door of the prison in the single word, *Vixerunt*—"They are no more." As the Consul started home, he was accompanied by a throng of citizens who gathered about him partly because of natural excitement and partly in order to protect him against possible attack. Where he lived before and during the consulship is not known.

Cicero's home from the year 62 B.C. to his death was high on the steep incline of the Palatine Hill, diagonally across the Forum from the prison; in his own words, *in conspectu prope totius urbis domus est mea*—"in sight of almost the entire city is my home." He acquired it in 62 from Marcus Crassus for about $150,000; it was pillaged and destroyed by fire at the end of March, 58, after the decree for his banishment had been carried by Clodius and other enemies on the ground of his having put to death Roman citizens without due trial; and on his return, with the damages allowed him, was rebuilt. In the same Palatine neighborhood were the houses of Catiline and Clodius. The house of his life-long friend, Titus Pomponius Atticus, was on the Quirinal Hill near the Temple of Safety, not far from the present Palazzo Colonna, and, like the Colonna, had a garden.

Such are the Ciceronian places and monuments in Rome. Perhaps the houses of Cicero's brother Quintus, one near his own on the Palatine and the other on the rising land across the Forum to the northeast, called Carinae, should be added. An uncle of the Ciceros also had lived on the Carinae, and it is likely that when Marcus first came to Rome from Arpinum to be educated he lived with the uncle.

Outside of Rome, Cicero had a surprising number of properties, chiefly villas. Besides the old home in Arpinum, his inheritance, he acquired about 68 B.C. a country house in the vicinity of Tusculum, about whose furnishing with books and statuary we read much in his earliest letters; one at Antium by the sea, thirty-six miles from Rome, where we find him in 59 B.C. "delighting in my books, of which I have a great number at Antium, or counting the waves, for the weather is stormy and unsuitable for fishing"; one at Formiae, ninety-seven miles from Rome on a most beautiful bay, where we find him in April of the same year, a little after his visit to Antium, complaining in a letter to Atticus that he gets no news of Rome except from chance travellers, and begging for a "fat letter full of all you are doing and thinking"; one at Cumae, where in 55 B.C. he is "feasting on books—perhaps you thought, on the good things of Puteoli and the Lucrine Lake," by which he means oysters; one at Pompeii, a few miles from Stabiae and the villa of his friend Marius, who in 55 B.C. receives a letter from Cicero written at Rome, congratulating him on having missed the stupid plays and cruel gladiator shows given in Rome in honor of the completion of Pompey's theater and temple; one at Astura, near Antium, where he hides himself away after the death of Tullia in 45, and "buries himself in the thick and shaggy forest in the morning, not to come out until night"; and one at Puteoli, where on December 19, 45, he writes Atticus of having entertained Cæsar and his retinue at dinner. Probably no one of these places was either very large or very luxurious, but at the least they represent a great deal of property. Nor is one of them to be identified, though it is a sentimental pleasure to visit Tusculum and its theater, and to spend a day in those charming precincts, even if the home of Cicero was in all probability miles distant.

The most interesting and most beautiful of the Cicero neighborhoods to visit is the place of his birth and childhood in the valley of the Liris near Arpinum. The modern town of Arpino is reached by leaving the Naples line at Roccasecca, seventy-five miles from Rome, and continuing thirteen miles north out of the Sacco valley up the valley of the Liris. An alternative would be to alight at Frosinone, fifty-three miles from Rome, and take the autobus to Isola, near Arpino.

Arpinum was not the actual birthplace of Cicero, but was the largest neighboring town, four miles downstream on a height not far from the Liris. It was in the Volscian country, had been conquered by Rome two hundred years before Cicero's birth, and eighty-two years preceding that event had received full Roman citizenship.

Cicero was thus a mountaineer and a Volscian, and born a citizen of Rome at a time when many Italian towns were still not fully Romanized.

Arpino is a city of twelve to fifteen thousand inhabitants, and picturesquely situated. The train from Roccasecca, after five miles, approaches the Liris, now called Liri, at Arce, laboriously follows the left or eastern bank up steep grades for some seven miles through rocky landscape, and then, when the valley walls seem about to close and to bar further progress, quite suddenly emerges from a last tunnel into the wider and luxuriant portion of the lovely valley containing Arpino, Isola, and Sora.

Arpino is high on the rocky hill to the right, and reached by bus or zigzagging donkey road. A walk by the latter at the sunset hour through the steeply sloping olive orchards, with an ever widening and lengthening view up the green valley, is one of the greatest delights afforded by a land of delights.

At the entrance to the town, the streets begin to bear the names of Marius, Agrippa, and the Ciceros, and a façade fronting the public square is adorned with the busts of Marcus Tullius Cicero and the two others who conferred fame and honor on their native place. High above the present town is the arx or citadel of the ancient Arpinum, now nearly deserted. A monster prehistoric polygonal wall, extending along the crest and winding far down, forms a mighty barrier protecting the upper and lower towns on their mountain spur from the outside world.

From the heights of Arpino down the hard mountain road between hillside groves and orchards and hedges of roses three miles and a half to Isola, is a pleasant morning walk. In its earlier stages, before the walker has descended to the valley floor, the citadel of Sora is visible seven miles up the Liris where the valley narrows again—Sora, the native town of Regulus, most Roman of heroes, and of the Decii, father, son, and perhaps grandson, who successively at Vesuvius, Sentinum, and Asculum gave their lives in voluntary sacrifice on the field to secure victory for the Roman arms. At Isola the Liris divides, and the branches enclosing the rocky islet form two roaring cascades eighty feet high and of great volume. The Liris Valley in this neighborhood is busy with many paper mills.

Five miles to the west of Isola is Casamari, whose name perhaps indicates the birthplace of Marius, the conqueror of the Teutons and Cimbri in 102 and 101 B.C., when Cicero was four and five years old. The names of Marius, the Decii, and Regulus were among the great inspirations of Cicero's youth.

The Cicero estate was about one mile to the north of Isola, where the Fibrenus comes hurrying from the right and joins the Liris. It is reached from Isola by the level main road running

ARPINO

THE CHURCH OF SAN DOMENICO

THE FIBRENUS AT CICERO'S HOME

THE LIRIS AT CICERO'S HOME

between well watered fields and gardens whose luxuriant grains and grasses and vines and trees and vegetables are a riot of many shades of green. The birthplace of Cicero was in all probability a few rods beyond the Church and Monastery of San Domenico. Here, the Fibrenus divides into two arms, both of which flow into the Liris, forming a delta about 500 yards long and 300 wide, whose east end is regarded as the site of the house.

The home on the Liris was much beloved by Cicero, who returned again and again to enjoy its quiet and peace, to write, and to oversee the details of its management. The affectionate references to it in the essay *De Legibus* not only serve to identify its location but give us a pleasant picture of the busy orator at leisure with his brother and friend. *On the Laws* is a Platonic dialogue, and the setting is the landscape at the Liris and Fibrenus confluence. Marcus, Quintus, and Atticus appear first in the course of a ramble on the right bank of the Liris which has brought them to the neighborhood of Marius' birthplace. They then return to the Liris, where Marcus proposes that they continue their discussion "walking among these tall and stately poplars along the green and shady bank, and anon sitting." At the opening of the Second Book, Atticus suggests that they listen to the remainder of the discussion in a different place, the island in the Fibrenus.

"Now that we have walked up and down enough and you must also take up another head in your discourse, how would it be to change to another place, and listen to the rest of your talk on the island in the Fibrenus, seated? I think that is the name you gave the second stream you mentioned."

"By all means; for I often use that spot with the greatest pleasure, whether I have something to think over, or to write or read.

"For my part [says Atticus], now that I have chosen to come here, I can't feel delight enough, and I hold in contempt magnificent villas and pavements of marble and panelled ceilings. And really, the channels of water which your rich folk call their Niles and Euripuses—who, after seeing these surroundings of yours, would not laugh at them? So true it is that, just as when you were talking a little while ago about law and justice you referred all things to Nature, in the same way Nature dominates in those things also which are sought for the repose and delight of our minds. I used to marvel before—for I thought there was nothing in these places but rocks and hills, and indeed I was led on to think in that manner by your own talk and by your verses—I used to marvel, as I said, at your being so mightily pleased by this spot; but now, quite the contrary, I marvel that when you are not in Rome you can prefer any other."

"It is true [answers Marcus] that whenever I can get away for a few days, especially at this time of year, I do come out here to enjoy these charming and healthful surroundings, but it is not often I can get away. But of course there is another reason too that makes me delight in coming, a reason which you do not have."

"What, pray, is your reason?"

"Because, to tell the truth, this is the native soil of my brother here and myself; for in this spot were we born, of a very old stock, here is the altar of our line, here the center of our family interest, here the many relics of our ancestors. Not to go farther into that—the villa you see here owes its present improved state to the care of my father, a man of rather weak health who spent his time here principally in literary pursuits; but when I was born in this selfsame spot, during the lifetime of my grandfather, the villa was a humble one, like the famous home of Curius in the Sabine Hills. So you see there is something deeply hidden in my mind and heart that perhaps makes me enjoy the place more."

As this exchange of sentiments is in progress, the speakers have crossed the Liris by the bridge whose fragments are still to be seen just above the lower mouth of the Fibrenus, have approached and passed the Cicero home, and continued on the walk of a half hour or so which brought them along the shaded river bank to the island in the Fibrenus now called Carnello.

"But here we are on the island," says Atticus, breaking off his talk about Arpinum as Cicero's second *patria*.

"Really, nothing could be more charming. The Fibrenus is cleft here by a beak, as it were, and divided equally into two currents which glide rapidly along washing the banks on either side and soon flow together again, embracing just enough space for a moderate walk. This accomplished, as if its only duty and function were to provide this place for our discussion, it straightway plunges into the Liris, losing its own more obscure name, like one taken into a family of patrician rank, and makes the Liris much colder. For I have never felt the waters of a stream colder than this, though I have known many rivers."

With the exception of a very few fragments, the essay *On the Laws* is lost beyond the third of its six books. One of the fragments, preserved by Macrobius, four hundred and fifty years later, shows that in the Fifth Book the two brothers and their friend have discoursed for some time on the island and are to finish their talk on the banks of the Liris. It is an afternoon in the Italian midsummer. "Now that the sun is no longer straight above us and our place here is not entirely shaded by these young trees, would it not be better to go down to the Liris and pursue our discussion to its conclusion in the cool shade of the alders?"

The Cicero homestead, a hundred years after the murder of its owner, is heard of as the property of the poet Silius Italicus, A.D. 25-101, who deeply cherished the memories of both Cicero and Virgil. What its fate was in the later days of Rome and in the darker times that followed, nothing may be said except that it has disappeared; but the Church and Monastery of San Domenico, erected A.D. 1030, contain in their walls and floors so many fragments in the Roman villa style that it is entirely reasonable to suppose at least some of them parts of the Cicero home, many times altered and by that time long lying in ruins a few rods away.

THE CÆSAR COUNTRY

TO one acquainted with the course of Cæsar's life, the expression "Cæsar country" will hardly seem appropriate. Outside of Rome, there are no places in Italy which we associate intimately with thoughts of him. Unlike Cicero, he was born in the capital and died there, he had no favorite retreats in the country, he wrote nothing to indicate feeling for landscape or affection for a chosen spot, and the time he spent elsewhere than in Rome he spent beyond Italian borders.

Cicero belongs to Rome and Italy. His absences from them were confined to a year or so of study in Athens and the Greek cities of Asia, 79-78 B.C., a year's quæstorship in Sicily in 75, the year of exile in Thessalonica, 58-57, a year in Cilicia as governor in 51, and a year in Epirus before and after the battle of Pharsalia, 48-47; in all, somewhat more than five years of the sixty-three he lived.

An outline of Cæsar's career produces a different effect. Cæsar's absences began when he was twenty-two. From 80 to 74 B.C., most of the time he was in the East, serving in the army and navy in the war against Mithridates and the pirates and studying with Molo in Rhodes; in 68, he was quæstor in Spain, and returned by way of Transpadane Gaul, where he spent some time; in 61, he was proprætor in Spain. From 58 to 49, Cæsar was in Gaul, rarely setting foot in Italy, and probably not at all in Rome. From April to September, 49, he was in Spain campaigning against Afranius and Petreius, the supporters of Pompey, the chief engagement taking place at Ilerda. In January, 48, he left Italy for the campaign of eight months which ended in Pompey's defeat at Pharsalia in August; the remainder of 48 and the winter following, he spent in Egypt. From June to October, 47, he traversed Syria, Cilicia, Cappadocia, Pontus, Galatia, Bithynia,

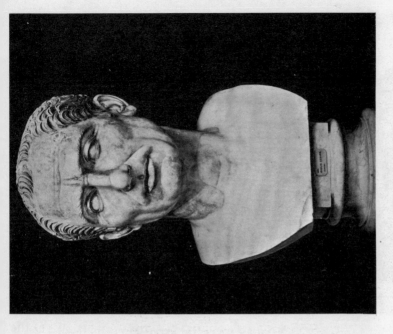

JULIUS CÆSAR

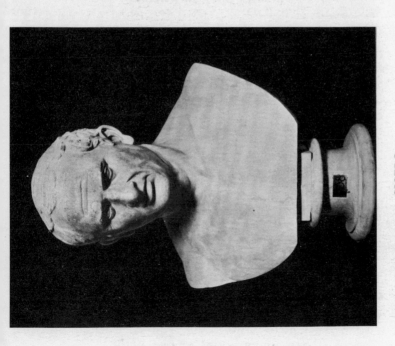

CICERO

ROMAN GATE IN AUTUN

THE RIVER DOUBS AT BESANÇON

and the Province of Asia, and returned to Tarentum, Brundisium, and Rome. After three months in the capital, he left in December for Africa, where in April, 46, he defeated the Pompeian army under Cato at Thapsus, leaving in June for his triumph in Rome. In 45, he was again in Spain, and on March 17 defeated the last Pompeian army at Munda. In September, he returned to Rome for the last time, with six months to live before the assassins' daggers on the Ides of March ended one of the most active lives the world has ever seen.

From this hasty sketch, it may be seen that of the years that Cæsar lived, twenty-three were spent away from Rome and beyond the borders of Italy. These twenty-three years occurred out of the thirty-six years after the year 80 B.C., when for the first time, at the age of twenty-two, he left Rome. Of the last sixteen years, practically fourteen were spent away from Rome, nine in Gaul and five in distant provinces. The Cæsar country is thus really the Roman territory he conquered or traversed and left ready for his successor to consolidate into the Roman Empire.

Yet there is a part of the Roman world outside of Rome in which the presence of Cæsar is felt by those familiar with his life almost as vividly as the presence of Cicero is felt in his Italian villa haunts. This is the land of ancient Gaul, now represented by France, the Low Countries, and part of Switzerland. In these territories Cæsar spent nine years, 58-50 B.C., with only short intervals of absence in northern Italy. They were the period from his forty-fourth to his fifty-third year, the most energetic and the wisest years of his life, and the period of his greatest service to the Roman Empire and the cause of civilization. A brief review of these years will indicate the interest that awaits the Cæsar student travelling in France and countries bordering upon it.

When Cæsar left Rome in 58 B.C., immediately after the exile of Cicero, it was to assume charge of Cisalpine Gaul and the Province. Cisalpine Gaul began at the latitude of Ariminum and the Rubicon and was bounded on the north by the Alps. The Province was beyond the Alps, and centered about the lower Rhône valley, the modern Provence. Cæsar's first operation began

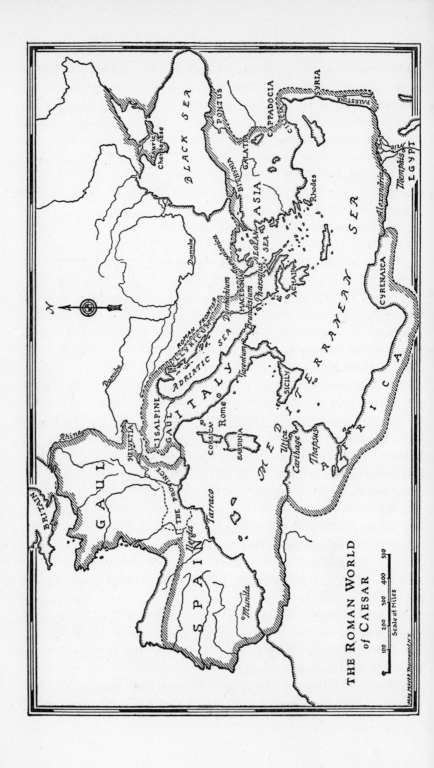

THE ROMAN WORLD of CAESAR

Scale of Miles

100   200   300   400   500

near Geneva, at the southwest end of the lake where the Rhône flows from it south and west on the way to Lyons. Here the Helvetii, who were migrating with the intention of seizing lands in Gaul, being turned back by Cæsar as they attempted to follow the river from Geneva on the left or southern bank, were compelled to go by the northern bank, where the path was narrower and less convenient. The traveller from Geneva on the beautiful route through Bellegarde, Culoz, and Ambérieu to the broad Rhône valley in France will find it easy to imagine the long train of the 368,000 Helvetii—warriors, old men, women, and children, with their wagons and beasts—dragging laboriously along the narrow north bank, and the joy with which they came into the wide fields beyond the mountains and directed their march to the north up the valley of the Saône into Burgundy on the way to new abodes farther west.

Cæsar, meanwhile, had gone back to Cisalpine Gaul for more soldiers, crossed the Alps again, and marched up the Rhône and Saône. On the Saône, and near Bibracte, a little to the south of modern Autun, he defeated and practically destroyed the whole Helvetian host.

The destruction of the Helvetii took place in the country of the Haedui, the Gallic allies of Rome. In modern Autun, a city of fifteen thousand situated a little north of where Bibracte stood, there is a statue of Diviciacus, who remained faithful to Cæsar in spite of his brother Dumnorix, and outside the city is a large concrete ruin eighty-eight feet high called with no good proof the tomb of Diviciacus. There are many remains of the times when Autun was Augustodunum, but all seem of later date than Cæsar. The tomb is one of them.

The Helvetian campaign began on March 24, 58 B.C., and was at an end about June 28. By September 18, Cæsar had moved north to Vesontio, the capital of the Sequani, and parleyed with Ariovistus the German, who had occupied and now claimed as his right the lands to the west of the Rhine. On this date Cæsar defeated and drove the Germans from Gaul.

Vesontio is modern Besançon, a city of sixty thousand about ninety miles east of Autun. It is a delight to find the *flumen Dubis* of Cæsar's account still called Doubs, and to study the position and character of the city with his description at hand.

The river Dubis, as if traced by a pair of compasses, surrounds almost the whole town. The rest of the circuit, not more than six hundred feet, where the river is interrupted, is occupied by a very high hill whose base is washed by the stream on both sides. The hill is walled as a citadel, and connected with the town. Hither Cæsar made haste, marching night and day, occupied the town, and stationed a garrison in it.

Early in 57 B.C. we find Cæsar on the Aisne, to the north of Reims, to the east of Soissons, and to the south of Laon. The Belgae, occupying Belgium, Holland, and northern France, had determined to drive him from Gaul, and met him in formidable numbers where stands modern Berry-au-Bac, only to be as completely routed as the Helvetii the year before. From here he advanced westward, receiving the submission of the Bellovaci and the Ambiani, fighting the famous battle with the Nervii on the Sambre a little west of Maubeuge, and pushing on to take a stronghold on the Meuse between Namur and Liège.

There are no monuments of Cæsarian interest to be seen in these regions, and the identification of the battlefields is not certain, but the country is the battleground of the World War, contains many famous cathedral towns, and is visited by many travellers. Its names, too, are of great interest to the reader of Cæsar. The Marne and the Aisne and the Seine are Cæsar's Matrona, Axona, and Sequana; Reims and Soissons get their names from the tribes of the Remi and the Suessiones, Beauvais and Amiens from the Bellovaci and the Ambiani; Laon was Lugdunum; the Meuse was the Mosa.

The operations in 56 B.C. began on the broken coast of the Veneti, where are the modern cities of Vannes, Auray, and Quiberon, on the south shore of Brittany between Brest and Nantes. After the defeat of the sea power of the Veneti in the battle of Auray, and the conquest of Viridovix and his army in the Cherbourg peninsula by Sabinus, Cæsar marched four hundred miles north into the country of the Morini and Menapii, corresponding to northern and southern Holland, and after his

STATUE OF AMBIORIX AT TONGRES

STATUE OF VERCINGETORIX AT ALESIA

ROMAN ARCH AT FANO, ANCIENT FANUM

ROMAN BRIDGE AT RIMINI, ANCIENT ARIMINUM

return quartered for the winter in the territory between the Seine and the Loire.

In 55 B.C. occurred the famous demonstration against the Germans across the Rhine. Starting from the country of the Eburovici, modern Évreux, Cæsar advanced to the Rhine between Bonn and Coblenz, annihilated the Usipetes and Tencteri near the latter place, in ten days built the renowned bridge across the Rhine, perhaps between Coblenz and Andernach, crossed into the country of the Germans, ravaged the lands of the Sugambri, returned to the southern bank, destroyed the bridge, and made his first expedition to Britain. After a winter in Illyricum, he made the second expedition in 54, returning in September. It was almost a hundred years before another Roman army crossed the Channel.

The year 54 B.C. is famous also for the disaster to Sabinus and Cotta. After the return from Britain, the seven legions on duty in this northwest region were distributed for the winter as follows: at Samarobriva, or Amiens, Cæsar's headquarters, and about Beauvais, three; near Namur, among the Nervii, one, under Quintus Cicero; in the country of the Treveri, one; among the Morini, one; and at Aduatuca, among the Eburones, somewhere near Aix-la-Chapelle, one. The last, under the joint command of Sabinus and Cotta, having been persuaded by Ambiorix to leave its quarters, was annihilated by the forces of the Eburones in ambuscade. The siege of Quintus Cicero's camp by the Eburones and the Nervii followed, but the garrison, after an obstinate defense in which only one man in ten escaped wounds or death, was rescued by Cæsar. A statue of Ambiorix has recently been erected in Tongres, one of the places thought to represent the ancient Aduatuca.

The year 53 B.C. was spent by Cæsar in operations against the Senones, from whom Sens, seventy miles southeast of Paris, received its name; against the Treveri, whose name is preserved in Trèves: the Carnutes, in the neighborhood of Orléans; and the Nervii and Eburones. The attempt to capture Ambiorix never succeeded. The troubles of 53 were largely due to the defeat of Sabinus and Cotta, which proved that the Roman legion was not invincible.

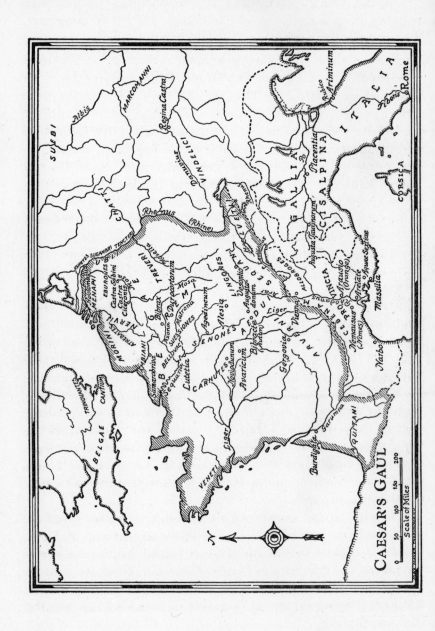

CAESAR'S GAUL

Scale of Miles
0   50   100   150   200

The full consequences of the fall of Aduatuca, however, were manifest in 52 B.C. in the great rebellion led by Vercingetorix. The principal towns and battlefields of this campaign are to be identified without difficulty. Gergovia, the home of Vercingetorix and the scene of his defeat of Cæsar, was on an isolated plateau twenty-four hundred feet high four miles south of modern Clermont-Ferrand, in Auvergne, a hundred miles west of Lyons. Avaricum, taken by Cæsar after a long and cruel siege, is the lofty modern Bourges, one of the great cathedral towns. At Gergovia, the next important scene of conflict after Avaricum, excavations have revealed the lines of ancient streets, and the modern Arverni have erected among them a large and ugly monument inscribed: *In his locis Dux Arvernorum Vercingetorix Cæsarem invadentem profligavit*—"In These Places Vercingetorix, Leader of the Arverni, Defeated Cæsar the Invader." In the city of Clermont-Ferrand there is a statue of the chieftain in full career on horseback.

Alesia, the famous siege of which resulted in the surrender of Vercingetorix and the end of the rebellion, has been identified as the hill of Auxois, about thirteen hundred feet high, on whose slope lies the village of Alise-Ste. Reine, one hundred and sixty miles southeast of Paris on the line to Dijon. Excavations around the hill and on its summit have brought to light the circumvallations of Cæsar, many Roman and Gallic weapons, and hundreds of coins from a score of Gallic states, including a hundred belonging to the Arverni and one bearing the face and name of Vercingetorix. The excavations were undertaken by Napoleon the Third, with Colonel Stoffel as military critic. A colossal statue of Vercingetorix stands on the hill, and is visible from the train.

The year 51 B.C., marked by severe punitive measures against several nations, ended with the permanent quieting of Gaul. Cæsar's movements in 50 are not well known, but his tasks now were those of administration rather than war. When we see him at the head of an army again, it is early in January, 49, at the Rubicon. The Senate has not been able to meet his terms, and the civil war begins.

. XI .

CÆSAR AND CICERO IN ITALY

THE senatorial party, and conservatives in general, had long disliked and distrusted Cæsar. He was thought to know more about the conspiracy of Catiline than was creditable, and had obstinately opposed the vote for death to the conspirators; he was notoriously in sympathy with radical measures; he was feared as a potential challenger of the Senate's power before his election to the consulship, and proved to be as high-handed after it as was expected; and during his nine years in Gaul he had created a veteran army devoted to him and depending on him for support. With Gaul set in order, both general and army were ready for further action. The Senate and its friends among the sober-minded citizenry looked back to the times of Sulla and Marius and the eighty troubled years since with the Gracchi armed violence had become a factor in government, and feared the return of dictatorship.

They had felt the same fear of Pompey when he returned in 62 B.C. from the wonderful successes of the war against Mithridates and the freebooters on the sea. They did not wholly trust him even yet, but it was their time of need, and they found themselves through force of circumstances looking to him for leadership and armed protection. It was a time of need no less for Pompey. With the death of Cæsar's daughter Julia, the wife of Pompey, in 53 B.C., the tendency toward estrangement between the two great men of action, already far developed by the steady increase of Cæsar's power in Gaul, had rapidly grown more pronounced. When the Senate in its fear of the Gallic conqueror had voted conditions which neither Cæsar's dignity, ambition, nor safety allowed him to accept, when all attempts at agreement had failed and the legions had crossed the Rubicon, it was natural that Pompey should assume the military leadership of the Government party.

Whether or not Pompey was acting in his own interest as well as in that of the Senate, is a question whose answer is suggested by the closing paragraph of a letter from Cælius to Cicero, written at Rome in September, 50 B.C., four months before the crisis:

You want to know what I think is going to happen. If one or the other of them doesn't go off to a war against the Parthians, I can see a big quarrel coming, with the power of the sword to settle it. They are both full of determination and provided with forces. If it could only be without danger on your part I'd say Fortune was making ready a grand and a delightful spectacle for you.

The Rubicon, a little to the north of Ariminum, was the legal boundary between Roman territory and Cæsar's province of Cisalpine Gaul. To cross it, with his men, as Cæsar did sometime in the second week of January, was armed defiance of the Senate.

Cicero, who had left Rome in May, 51 B.C., to assume his duties as governor of Cilicia, landed in Italy on his return on November 25, 50 B.C., and arrived at Rome on January 4, 49 B.C. As he hoped for the honor of a triumph because of his military achievements the year before, and as a triumph could not be granted to one who had already entered the city and thus laid down the imperium, he was still outside the walls of Rome when the Senate formally voted armed resistance to Cæsar and assigned the various districts of Italy to magistrates for the purpose of recruiting.

Cicero's assignment was Capua and the adjacent territory of Campania, and he finally accepted the charge only after resigning and being persuaded by Pompey in person. On January 18 he left Rome, was at his Formian estate about the 20th, and on the 25th reached Capua. On January 27 he reviews the situation to his secretary, Tiro:

Things have come to such a pass that unless some god or some lucky chance rescues us we cannot hope for a remedy. For my part, as soon as I arrived at Rome I did not cease from feeling and saying and doing everything that would bring about an agreement; but a strange madness had fallen upon not only the bad but even upon those who are thought good, so that they were eager to fight though I kept declaring that nothing was worse than civil war.

Meanwhile Cæsar was advancing along the east coast, taking or winning city after city: Ariminum, Pisaurum, Fanum, Ancona, Auximum, Cingulum, Asculum, with Arretium in central Italy. Pompey and the consuls, having but two legions to Cæsar's rapidly assembled six, had first withdrawn to Campania, and then fixed their headquarters at Luceria.

On February 14 Cæsar arrived at Corfinium, eighty miles north-west of Luceria, and on the 20th received the surrender of this stronghold. Domitius and the garrison he allowed to go free, and the captured soldiers joined his ranks as he continued the march.

This leniency of the victor, and the response it met on the part of the vanquished, if we may take Cicero as proof, did much to change the thought of the public toward Cæsar. On February 8 or 9 he had written to Atticus:

I see there is not a foot of ground in Italy which is not in Cæsar's power. I have no news of Pompey, and I imagine he will be captured unless he has taken to the sea. What incredible despatch! While our leader—but it grieves me to blame him, as I am in an agony of suspense on his account. There is reason for you to fear butchery, not that anything could be less advantageous to secure Cæsar a lasting victory and power; but I see on whose advice he will act. I hope it will be all right.

On March 1, his tone has changed. He writes again from Formiae:

Do you see the kind of man into whose hands the State has fallen? What foresight, what energy, what readiness! Upon my word, if he refrain from murder and rapine, he will be the darling of those who dreaded him most. The people of the country towns and the farmers talk to me a great deal. They care for nothing at all but their lands, their little homesteads, and their tiny hoards. And see how public opinion has changed. They fear the man they once trusted, and adore the man they once dreaded.

On March 9 Cæsar and his six legions reached Brundisium, whither Pompey had retreated from Luceria after the news from Corfinium. On the 17th, he evaded the blockade of Cæsar and sailed for Dyrrachium, the chief port on the east shore of the Adriatic, at the head of the great highway, and the only one, lead-

The ITALY
of CICERO, CAESAR,
VIRGIL and HORACE

Scale of Miles
50   100   150

GALLIA
CISALPINA

Turin
Padus R.   Cremona
Placentia   Verona
Parma   Mutina   Mantua   Atesis   Patavium
Bononia

MARE ADRIATICUM

Pistoria   Faesulae   Rubico
Arnus R.   Florentia   Ariminum
Arretium   Pisaurum
Metaurus R.   Fanum
Ancona
Auximum
Cingulum

Fisculum

CORSICA

Rome   Anio   Tusculum
Ostia   Arpinum   Luceria   Dyrrhachium
Antium   Formiae   Canusium
MARE   Sinuessa   Beneventum   Barium
Cumae   Napolis   M. Vultur   Rubi
Puteoli   Pompeii   Venusia   Brundisium
TUSCUM   M. Vesuvius   Tarentum

SARDINIA

EPIRUS

Drepanum
SICILIA

Siracusa

Carthage

AFRICA

Mt. Soracte
Scale of Miles
10   20   30   40

ROME   Fidenae
VIA AURELIA   Gabii   Tibur   Liris
Tusculum   Pedum   Praeneste   VIA LATINA
Ostia   L. Albanus   Alban Mts.   Sora   Fibrenus
Antium   Tolerus   Isola   San Domenico
Astura   VIA APPIA   Arpinum   Arce   Venafrium
MARE   Antium   Circeii   Anxur   Formiae
TUSCUM   Caieta   Sinuessa
LATIUM

MAX MAYER, THORNWOOD N.Y.

ing across Macedonia through Thessalonica to the Hellespont. Cæsar now turned about and marched for Rome, the first step in the plan he had formed of establishing his power in Italy and the West before pursuing Pompey in the East.

At about this time, and probably after facing about, Cæsar writes to Cicero, sending the letter by one Furnius:

Though I have only had a glimpse of our friend Furnius, and have not yet been able conveniently to speak to him or hear what he has to say, being in a hurry and on the march, yet I could not neglect the opportunity of writing to you and sending him to convey my thanks. Be sure I have often thanked you and I expect to have occasion to do so still more often in the future: so great are your services to me. First I beg you, since I trust that I shall quickly reach Rome, to let me see you there, and employ your advice, favor, position, and help of all kinds. I will return to what I began with: pardon my haste and the shortness of my letter. All the other information you may get from Furnius.

Cicero replied from his Formian villa on the 19th of March in a letter indicating the conflict of spirit he was undergoing. He had long been more the personal friend of Pompey than of Cæsar, and his one-time thought of Pompey as the possible ideal leader of an ideal party composed of the senatorial and equestrian orders had been long in leaving him. But now Pompey has left Italy and in a manner abandoned his party, and Cæsar no longer seems "the barbarian" of the days before Corfinium:

On reading your letter, which I got from our friend Furnius, in which you told me to come near Rome, I was not much surprised at your wishing to employ "my advice and my position"; but I asked myself what you meant by my "influence" and "help." However, my hopes led me to think that a man of your admirable statesmanship would wish to act for the comfort, peace, and agreement of the citizens, and for that purpose I considered my own character and inclination very suitable. If that is the case, and if you are touched by the desire to protect our friend Pompey and reconcile him to yourself and the State, I am sure you will find no one more suited for the purpose than I am.

I have always advocated peace both with Pompey and the Senate ever since I have been able to do so, nor since the outbreak of hostili-

TARANTO, ANCIENT TARENTUM

RUINS OF JULIUS CÆSAR'S FORUM

PORTICO IN CÆSAR'S FORUM, WITH TEMPLE OF
VENUS GENETRIX

ties have I taken any part in the war; I have considered that the war
was attacking your rights in that envious and hostile persons were opposing a distinction conferred on you by the grace of the Roman people. But, as at that time I not only upheld your rights but urged others
to assist you, so now I am greatly concerned with the rights of Pompey.
It is many years since I chose you two men for my special respect, and
to be my closest friends, as you are. So, I ask you, or rather beseech
and entreat you with all urgency, that in spite of all your anxieties
you may devote some time to considering how I may be enabled by
your kindness to be what decency and gratitude, nay good-feeling, require, in remembering my great debt to Pompey.

If this mattered only to myself, I should yet hope to obtain my request; but to my mind it touches your honour and the public weal that
I, a friend of peace and of both of you, should be so supported by you
that I may be able to work for peace between you and peace amongst
our fellow-citizens. I thanked you formerly in the matter of Lentulus,
for having saved him, as he had saved me. Yet on reading the letter
he has sent me full of thankfulness for your generous kindness, I feel
that his safety is my debt as much as his. If you understand my gratitude
to him, pray give me the opportunity of showing my gratitude to
Pompey too.

On March 20, still at Formiae, Cicero writes the following to
Atticus, enclosing a letter from Cæsar:

Though I have nothing to write to you, still, not to miss a day, I
send this letter. On the 27th of March Cæsar will stop at Sinuessa, they
say. He sent me a letter dated the 26th, in which he looks forward to
my "resources," not, as in the former letter, to my "help." I had written praising to the skies his kindness, his clemency at Corfinium. He
replied as follows:

"Cæsar Imperator to Cicero Imperator, Greeting.

"You are right to infer of me (for I am well known to you) that there
is nothing further from my nature than cruelty. Whilst I take great
pleasure from that fact, I am proud indeed that my action wins your
approval. I am not moved because it is said that those whom I let go
have departed to wage war on me again, for there is nothing I like
better than that I should be true to myself and they to themselves. I
could wish you to meet me at Rome that I may avail myself of your
advice and resources, as usual, in everything."

Two days afterward, according to expectation, Cæsar paid a
visit to Cicero at his Formian villa, which Cicero describes to

Atticus in a letter written on the 29th of March, the day following:

In both respects I followed your advice. I spoke so as to gain Cæsar's respect rather than his gratitude; and I persisted in my resolve not to go to Rome. We were mistaken in thinking he would be easy to manage. I have never seen anyone less easy. He kept on saying that my decision was a slur on him, and that others would be less likely to come, if I did not come. I pointed out that my case was very unlike theirs. After much talk he said, "Well, come and discuss peace." "On my own terms?" I asked. "Need I dictate to you?" said he. "Well," said I, "I shall contend that the Senate cannot sanction your invasion of Spain or your going with an army into Greece, and," I added, "I shall lament Pompey's fate." He replied, "That is not what I want." "So I fancied," said I; "but I do not want to be in Rome, because either I must say that and much else, on which I cannot keep silent, if I am present, or else I cannot come." The upshot was that I was to think over the matter, as Cæsar suggested, with a view to closing our interview. I could not refuse. So we parted. I am confident then he has no liking for me. But I like myself, as I have not for a long time.

For the rest, ye gods what a following! What *âmes damnées*, in your phrase! Celer is an hero to the rest. What an abandoned cause, and what desperate gangs! What can one think of a son of Servius and a son to Titinius being in an army which beset Pompey? Six legions! He is very wide-awake and bold. I see no end to our evil days. Now assuredly you must produce your advice. This was the limit we contemplated.

Cæsar's *finale*, which I had almost forgotten, was hateful: "If I may not use your advice, I shall use the advice I can and go to any length." You will say: "You have seen him to be as you have described him: and did you heave a sigh?" Indeed I did. You ask for the rest of our talk. What more is there to tell? He went straight to Pedum, I to Arpinum. From thence I await the "twittering swallow" you talk of. You will say you prefer me not to dwell on past mistakes. Even Pompey, our leader, has made many.

But I await a letter from you. There is no room now, as before, for your "await the event." The limit we fixed was that interview; and I have no doubt I annoyed Cæsar; so I must act the more quickly. Please send me a letter and deal with *la haute politique*. I await a letter from you now very anxiously.

Cæsar arrived in Rome on March 31, and in about five days was on the way to Spain to clear it of the Pompeian forces. Before his departure, he had written Cicero regarding their discussion at Formiae. Cicero sends news of this to Atticus in a letter of April 7: "Cæsar has written to excuse me for not coming to Rome, and says that he takes it in good part." On April 16, Cæsar sends a final letter before leaving Italy:

Cæsar Imperator to Cicero Imperator, Greeting.
Although I had concluded that you would do nothing rashly or imprudently, nevertheless I have been so stirred by what people say that I thought it best to write to you and ask you in the name of our goodwill to each other not to go anywhere, now that fortune inclines my way, where you did not think it necessary to go before anything was certain. For you will have done a serious injury to our friendship and consulted your own interest very little, if you show that you are not following fortune (for everything that has happened seems most favorable to me and most unfavorable to Pompey), nor yet following the right cause (for the cause was the same then, when you thought fit to hold aloof from it), but that you have condemned some act of mine, the greatest harm you could do me. Do not take such a step, I pray you by the right of our friendship. Finally what better befits a good and peaceful man and a loyal citizen than to keep out of civil disturbance. There are some who approved such a course, but could not follow it because of the danger. But you may examine the evidence of my life and the opinion given by my friendship; you will find no safer or more honorable course than to keep quite clear of the quarrel.
April 16 on the march.

But neither natural attraction to Cæsar nor fear of his displeasure could stand against Cicero's feeling of duty toward Pompey and what he conceived to be the patriotic cause. On June 7 the four Ciceros, Marcus and Quintus and their two sons of the same names, set sail from Caieta, a few miles away from Formiae, for the estate of Atticus in Epirus, from which Marcus Cicero went to join the Pompeians. After the battle of Pharsalia on August 9, the four went to Patrae, in Greece; and in the middle of the autumn Cicero crossed to Brundisium, where for some eleven months he awaited the disposition which events were to make of his fortunes.

About September 24, 47 B.C., after setting in order the affairs of the East, Cæsar arrived at Tarentum. On the 25th, he had a meeting with Cicero, which Plutarch describes:

But when it was announced that he had disembarked at Tarentum, and was proceeding by land thence to Brundisium, Cicero advanced to meet him, not being altogether without hope, but feeling shame in the presence of many persons at having to make trial of a man who was an enemy and victorious. But there was no necessity for him to do or to say anything unworthy; for when Cæsar saw Cicero coming to meet him far before all the rest, he got down from his carriage and embraced him, and walked several stadia in private conversation with him.

Cicero reached his Tusculan villa about October 8, and not long afterward was in Rome. In two months Cæsar had left for Africa, to return on July 25, 46 B.C. In September, 46, when with Cæsar's consent the Senate voted the recall of his bitter enemy, Marcus Marcellus, Cicero's feeling was so stirred by Cæsar's generosity that he broke his resolution to maintain silence under the new régime and delivered the eloquent oration Pro Marcello. Later, he appeared before Cæsar in behalf of Ligarius, who also was in exile.

Early in 45 B.C., Cæsar again left Rome for Spain, to win the battle of Munda, near Cordova, in March, to establish his authority, and to return to Rome in September. During this time Cicero had lost his dearly beloved Tullia. On December 19, 45, Cæsar and his retinue were entertained by Cicero in his villa at Puteoli, near Lake Avernus. As usual, Atticus received an intimate account of what has happened, and this time there is more than the usual vivacity.

O what a formidable guest! And yet one not to be regretted, because everything went off very pleasantly. But on his arrival at Philippus's— it was the 2d Saturnalia in the evening—the villa was so crammed with the soldiers that there was hardly a room available for Cæsar to have dinner in; and nothing strange, with two thousand men. I was really much disturbed at thought of how it would be with me next day, but Cassius Barba came to my rescue by detailing a guard, and having the men go into camp in the open, and my villa was protected. My famous guest spent the 3d Saturnalia at Philippus's up to about twelve, admitting nobody; going over accounts, I suppose, with Balbus. Then he went for a walk on the seashore. After two o'clock he went to the baths; then heard about Mamurra, and without a sign on his face. He had his rubbing up, came in to dinner. He was having a course of emetics, and so both ate and drank without concern and enjoyed him-

THE ROMAN FORUM, LOOKING EAST

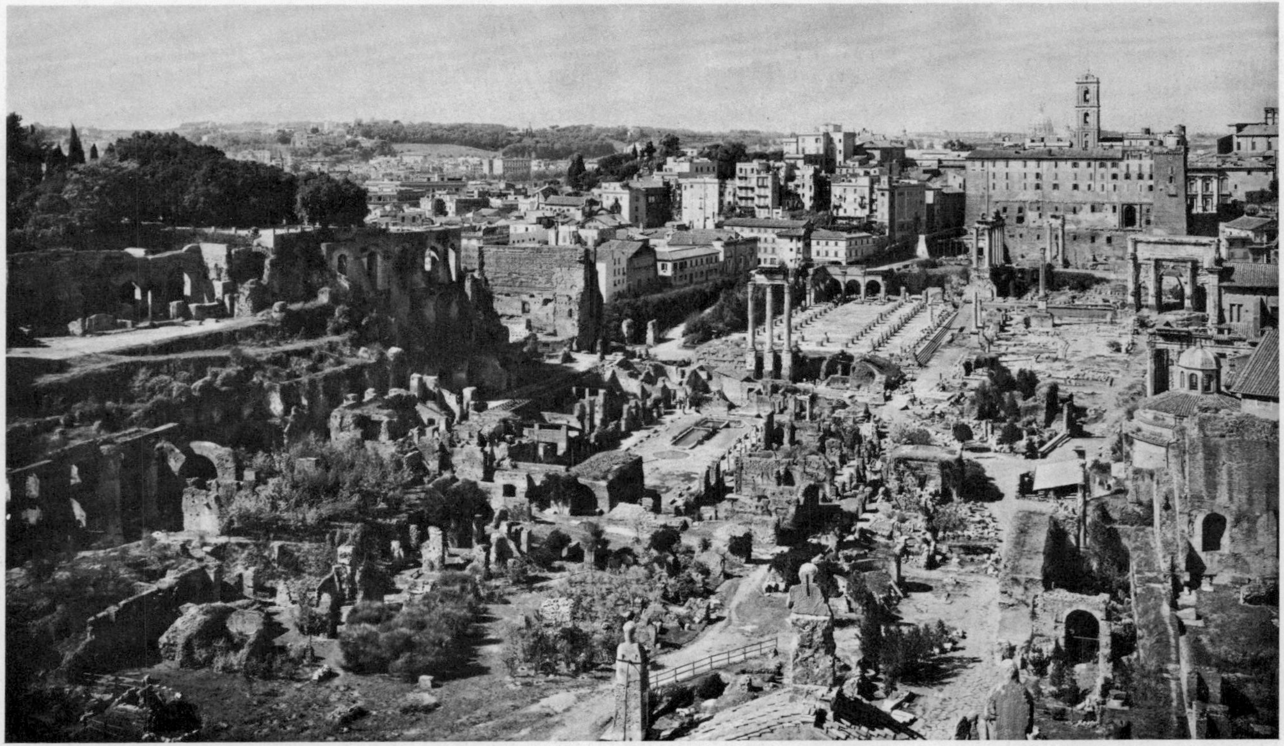

THE ROMAN FORUM, LOOKING WEST

self; a plentiful dinner and well served, and not only that, but "well cooked, and, if you ask, pleasantly seasoned with good talk." Besides, his retinue were provided for very plentifully in three dining rooms. His freedmen of less consequence and the slaves lacked nothing; for the more important were elegantly taken care of.

Why go on? We seemed quite human. Yet he is not the sort of guest you would say to, "Please drop in on your way back." Once will do. Nothing serious in our conversation; much literary talk. *Que voulez-vous?* He had a good time and it passed off pleasantly. He said he would be one day in Puteoli, a second day near Baiae.

There you have the story of my entertainment of him, or rather his quartering on me—disagreeable, I told you, not troublesome. I am to be here a short time, and then go to my Tusculan place. As he passed Dolabella's house, the whole troop of men-at-arms divided to right and left of his horse, and did this nowhere else. This I got from Nicias.

This was two days less than three months before the Ides of March.

. XII .

CÆSAR IN ROME

WE have seen how comparatively few, after his reaching manhood, were Cæsar's years in Rome. The thirteen years of his presence there at intervals from 80 B.C. to 44 B.C. were hardly more than enough to keep him from becoming a stranger in his native city; and the two years or less of his Roman residence during the last sixteen years of his life were composed of periods varying from the eleven days he spent in Rome on his return from Spain in 49 B.C. before starting for the East in pursuit of Pompey, to the six months preceding his assassination. The building and the beautification he planned for the city were hardly begun when he died. It was Augustus who became the great builder of the age, and Augustan buildings are the chief memorials of Cæsar visible in Rome today.

"He lived at first in the Subura in a modest house," says his biographer, Suetonius, "but, after he was elected pontifex maximus, in the Domus Publica on the Sacred Way. Many record that he was most fond of elegance and luxury; that he began from the foundations and finished at great expense a country house on his property at Nemi, and then tore the whole thing down because it did not come out to suit him in every detail."

By the Domus Publica is meant the official residence of the pontifex maximus, which was near the Regia at the east end of the Forum. The reference to the villa at Nemi gains interest from the recent draining of Lake Nemi in order to recover the two ships dating from the times of Caligula or Tiberius. The region is a lovely place, and was much used by prominent Romans.

Whether or not Cæsar retained his house in the Subura after taking up residence in the Domus Publica cannot be determined. The Subura had the name of being one of the noisier and less desirable parts of the city. It was immediately to the northeast of the Forum, and led to the rising ground known as Carinae, "The Keels." Marius, the famous uncle of Cæsar, had lived in the Subura, and Quintus Cicero and Pompey lived on the Carinae. Mark Antony afterward owned Pompey's house.

While Cæsar still resided in the Subura, probably in the early part of the year 67 B.C., he delivered from the Rostra the funeral orations of Julia, his aunt, the widow of Marius, and of his own wife Cornelia, the daughter of Cinna. The Rostra at this time was in front of the Senate House in the northwest corner of the Forum, and was the place also of Cicero's orations to the people.

The Forum was again the scene of public appearances by Cæsar in 65 B.C., when he gave on a grand scale the popular entertainments customary with ædiles. He erected temporary colonnades for his shows both in the Forum and on the Capitol, and gave wild-animal hunts and drama. At the southeast corner of the Forum stood the Temple of Castor and Pollux, commonly known as the Temple of Castor, which was the subject of a *bon mot* of Bibulus, Cæsar's colleague in the ædileship. The latter, who was entirely overshadowed by Cæsar even in the entertainments for which he paid an equal share, humorously remarked that in the ædileship with Cæsar he was in the same case as Pollux in his partnership with Castor; that Cæsar, like Castor, got all the credit. Six years later, when Bibulus and Cæsar were colleagues in the consulship, Bibulus was again the Pollux of the combination, and the wits referred to acts "done in the consulship of Julius and Cæsar."

For Cæsar as well as Cicero, the year 63 B.C. was a year of great events. It was in this year that he was elected pontifex maximus and prætor, and spoke in the Senate urging the milder penalty for the conspirators. We may imagine him often in the Forum this year and the next—coming down on the day of his election as pontifex, after declaring to his mother that he would not return unless victorious; mingling with the crowds as they listened to Cicero's speeches from the Rostra against Catiline; entering the Temple of Concord to take part in the debate; presiding over trials in the tribunals in open air or in the basilicas; going to and from the Domus Publica. It was in the Domus Publica on the night of

December 5, 62 B.C., that the notorious Clodius was detected at the rites of the Bona Dea is disguise as a woman, thus bringing suspicion on Cæsar's wife Pompeia, whom he had married after the death of Cornelia, and whom he promptly divorced, though testifying that he had found nothing wrong in her conduct, "because I maintain that the members of my household must be no less free from suspicion than from guilt."

On his return from Spain in 60 B.C. occurred the famous consular election in which both Bibulus and Cæsar resorted to bribery, the former being financially supported in his course by the aristocracy, and even by the incorruptible Cato, because of their fear of what Cæsar might do if not checked by a colleague in opposition. An innovation of the year was the daily publication of the proceedings of Senate and popular assembly, which may be thought of as posted in the Forum or circulated in sheets, the Roman form of newspaper.

The determination and vigor of the democratic consul were sometimes manifest in public. When Bibulus obstructed his legislation by the long continued announcing of adverse omens, Cæsar forcibly drove him out of the Forum; and when Cato, with the same purpose, made long speeches in the Senate, Cæsar had a lictor arrest him and take him off to prison. Displeased with Cicero, according to Suetonius, he allowed the orator's mortal enemy to bring about his banishment. About this time he married Calpurnia and betrothed his daughter Julia to Pompey.

The next time we see Cæsar in the city is on March 31, 49 B.C., after nine years in Gaul, the return to Italy, and the pursuit of Pompey to Brundisium. On this occasion he summoned and addressed the Senate, appointed Æmilius Lepidus prætor to govern the city as prefect and Marcus Antonius proprætor to command the army in Italy, seized the contents of the treasury, and in five days was on the way to Spain. The treasury was at the west end of the Forum in the Temple of Saturn, the late restoration of which is represented by the lofty ruins so familiar in Forum views. Cæsar is said to have been confronted at the door of the inner chamber by the tribune Metellus, whom he commanded to hand over the keys, adding, "and you know it would be easier for me to have you killed than to give this order." What he found in the treasury was 15,000 bars of gold, 30,000 of silver, and about 30 million sesterces, or $1,500,000.

The return of Cæsar from Spain to Rome, where as dictator he provided for the elections at which his election as consul took place, with Servilius Isauricus as colleague, was followed soon by his embarcation at Brundisium for Dyrrachium. His return from Pharsalia and in the East in October, 47 B.C., a year and a half later, was followed in two months by the expedition to Africa. It was the summer of 46 B.C. before the capital had the first deliberate sight of its master, but even then it was only for six months. The second expedition against the Pompeians in Spain took him away from Rome during the winter and summer of 45 B.C., and when he returned, in September, it was to spend in the city the last six months of his life.

The signs of Cæsar's mastery most visible to Roman eyes were the five triumphs with which he celebrated the end of his wars. The first four occurred in 46 B.C. on his return from Africa, and the fifth in 45 B.C. on the second return from Spain. Suetonius tells of them:

Having ended the wars, he celebrated five triumphs, four in a single month, but at intervals of a few days, after vanquishing Scipio; and another on defeating Pompey's sons. The first and most splendid was the Gallic triumph, the next the Alexandrian, then the Pontic, after that the African, and finally the Spanish, each differing from the rest in its equipment and display of spoils. As he rode through the Velabrum on the day of his Gallic triumph, the axle of his chariot broke, and he was all but thrown out; and he mounted the Capitol by torchlight, with forty elephants bearing lamps on his right and his left. In his Pontic triumph he displayed among the show-pieces of the procession an inscription of but three words, "I came, I saw, I conquered," not indicating the events of the war, as the others did, but the speed with which it was finished.

Cæsar's long absences from Rome did not prevent him from active interest in its improvement. The Forum Julium, named after him, with its temple of Venus Genetrix, the ancestral deity of his family, begun at the close of the Gallic wars, was dedicated by him on September 26, 46 B.C., on the last day of his four triumphs. The Julian Basilica also, though still unfinished, was dedicated on the same day, and given final form by Augustus after damage by fire. Both these additions to the city's great buildings are represented by ruins: the Basilica by a vast platform 300 by 150 feet, one of the most prominent features of the Forum Romanum, and the Forum Julium by the ruins excavated in 1931-32, chief of which are the magnificent fragments of the temple. Cæsar had many other undertakings planned for the city, among them the world's largest temple to Mars and a colossal theater against the Capitoline Hill.

The student of Latin visiting Rome with Shakespeare's *Julius Cæsar* in his hand will find the figure of Cæsar suddenly much more real, and the play suddenly much more interesting. The Forum is the best place in which to read it.

It is in the Forum that Cæsar, Antony, and Calpurnia appear on "the feast of Lupercal," when Cæsar bids Calpurnia "stand directly in Antonius' way" as he runs the ceremonial course around the Palatine Hill, so that she may be touched by him and relieved of barrenness. There, too, the soothsayer appears, with his "Beware the Ides of March!" When Cæsar and his train have passed through the Forum to the Palatine, where the ceremony is to be held, Brutus and Cassius remain behind in the fine dialogue of Scene 2, in which occur the lines on the Tiber:

> I was born free as Cæsar; so were you.
> We both have fed as well, and we can both
> Endure the winter's cold as well as he;
> For once, upon a raw and gusty day,
> The troubled Tiber chafing with her shores,
> Cæsar said to me, "Darest thou, Cassius, now
> Leap in with me into this angry flood,
> And swim to yonder point?" Upon the word,
> Accoutred as I was, I plunged in
> And bade him follow. So indeed he did.
> The torrent roared, and we did buffet it
> With lusty sinews, throwing it aside
> And stemming it with hearts of controversy;
> But ere we could arrive the point proposed,
> Cæsar cried, "Help me, Cassius, or I sink!"
> I, as Æneas, our great ancestor,

Did from the flames of Troy upon his shoulder
The old Anchises bear, so from the waves of
 Tiber
Did I the tired Cæsar.

When Cæsar returns, the two conspiring critics notice his face:

But, look you, Cassius,
The angry spot doth glow on Cæsar's brow,
And all the rest look like a chidden train.
Calpurnia's cheek is pale; and Cicero
Looks with such ferret and such fiery eyes
As we have seen him in the Capitol,
Being crossed in conference by some senators.

Cæsar has been thrice offered the crown by Mark Antony, and has "put it by thrice, every time gentler than the other"—"but, for all that, to my thinking, he would fain have had it." Soon we shall hear Antony in his funeral oration:

You all did see that on the Lupercal
I thrice presented him a kingly crown,
Which he did thrice refuse: was this ambition?

Shakespeare assumes in *Julius Cæsar* that the Senate meets on the Capitol. "Comes Cæsar to the Capitol tomorrow?" inquires Cicero, later; and on the fatal day Casca cries to those who are stopping Cæsar on his way to the Senate:

What, urge you your petitions in the
 street?
Come to the Capitol.

In *Hamlet,* too, we find old Polonius and the Prince in a similar mistake:

Ham. My lord, you played once i' the university, you say?
 Pol. That did I, my lord; and was accounted a good actor.
Ham. What did you enact?
 Pol. I did enact Julius Cæsar: I was killed i' the Capitol: Brutus
 killed me.
Ham. It was a brute part of him to kill so capital a calf there. Be the
 players ready?

Neither at the time of Julius Cæsar's death nor at any other time did the Senate meet in the Capitol, meaning on the Capitoline Hill. In the year 44 B.C. it was meeting in the Curia Pompeia, or Pompey's Hall, which was a building or annex in the group dedicated in 55 B.C., comprising the Theater of Pompey and the Temple of Venus, the steps of the temple being constructed on a gigantic scale and in a curve in order to serve as the seats of the theater and thus evade the law against the construction of a permanent theater. The regular Senate House had burned in 52 B.C., had been rebuilt, and during Cæsar's last days was in process of being replaced by the new Curia Julia, named after Julius. The erection of this Senate House, interrupted by the Dictator's death, was completed by Augustus, by whom it was dedicated in 29 B.C., fifteen years later.

On the 18th of March, 44 B.C., Cæsar was to have left Rome for the East in a campaign against the Parthians, who nine years before had defeated and destroyed the army of Crassus, and from whom the Roman boundaries were never safe. The conspirators, knowing that it would be useless to attempt his life once he was out of Rome and at the head of his army, appointed the 15th of March for their undertaking.

. XIII .

THE IDES OF MARCH

ON the evening of the 14th of March, 44 B.C., Cæsar dined with Lepidus in company with Decimus Brutus. As they talked of the manner of death each would prefer, Cæsar is said to have looked up from the letters he was busy with and to have declared, "That which is sudden and unexpected."

The night as represented in the play of Shakespeare was a dreadful one. Marcus Brutus was filled with the unrest and apprehension that precede great ventures:

> Since Cassius first did whet me against Cæsar,
> I have not slept.
> Between the acting of a dreadful thing
> And the first motion, all the interim is
> Like a phantasma or a hideous dream:
> The Genius and the mortal instruments
> Are then in council; and the state of man,
> Like to a little kingdom, suffers then
> The nature of an insurrection.

Casca, who had accompanied Cæsar home and afterward gone to plot with his enemies, met Cicero on the way.

> *Cic.* Good even, Casca: brought you Cæsar home?
> Why are you breathless, and why stare you so?
> *Casca.* Are you not moved, when all the sway of
> earth
> Shakes like a thing unfirm? O Cicero,
> I have seen tempests when the scolding winds
> Have rived the knotty oaks, and I have seen
> The ambitious ocean swell and rage and foam,
> To be exalted with the threatening clouds;
> But never till to-night, never till now,
> Did I go through a tempest dropping fire. . .

> Against the Capitol I met a lion,
> Who glared upon me, and went surly by,
> Without annoying me . . .
> And yesterday the bird of night did sit
> Even at noonday upon the market-place
> Hooting and shrieking.

Cicero and Casca go their separate ways. Cicero is known to be no friend of the Cæsarian régime, but the plotters are rightly of opinion that a man of his prominence, a lifelong acquaintance of Cæsar and sometime admirer of his qualities, is not likely in the sixty-second year of his life to prove a good conspirator in their violent cause. Casca and his friends discuss him but briefly:

> *Cas.* But what of Cicero? Shall we sound him?
> I think he will stand very strong with us.
> *Casca.* Let us not leave him out.
> *Cin.*   No, by no means.
> *Met.* O let us have him, for his silver hairs
> Will purchase us a good opinion,
> And buy men's voices to commend our deeds:
> It shall be said, his judgment ruled our hands;
> Our youths and wildness shall no whit appear,
> But all be buried in his gravity.
> *Bru.* O name him not: let us not break with him;
> For he will never follow anything
> That other men begin.
> *Cas.*   Then leave him out.
> *Casca.* Indeed he is not fit.

Another Shakespearean reflection of the stories told afterwards about this portentous night is in Horatio's speech to Bernardo and Marcellus as the three keep watch on the platform before the castle of Elsinore the night of the Ghost's appearance:

> In the most high and palmy state of Rome,
> A little ere the mightiest Julius fell,   ·
> The graves stood tenantless, and the sheeted
>   dead
> Did squeak and gibber in the Roman streets.

In Cæsar's own house, too, there were signs. This, we may assume, was the Domus Publica, already mentioned as being near the Regia at the southeast corner of the Forum. Cæsar himself

appears in the early hours of the morning while the thunder and
lightning still play, and cries:

> Nor heaven nor earth have been at peace
>   tonight:
> Thrice hath Calpurnia in her sleep cried out,
> "Help, ho! they murder Cæsar."

Calpurnia's dreams have been of streaming blood and falling
roofs. In the midst of all the heavenly din, the holy spear of Mars
in the Regia has been heard to clash against the shield. Cæsar has
had an attack of faintness.

When, added to all this, Calpurnia is told of dreadful portents,
she is filled with dismay and will not consent to Cæsar's going
forth to the meeting of the Senate:

> Cæsar, I never stood on ceremonies,
> Yet now they fright me. There is one within,
> Besides the things that we have heard and seen,
> Recounts most horrid sights seen by the watch.
> A lioness hath whelpèd in the streets;
> And graves have yawned, and yielded up their
>   dead;
> Fierce fiery warriors fought upon the clouds,
> In ranks and squadrons and right form of war,
> Which drizzled blood upon the Capitol;
> The noise of battle hurtled in the air,
> Horses did neigh, and dying men did groan,
> And ghosts did shriek and squeal about the
>   streets.
> O Cæsar, these things are beyond all use,
> And I do fear them.

But the man who for fifteen years has taken no thought for
safety in his career

> Of moving accidents by flood and field,
> Of hair-breadth scapes i' the imminent
>   deadly breach,

is not the one to entertain the thought of fear now:

> *Cæs.*   What can be avoided
> Whose end is purposed by the mighty gods?

> Yet Cæsar shall go forth; for these predictions
> Are to the world in general as to Cæsar.
> *Cal.* When beggars die, there are no comets seen;
> The heavens themselves blaze forth the death of
> princes.
> *Cæs.* Cowards die many times before their death;
> The valiant never taste of death but once.
> Of all the wonders that I yet have heard,
> It seems to me most strange that men should fear;
> Seeing that death, a necessary end,
> Will come when it will come.

Not even when the augural victim is found to be without a heart, will Cæsar alter his purpose:

> Cæsar should be a beast without a heart,
> If he should stay at home to-day for fear.
> No, Cæsar shall not: Danger knows full well
> That Cæsar is more dangerous than he.
> We are two lions littered in one day,
> And I the elder and more terrible:
> And Cæsar shall go forth.

Cæsar does go forth. We see him step from the portals of the Domus Publica to the Sacred Way, advance with his retinue of attendants and pretended friends between the Regia and the Temple of Vesta, cross the Forum, and at its northwest corner near the Tullianum enter the narrow, steep, and winding street called then Lautumiae, "The Quarries," and afterwards Clivus Argentarius, "Silversmith Street," or possibly "Bankers' Street," whose pavement, since early 1932 again trodden of men, led to the Campus Martius and the Curia Pompeia, where the Senate awaited its presiding officer and the conspirators their victim. Many fragments of Pompey's buildings are still extant, though hidden in modern buildings and under the pavement. They prove the theater to have been enormous: nearly 500 feet in diameter, with a stage nearly 300 feet long, and a capacity of at least 10,000.

As Cæsar nears the door of the Senate, his eye falls on the soothsayer, and they engage in the brief dialogue:

> The Ides of March are come.
> Ay, Cæsar; but not gone.

CLIVUS ARGENTARIUS, 1932

ALTAR OF JULIUS CÆSAR

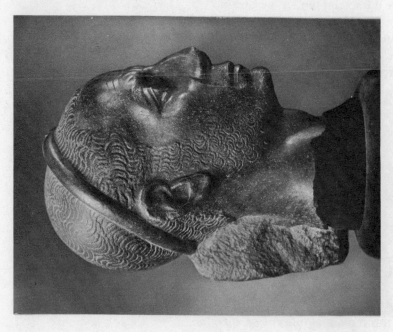

Let Suetonius tell what followed:

As he took his seat, the conspirators gathered about him as if to pay their respects, and straightway Tillius Cimber, who had assumed the lead, came nearer as though to ask something; and when Cæsar with a gesture put him off to another time, Cimber caught his toga by both shoulders; then as Cæsar cried, "Why, this is violence!" one of the Cascas stabbed him from one side just below the throat. Cæsar caught Casca's arm and ran it through with his stylus, but as he tried to leap to his feet, he was stopped by another wound.

When he saw that he was beset on every side by drawn daggers, he muffled his head in his robe, and at the same time drew down its lap to his feet with his left hand, in order to fall more decently, with the lower part of his body also covered. And in this wise he was stabbed with three and twenty wounds, uttering not a word, but merely a groan at the first stroke, though some have written that when Marcus Brutus rushed at him, he said in Greek, "You too, my child?"

All the conspirators made off, and he lay there lifeless for some time, until finally three common slaves put him on a litter and carried him home, with one arm hanging down. And of so many wounds none turned out to be mortal, in the opinion of the physician Antistius, except the second one in the breast.

In the play, when all have fled from the Senate but the conspirators, Mark Antony appears. Dazed, not yet quite knowing what course to pursue, he asks and receives their consent for him to

> Produce his body to the market-place;
> And in the pulpit, as becomes a friend,
> Speak in the order of his funeral.

His speech is to follow that of Brutus.

> *Bru.*   And you shall speak
> In the same pulpit whereto I am going,
> After my speech is ended.
> *Ant.*   Be it so;
> I do desire no more.
> *Bru.* Prepare the body then, and follow us.

But before Antony follows, he addresses the dead Cæsar in one of the most magnificent of speeches:

O pardon me, thou bleeding piece of earth,
That I am meek and gentle with these butchers!
Thou art the ruins of the noblest man
That ever lived in the tide of times.
Woe to the hand that shed this costly blood!
Over thy wounds now do I prophesy—
Which, like dumb mouths, do ope their ruby lips
To beg the voice and utterance of my tongue—
A curse shall light upon the limbs of men;
Domestic fury and fierce civil strife
Shall cumber all the parts of Italy;
Blood and destruction shall be so in use,
And dreadful objects so familiar,
That mothers shall but smile when they behold
Their infants quartered with the hands of war;
All pity choked with custom of fell deeds;
And Cæsar's spirit, ranging for revenge,
With Ate by his side come hot from hell,
Shall in these confines with a monarch's voice
Cry "Havoc," and let slip the dogs of war,
That this foul deed shall smell above the earth
With carrion men, groaning for burial.

The Liberators, as they called themselves, not finding the citizenry so ready to rise in their favor as they had thought, took refuge on the Capitoline Hill. The city was in confusion, no one knowing what to expect or what to do. The Senate was convoked now here, now there, and became coherent enough to pass an act of amnesty; the conspirators came down from the Capitol, and parleys were held; Cæsar's will was made public, leaving to the people in common his gardens by the Tiber, and to each citizen three hundred sesterces; and after two or three days the funeral took place.

The funeral ceremony was to be in the Forum, and the burning of the body and the funeral games were to take place in the Campus Martius; but in the great excitement of the day the populace, as frequently happens at political funerals, suddenly took matters into its own hands. According to one account, Antony, as he delivered the funeral oration from the Rostra where the body lay, suddenly exposed to view a waxen image of Cæsar with all his wounds, reciting as he did so the achievements and the sufferings of the dead Dictator with such effect that the crowd was wrought to frenzy, and riotously burned the body on the spot. Those who read in the actual Forum the funeral oration as imagined by Shakespeare may realize the pitch of emotion to which the people rose and the art of the speaker who could bring them to it:

> Friends, Romans, countrymen, lend me your ears;
> I come to bury Cæsar, not to praise him...
> He was my friend, faithful and just to me;
> But Brutus says he was ambitious...
> When that the poor have cried, Cæsar hath wept:
> Ambition should be made of sterner stuff...
> You all did love him once, not without cause;
> What cause withholds you, then, to mourn for him?
> O judgment! thou art fled to brutish beasts,
> And men have lost their reason. Bear with me:
> My heart is in the coffin there with Cæsar;
> And I must pause till it come back to me.
>
> .   .   .
>
> You will compel me, then, to read the will?
> Then make a ring about the corpse of Cæsar,
> And let me show you him that made the will.
>
> .   .   .
>
> If you have tears, prepare to shed them now.
> You all do know this mantle: I remember
> The first time ever Cæsar put it on;
> 'Twas on a summer's evening, in his tent,
> That day he overcame the Nervii.
> Look, in this place ran Cassius' dagger through;
> See what a rent the envious Casca made;
> Through this the well-beloved Brutus stabbed;
> And as he plucked his cursed steel away,
> Mark how the blood of Cæsar followed it,
> As rushing out of doors, to be resolved
> If Brutus so unkindly knocked, or no;
> For Brutus, as you know, was Cæsar's angel.
> Judge, O you gods, how dearly Cæsar loved him!
> This was the most unkindest cut of all;
> For when the noble Cæsar saw him stab,
> Ingratitude, more strong than traitors' arms,

Quite vanquished him; then burst his mighty heart;
And, in his mantle muffling up his face,
Even at the base of Pompey's statuë,
Which all the while ran blood, great Cæsar fell.

. . .

Good friends, sweet friends, let me not stir you up
To such a sudden flood of mutiny.
They that have done this deed are honorable.
What private griefs they have, alas, I know not,
That made them do it; they are wise and honorable,
And will, no doubt, with reasons answer you.
I come not, friends, to steal away your hearts;
I am no orator, as Brutus is,
But, as you know me all, a plain, blunt man,
That love my friend; and that they know full well
That gave me public leave to speak of him;
For I have neither wit, nor words, nor worth,
Action, nor utterance, nor the power of speech,
To stir men's blood: I only speak right on.
I tell you that which you yourselves do know;
Show you sweet Cæsar's wounds, poor, poor, dumb
        mouths,
And bid them speak for me; but were I Brutus,
And Brutus Antony, there were an Antony
Would ruffle up your spirits, and put a tongue
In every wound of Cæsar, that should move
The stones of Rome to rise and mutiny.

The funeral and its aftermath are described by Suetonius:

A pyre was erected in the Campus Martius near the tomb of Julia,
and on the Rostra a gilded shrine was placed, made after the model
of the Temple of Venus Genetrix; within was a couch of ivory with
coverlets of purple and gold, and at its head a pillar hung with the
robe in which he was slain. Since it was clear that the day would not
be long enough for those who offered gifts, they were directed to
bring them to the Campus by whatsoever streets of the city they
wished, regardless of any order of precedence. At the funeral games,
to rouse pity and indignation at his death, these words from the
Contest for the Arms of Pacuvius were sung:

"Saved I these men that they might murder me?"

and words of a like purport from the Electra of Atilius. Instead of a
eulogy the consul Antonius caused a herald to recite the decree of the

Senate in which it had voted Cæsar all divine and human honors at once, and likewise the oath with which they had all pledged themselves to watch over his personal safety: to which he added a very few words of his own.

The bier on the Rostra was carried to the Forum by magistrates and ex-magistrates; and while some were urging that it be burned in the Temple of Jupiter on the Capitol, and others in the Hall of Pompey, on a sudden two beings with swords by their sides and brandishing a pair of darts set fire to it with blazing torches, and at once the throng of bystanders heaped upon it dry branches, the judgment seats with the benches, and whatever else could serve as an offering. Then the musicians and actors tore off their robes, which they had taken from the equipment of his triumphs and put on for the occasion, rent them to bits and threw them into the flames, and the veterans of the legions the arms with which they had adorned themselves for the funeral; many of the women, too, offered up the jewels which they wore and the amulets and robes of their children.

At the height of the public grief a throng of foreigners went about lamenting each after the fashion of his country, above all the Jews, who even flocked to the place for several successive nights.

Immediately after the funeral the commons ran to the houses of Brutus and Cassius with firebrands, and after being repelled with difficulty, they slew Helvius Cinna when they met him, through a mistake in the name, supposing that he was Cornelius Cinna, who had the day before made a bitter indictment of Cæsar and for whom they were looking; and they set his head upon a spear and paraded it about the streets. Afterwards they set up in the Forum a solid column of Numidian marble almost twenty feet high, and inscribed upon it, "To the Father of his Country." At the foot of this they continued for a long time to sacrifice, make vows, and settle some of their disputes by an oath in the name of Cæsar.

The rostra from which Antony spoke must have been the regular Rostra of the Republic, in front of the Senate House. Cæsar's plan to move it to the west end of the Forum, where its remains are now to be seen, was executed by Augustus. The place where the pyre was hastily built and the body burned was at the opposite end of the Forum, in front of the Regia, where stand now the ruins of the Temple of Julius Cæsar, erected by Augustus and dedicated August 18, 29 B.C.

At the base of the front wall of this temple, in a niche discovered nearly thirty years ago, is the core of a round stone base which supported the column or altar at which the spirit of Cæsar was worshiped, and which marks the spot where the remnants of its mortal casing were gathered after the blazing pyre had sunk to glowing embers and embers had cooled to ashes. This is the most moving monument in the Roman Forum.

Suetonius continues:

He died in the fifty-sixth year of his age, and was numbered among the gods, not only by a formal decree, but also in the conviction of the vulgar. For at the first of the games which his heir Augustus gave in honor of his apotheosis, a comet shone for seven successive nights, rising about the eleventh hour, and was believed to be the soul of Cæsar, who had been taken to heaven; and this is why a star is set upon the crown of his head in his statue.

In the Barracco Museum in Rome, a black basalt head with a star upon it is regarded as a portrait of Julius Cæsar. It was found in Egypt, and shows a beard of some two weeks' growth, which with the ancients was sometimes a sign of mourning. Because of the beard and the star and the discovery of the head in Egypt, the portrait is thought to represent Cæsar at the beginning of his sojourn in Egypt, after the death of Pompey, once his son-in-law.

These were tragic times. "Hardly any of his assassins survived him for more than three years, or died a natural death," concludes Suetonius' *Life*. "They were all condemned, and they perished in various ways—some by shipwreck, some in battle; some took their own lives with the selfsame dagger with which they had impiously slain Cæsar."

THE SEVENTH OF DECEMBER

FOR the Roman Republic, the two years that followed the death of Cæsar were as the final act in a great tragedy. Cicero himself was involved in the ruin of the times. Guiltless of conspiracy, personally grieved at the death of Cæsar and yet unable not to approve what he thought the liberation of the State from tyranny, it was not on the field or in arms that he met his end, but in courageous civic opposition to the high-handed measures of Cæsar's temporary successor, Mark Antony.

Disappointed and despairing of the restoration of the Republic, after four months of Antony's régime Cicero left Rome for the south of Italy, intending to visit Marcus Junior, then a student in Athens, and to return at the beginning of the following year, when he hoped that the installation of Hirtius and Pansa as the first regular consuls after many years would bring back the old senatorial régime. After he had sailed from Syracuse on August 1, however, and had been driven by adverse winds to the Italian coast, hearing of a better attitude on the part of Antony, he faced about, and on August 31 was once more in Rome.

The smouldering enmity between the new autocrat and Cicero suddenly burst into flame. From September 2, 44 B.C., the date of the *First Philippic*, to April 21, 43 B.C., the date of the *Fourteenth* and last, the deadliness of their enmity increased. When Cicero composed the *Second Philippic*, in September, he knew the character of the man to whom the speech would be a challenge, and he knew the dangers of the course on which he had entered.

I defended the State when I was young, I will not fail it now that I am old. I despised the sword of Catiline, I will not quail before yours. I will offer my body freely if my death can bring back liberty to the State. . . . Death is even desirable to me, Senators, after the honors

I have gained and the deeds I have done. I ask for only these two things: first, that dying I may leave the Roman People free—the immortal gods can grant me nothing that I desire more; second, that the rewards of each man may be in proportion to what he has deserved of the Republic.

The publication of the speech in December, as a pamphlet, was the act that determined Cicero's death in case Mark Antony came back to power.

When Antony in May, 43 B.C., finally came to terms with Plancus and Lepidus, who with their armies had been watching from the Gallic provinces the course of events, and when in October Antony and Lepidus had come to terms with Cæsar's nephew and heir Octavian, the young Augustus, and the Second Triumvirate was formed, the doom of Cicero was one of the first to be pronounced in the murderous proscription that followed.

We are told by Plutarch that for two days Octavian resisted the demands of Antony for Cicero's death. We may easily imagine the elder triumvir's unrelenting insistence. Again our Shakespeare helps us to realize the times:

> *Ant.* These many, then, shall die; their names are
> pricked.
> *Oct.* Your brother, too, must die; consent you, Lepidus?
> *Lep.* I do consent.
> *Oct.*   Prick him down, Antony.
> *Lep.* Upon condition Publius shall not live,
> Who is your sister's son, Mark Antony.
> *Ant.* He shall not live; look, with a spot I damn him.

The death of Cicero, on December 7, 43 B.C., was one of the most deeply felt events of ancient times. Of the one hundred and seven books of Livy which the world has let perish, almost the only fragment to survive is the account of it preserved by the elder Seneca from Book CXX:

Just before the arrival of the triumvirs Marcus Cicero left the city, considering it certain that he had no more chance of being saved from the vengeance of Antony than Brutus and Cassius had of escaping that of Octavius—which was the fact. He fled first to his Tusculan

GAETA, ANCIENT CAIETA

THE MONASTERY OF SAN DOMENICO

THE LIRIS AT SORA

villa, and thence proceeded by cross-roads to that of Formiae, in order to take ship at Caieta. There, after advancing several times seaward, he was driven back by adverse winds, and again he found himself unable to endure the tossing of the ship on the gloomy rolling waves, and he began at length to grow weary both of flight and of life. So he returned to his upper villa, which was a little more than a mile from the shore, saying, *"Moriar in patria saepe servata"*—"I will die in my own land that I have often saved."

It is well established that his slaves were ready to fight for him bravely and faithfully, but that he ordered them to put down the litter and endure with patience whatever an adverse fate should compel. As he leaned out of the litter and offered his neck, unmoved, his head was cut off. Nor did this satisfy the senseless cruelty of the soldiers. They cut off his hands, also, for the offence of having written something against Antony. Thus the head was brought to Antony and placed by his order between the two hands on the Rostra, where, often as consul, often as a consular, and, that very year against Antony, he had been heard with admiration of his eloquence, the like of which no other human voice ever uttered. The people, raising their eyes bedimmed with tears, could scarcely bear the sight of his dismembered parts.

He lived sixty-three years, so that in the absence of violence his death could not have been considered premature. His genius served him well, both in his works and in the rewards thereof. He enjoyed the favors of fortune for a long time, yet in the intervals of his protracted career of prosperity he suffered some severe blows, exile, the ruin of the party he had espoused, the death of his daughter, and his end so sad and bitter, none of which calamities did he bear as became a man except his death, which to one who weighs the matter impartially must seem the less undeserved, since he suffered nothing more cruel at the hands of his victorious enemy than he would himself have inflicted if fortune had put the same power in his hands. Yet if we weigh his virtues and his faults he must be pronounced a great, energetic, and ever memorable man, to fitly sound whose praises another Cicero would be needed.

We need not take too literally the criticism here expressed as to Cicero's behavior during exile and bereavement. He was a man of emotional temperament, the blows were heavy, he was a letter-writer, and he had a friend from whom he withheld no thought he had and no pang he felt in the course of those crushing trials. Livy's appreciation as a whole is pleasing to the admirer of Cicero, and many others extant are equally so.

The proscription was the cause of dreadful scenes in Rome. Says Appian of Alexandria, writing *The Civil Wars* about two hundreds years afterward:

When the lists were published, the gates and all the other exits from the city, the harbor, the marshes, the pools, and every other place that was suspected as adapted to flight or concealment, were occupied by soldiers; the centurions were charged to scour the surrounding country. All these things took place simultaneously. Straightway, throughout city and country, wherever each one happened to be found, there were sudden arrests and murder in various forms, and decapitations for the sake of the rewards when the head should be shown; also undignified flights in strange costumes, of persons hitherto well dressed. Some descended into wells, others into filthy sewers. Some took refuge in chimneys. Others crouched in the deepest silence under the thick-set tiles of their roofs. Some were not less fearful of their wives and ill-disposed children than of the murderers. Others feared their freedmen and their slaves; creditors feared their debtors and neighbors feared neighbors who coveted their lands. There was a sudden outburst of previously smouldering hates.

The younger Marcus Cicero was in Greece when his father met the tragic end. The two Quintus Ciceros fell victims to the same bitter fortune.

Cicero's brother, Quintus, was captured, together with his son. He begged the murderer to kill him before his son, and the son prayed that he might be killed before his father. The murderers said that they would grant both requests, and, dividing themselves into two parties, each taking one, killed them at the same time according to agreement.

Augustus himself, if we are to believe Plutarch, was among the chief of those who appreciated Cicero as man and orator. Writes the biographer in his *Cicero:*

It happened many years after that Augustus once found one of his grandsons with a work of Cicero in his hands. The boy was frightened, and hid the book under his gown; but Cæsar took it from him, and, standing there motionless, he read through a great part of the book. Then he gave it back to the boy, and said: "This was a great orator, my child; a great orator, and a man who loved his country well."

The Seventh of December, 43, and the Ides of March, 44, were the last days of two of Rome's and the world's greatest men. They were both men of the public career and identified with the State; they were both men of action, and both men of mind; they were friends by nature, and foes by circumstance; they both met tragic ends while still in the full tide of action and intellect; they both lived on in the life of after times—the one in his contributions chiefly as the man of decision and action, as the soldier and statesman; the other in his inspirations as orator and patriot, moralist, student, and stylist. There is no need to argue which was the greater, either in their own day or in the days that received the fruits of their lives as heritage. Their ways and works, though separate and, when the crisis came, opposed, were yet one in the working out of Roman destiny and in the creation of the culture that rules the modern world.

> That Julius Cæsar was a famous man;
> With what his valor did enrich his wit,
> His wit set down to make his valor live:
> Death makes no conquest of this conqueror.

To balance the compact eloquence of Shakespeare, we may set down the enthusiasm of Pliny the Elder for Cicero a century after his death:

Hail, thou Father of eloquence and of Latin letters, first of all to be called Father of His Country. Well did Cæsar the Dictator, though an enemy, once write of thee, "Thy honor is greater than all triumphs, just as to enlarge the bounds of Roman thought is nobler than to extend the limits of Roman power."

Of modern tributes to Cicero, the most eloquent is in the single line of Lord Byron describing Servius Sulpicius, Cicero's colleague of the bar. With his mind filled with thoughts of Cicero not as the orator and public man, but as the essayist on friendship, old age, ethics, and immortality, and as the bereaved father receiving the famous letter of consolation from Servius, the poet immortalizes the names of both in the stately and beautiful expression,

The Roman friend of Rome's least mortal mind.

The stanzas from *Childe Harold* in which this gem is set should be among the mental furnishings of every lover of Cicero. When Tullia died, in the early part of 45, Servius Sulpicius was governor of Greece. He had contemplated with philosophic sadness on his voyagings the decayed cities of Ægina, Corinth, Megara, Athens, and its port Piræus—the glory that once was Greece. When he writes to the stricken Cicero consoling him for the death of his daughter, he remembers the experience:

As on my return from Asia I sailed from Ægina toward Megara, I began to look on the places round about me. Behind me was Ægina; in front, Megara; on the right, Piræus; on the left, Corinth—cities at one time most flourishing, but now prostrate and decayed before my eyes. I began to ponder thus: "Ah me! shall we poor little mortals feel ourselves aggrieved if one of us has died or been slain, whose life must be brief, when in one place the dead bodies of so many cities lie prostrate before us? Will you not remember that you are a mortal man, Servius, and restrain yourself?"

Byron sailed the same waters, and knew the letter of Servius Sulpicius:

> Wandering in youth, I traced the path of him,
> The Roman friend of Rome's least mortal mind,
> The friend of Tully: as my bark did skim
> The bright blue waters with a fanning wind,
> Came Megara before me, and behind
> Ægina lay, Piræus on the right,
> And Corinth on the left; I lay reclined
> Along the prow, and saw all these unite
> In ruin, even as he had seen the desolate sight.
>
> For time hath not rebuilt them, but upreared
> Barbaric dwellings on their shattered site,
> Which only makes more mourned and more endeared
> The few last rays of their far-scattered light,
> And the crushed relics of their vanished might.
> The Roman saw these tombs in his own age,
> These sepulchres of cities, which excite
> Sad wonder, and his yet surviving page
> The moral lesson bears, drawn from such pilgrimage.

. XV .

CICERO AND STYLE

THE Emperor Augustus called Cicero "a great orator" and "a master of words." Julius Cæsar courted his eloquence, Mark Antony feared it. The historian Livy recognized his genius, and pronounced him "an ever memorable man, to fitly sound whose praises another Cicero would be needed." Velleius Paterculus, an officer under Tiberius, pays tribute to his "heavenly eloquence" and the "fame and glory of his deeds and words," declaring that "sooner shall the race of man fail in the world than his name decay." Pliny the Elder saluted him as "Father of eloquence and Latin letters," as well as "Father of his Country." The Younger Pliny tried to fancy himself in letter-writing and before the jury a second Cicero. Tacitus begins his literary career as an imitator of his style, and in the *Dialogue on Orators* says that "out of much learning in a great many subjects, and out of a universal knowledge, wells forth in its richness that wonderful eloquence of his." Martial the epigrammatist and Juvenal the satirist assume his supremacy. Quintilian, the great professor of Rhetoric, declares in *The Training of the Orator* that he "would set Cicero against any one of the Greek orators without fear of refutation." "For posterity," he says, "the name of Cicero has come to be regarded not as the name of a man, but as the name of eloquence itself. Let us therefore fix our eyes on him, take him as our pattern, and let the student realize that he has made real progress if he is a passionate admirer of Cicero." Quintilian also refers to the "sovereignty" at the bar which was acknowledged in the orator's own day. He was known as an advocate who won his cases. Fronto, tutor of Marcus Aurelius and ambitious to found a new style, nevertheless calls Cicero the "highest and supreme expression of the Roman tongue." Minucius Felix, the first of the Latin Christian essayists, begins the *Octavius* with a sentence instantly recalling the first phrases of Cicero's *On the Orator*. Augustine, Ambrose, Lactantius, and Jerome look back on him with a gratitude for his almost Christian content which we may assume was equalled by their admiration for his eloquence. Lactantius was honored by the name of "the Christian Cicero." We need not trace the influence of the Ciceronian manner of writing and speaking down through the Renaissance, when it was admired by Petrarch and Erasmus, or to later times when it was the model of orators and authors among the nations of Europe and America. "All the great letter-writers of more modern ages," writes Mackail, "have more or less, consciously or unconsciously, followed the Ciceronian model." The majority of critics familiar with the history of style would agree with Dimsdale, that Cicero "achieved a style which is the basis of modern European prose."

If this seems at first a sweeping statement, a moment's reflection will remove any doubt of its truth. In the first place, it must be remembered that "modern European prose," which is also the prose of the North and South American nations, and of other far-away offshoots of European civilization, means the language written and spoken by educated people; that is, the prose of historians, essayists, novelists, scholars, lawyers, orators, teachers, and preachers, and of polite intercourse. In the second place, the language habits and inspirations of these classes are a product of the schools, and the schools are the tradition of language teaching based on the Latin tongue. The Latin language is not only one of the most prominent subjects in the educational systems of today, but it has not entirely ceased to be the medium of spoken and written instruction. It is not many generations since it was the frequent medium of the schools, and it is not many centuries since it was the universal language of the learned and the learning world. Dante and Petrarch in the fourteenth century were innovators when they wrote in Italian.

The language of the cultivated man in Europe for a thousand years after Cicero was Latin, and the model for his prose, as well as much of the matter of his instruction, was Cicero. Just as the various romance languages, not excluding English, which would be termed more correctly Anglo-Latin, are descended from the

Latin tongue, so are their styles descended from and based on the Latin style; and the Latin style is more universally represented by Cicero than by any other author. Even in European countries whose language is not of Latin origin, the use of Latin in schools and in intellectual and ecclesiastical circles impressed the Latin style in greater or less degree upon the native language. The stream of culture up to modern cosmopolitan times has been narrow and quite sharply defined, and today is only less so in the many national channels into which it has divided. We flatter ourselves by thinking we are independent, but the analysis of our culture and the tracing of our linguistic and literary habits bring us quickly to the Latin language and to its great master.

This does not mean either that Cicero's excellence as a stylist has been undisputed or that the prose of the twentieth century is always consciously imitative of the Ciceronian style. Cicero's greatest admirer in antiquity reminds his readers that not even the greatest writers are free from fault. Let us concede with Quintilian that Cicero is not perfection, and let us agree also that Ciceronian prose is not the most perspicuous medium of communication with the masses of today.

Let us nevertheless look into the nature of the Ciceronian style. This will bring into relief the virtues claimed for it and the vices charged against it. It will also demonstrate—what is of great moment in the formation of a final estimate—that the vices and virtues of Ciceronianism are often identical, and that mere prejudice, or slight variation of temperament in the critic, may serve to render the virtue into a vice, or to make of the vice a virtue.

Our inquiry must really be, then, as to whether the charges against Ciceronianism are valid in the greater degree, or only in the less.

Perhaps it will help to an easier grasp of the nature of Cicero's art if we select the quality which embraces most of its virtues, and about it as a center construct an appreciation.

This quality is nothing more mysterious than a marvellous fluency. Whether in oration, essay, or formal epistle, Ciceronian eloquence is a full-flowing, unceasing current, smooth, steady, reposeful.

By fluency, too, we must understand not only fluency of language, but fluency of thought. There is fluent thinking, as well as fluent writing or speaking, and the one is necessary to the other. There is thinking which streams easily and continuously, and there is thinking which leaps, or halts, or strays and loses time in getting back again, or never gets back. Cicero's thought is copious, continuous, logical. His mental processes are easy-running. There are no breaks, no jolts; there is no getting lost. When we are led aside from the main path, it is with full consciousness that the path is still there, and that we are soon to be brought safely back to it.

Here perhaps a caution should be uttered. The virtue of fluent thought is that it is clear and easily followed. Further, that which is clear and easily followed is not always duly credited with depth. Cicero, like others who have made themselves readily understood, has not escaped the charge of superficiality.

When we think of the philosophical essays, of the many rich *loci communes,* or universalities, imbedded in the orations, or of the compression of Plato's whole doctrine of the immortality of the soul into a few lines of *De Senectute,* we are not disposed to accept this criticism. However, even granted that Cicero's thought does seem to lie on the surface, it may be asked, in turn, What constitutes depth? Anyone may easily call to mind, for example, thinkers in the religious life of the past century who seemed to the onlooker of their day, in Mrs. Browning's Lucretian phrase, to drop their plummets "down the broad, deep universe . . . finding no bottom"; yet their doctrines are clear enough now, and the expressions of the average religious journal of today make them appear even conservative. We have adopted their thought and are familiar with it. The preacher who should deliver the content of their sermons today would be called platitudinous. The deep things of Cicero's day have for the most part long been common property. And besides, there is often a confusion of depth of thought with thought only partially expressed. Omit to express a link here and there in the logical process, and it is conceivable that the reader will think one is deep, when, as a matter of fact, one is only careless, lazy, or stupid. The deepest thought is but the final link in a long, logical chain. Take time, let every successive link be traced, and a natural and easy progress brings us to the end— granting, of course, the possession of the experience necessary to understanding.

But this brings us back to language. Ciceronian fluency of thought finds a perfect medium of expression in Ciceronian fluency of language. The full, streaming, logical process is clothed in full, streaming, verbal dress. All is clearness, limpidity, ease. To adapt a famous phrase, *Ce qui n'est pas éclair, n'est pas de Cicéron.* Few writers so effectively conserve the energy of the reader by leading him gently and noiselessly and effortlessly from the beginning to the end of his thought. There are no haltings, no leaps and jerks, no gaps. All is amplitude and fulness. Cicero does not scruple to use all the words he needs. The epigrammatic comparison of him with Demosthenes by Quintilian is more accurate than most epigrams. "From the one you can take nothing away, to the other you can add nothing."

As might be expected, such fulness invites the charge of redundancy. Let us examine this charge also.

It may, indeed, be conceded that many a word could be omitted from Cicero's orations without very appreciably interfering with the sense. The orator's delight in fulness leads him to employ pairs of words and phrases where the second member balances the first, and often seems to repeat it. In most cases, however, a little examination will show that expressions which are apparently synonymous are not so in reality. Cicero's method here is not repetition, but amplification, and the result is a sense of richness and abundance of resource. Such phrases as the following are not examples of tautology: *singulari eximiaque virtute,* "singular and exceptional virtue"; *animos excitare atque inflammare,* "to arouse our souls and to set them on fire"; *sententiis nostris consultisque,* "our verdicts and decrees"; *maerorem atque luctum,* "grief and mourning." The repetition of idea is only partial. The risk of redundancy is worth running for the sake of the harmony of the language and the sense of equipoise in the thought. Pairs like this may be compared with two circles which slightly intersect each other; there is common ground, but the areas are by no means identical. They are, indeed, often entirely separate, but there is always a balance of thought and sound.

So also when Cicero employs a series of words—*consilio, auctoritate, sententia,* "counsel, authority, judgment"; *mente, ratione, cogitatione,* "mind, reason, consideration"; *inconstantia, levitate, mobilitate,* "inconstancy, lightness, fickleness." We might omit some of these terms, to be sure, and still be understood. Sometimes, it may be conceded, we should be glad to omit; but not often, and then, perhaps, not wisely—for the question of harmony and rhythm is also to be considered, and sentiment. Consider, for example, the rich vowel and consonantal harmonies, the rhythmical quality, and the fitness of language to content in the following sentence: *Horae quidem cedunt et dies et menses et anni, nec praeteritum tempus umquam revertitur, nec quid sequatur sciri potest,* "The hours go on and on, and the days and the months and the years, nor does time once gone by ever return, nor can what is to follow be known." To the "simple-primrose" kind of people, it would have been perhaps just as satisfying had Cicero merely said, *Tempus fugit,* and not concerned himself with the elegant, ample, and reposeful sentence of the stylist expressing so perfectly the sense of long continued passage of time and the impossibility of its recall.

When there occurs actual repetition of words, there is of course no question of tautology, for this is one of the ordinary factors in rhetorical art. *Unum sentitis omnes, unum studetis. . . . Quem umquam iste ordo patronum adoptavit? Si quemquam, debuit me. Sed me omitto. Quem censorem? Quem imperatorem?* No apology is necessary for this kind of repetition.

But the most effective of all Cicero's devices for fluency is to be seen in his use of the connective. "In literature," says Balzac, "the art lies entirely in the gracefulness of the transitions." This is exaggeration, but it contains a great principle of style. Cicero is master of the art of graceful transition. Nothing can be more admirable than the skill and ease with which one sentence is made to follow another. All the fine variety of Latin conjunctions and relative pronouns and adverbs is pressed into service with unequaled dexterity. Almost any page of any work shows it. *Enim,*

quamquam, enim, et tamen, quarum, autem, enim, etsi, sed,
quidem, igitur, sed, autem, apud quem, qui si, sed, enim, is the
array that makes the first paragraphs of *De Senectute* flow; some
of them adversative, some continuative, some relative, some
stronger, and some weaker, and all serving to gather up and present in review before the mind, so to speak, the contents of the
sentence or clause immediately preceding before going on to the
next. Examine the following paragraph. What a wealth of words,
what easy connection, and what fluency and fulness as a result!
About one word in five is not strictly necessary, yet not a word in
the passage is actually superfluous. The roman type indicates connection or transition, and the parentheses inclose words not
strictly necessary.

(Hoc) enim *onere, quod mihi (commune) tecum est, (aut iam)*
urgentis aut (certe) adventantis senectutis (et) te et me (etiam ipsum)
levari volo; etsi *te* (quidem) *id (modice et) sapienter (sic) ut omnia*
(et) ferre et laturum esse (certo) scio. Sed *(mihi), cum de senectute*
vellem aliquid scribere, (tu) occurrebas dignus (eo) munere quo
uterque (nostrum communiter) uteretur. Mihi (quidem) *ita iucunda*
(huius) libri confectio fuit, ut non modo (omnes) absterserit senectutis
molestias, sed effecerit (mollem etiam et) iucundam senectutem.
Numquam igitur *(digne) satis laudari philosophia poterit,* cui *qui*
pareat omne tempus aetatis sine molestia possit degere.

For of this burden, old age, which you and I bear (in common),
and which is (either already) weighing us down or (at any rate) advancing on us, I wish (both) you and (also) me (myself) to be light-
ened; although I know (of a surety) that you (indeed) are (both)
bearing it and will bear it, (in like manner) as you bear all things,
with self-control and philosophically. But when I decided to write
something on old age, you occurred (to me) as worthy of an undertaking (such as) both (of us in common) could profit by. For me,
(to be sure,) the writing of the (present) book has been so delightful
that it has not only brushed away (all) the vexations of old age, but
has even rendered it (easy and) pleasant. Never (therefore) will it be
possible for philosophy to be (worthily) enough praised, for he who
obeys her may pass without trouble every period of life.

The continuity and fulness of Cicero's language are second only
to the continuity and fulness of his thought.

Again, Cicero's language is not only full and fluent, but painstaking and pure. Language is, after all, so imperfect a medium, and so dependent for efficiency upon the attention and experience of the auditor and reader, that the loss of thought in greater or less measure during transit is inevitable. Yet the loss may be reduced to a negligible amount, and in Cicero it is so reduced. His language conveys to us what he thinks—not more, and not less.

There are great differences possible in this respect. Most writers of our own day, and perhaps most writers of antiquity—certainly most writers of today, and most speakers—appear to be content with the use of such language as will enable the reader or listener to understand if he brings good will to the task. The crying literary sin of the generation is looseness. It is excused and encouraged by manuals of English which seem to justify any usage if it is only susceptible of psychological explanation, by dictionaries which permit spelling according to the taste of the individual, by reformers who deny all authority to tradition, by a press which is in constant feverish hurry and accommodates its standards to the supposed tastes of the average reader, by successful so-called literary men and women who have gone far toward drowning literature and the taste for literature in a flood of journalism, by a public sentiment which resents any mode of expression superior to its own, by an educational system which has surrendered to the democratic average.

There is a vast difference between language which allows one to understand and language which compels one to understand, whether one will or not; yet the conception of this difference may be said practically not to exist. A novelist of some fame states in a public lecture that he regards form and style as not half so important as content. This is not meant to be an exhortation to looseness, but it has that practical effect. Why should a college student be inspired to strive for refinement of style when a financially successful literary man attaches to it little importance? Our undergraduates are surprised and indignant when it is pointed out to them that what they really have written is not what they think they have written.

The fulness, fluency, and perspicuity of Cicero must share with his clear and fluent logical processes something of the responsi-

bility for having invited the charge of superficiality. But here
again we must be on our guard. Almost any thought which is
poorly expressed is obscure, and obscurity, in that it does not yield
to vision, shares to some extent the character of depth. One may
look into a certain river source in Florida that is sixty feet deep
and see bottom with utter distinctness; and again, one may look
almost any day into a puddle three inches deep whose bottom is
utterly indistinguishable. It depends upon the medium. Many a
writer has a reputation for depth who is only muddy—intellectually, stylistically, or both.

But fulness of thought and language and gracefulness of transition are not the only qualities which make for fluency. Words are
chosen by the stylist not for their meaning alone, but for the
charm of their vowel and consonantal qualities, and for their
rhythmical composition. The modern ear is more or less unappre-
ciative of the magic of harmonious sound in prose; at least, it is
not often consciously appreciative. Harmony is nevertheless a
factor which must be taken into account.

Two recent authors have expressed themselves eloquently on
the subject of harmonious and rhythmical diction.

Says Robert Louis Stevenson:

Each phrase of each sentence, like an air or recitative in music,
should be so artfully compounded out of long and short, out of ac-
cented and unaccented, as to gratify the sensual ear. And of this the
ear is the sole judge. It is impossible to lay down laws. . . . Each phrase
in literature is built of sounds, as each phrase in music consists of
notes. One sound suggests, echoes, demands, and harmonizes with
another; and the art of rightly using these concordances is the final
art of literature. . . . We begin to see now what an intricate affair is
any perfect passage; how many faculties, whether of taste or pure
reason, must be held upon the stretch to make it; and why, when it is
made, it should afford so complete a pleasure.

And the Spanish novelist Valdés:

Here comes a period, ample, polished, and sonorous, of the kind
that the pseudo-classicist is always seeking without knowing what he
is after; after that, another, short and palpitating as the heart that
dictates it. Here appears one, gentle and honeyed, like the love-making

compliment of a youth, and then, at full speed there rises after it another, dry and harsh, that cuts it short. Prose, in a word, hates monotony like death, and takes pains to demonstrate the fact on every possible occasion. Perhaps this is why it rarely rises to the sky. The sky is charming, but it is monotonous. . . .

Prose, too, is not absolutely without rhythm. Its rhythm is much more deep and mystical than that of metrical language, but, for all that, it is not without existence. A delicate ear perceives it as the bland and hidden music from within a dark forest. Who would venture to deny rhythm, number, and harmony to the prose of Cervantes, Fénélon, or Manzoni? I would not be the one to assume such responsibility. The fact is, that the rhythm of prose is not uniform and continuous like that of verse. The winds of thought agitate it at their caprice, and cause it to vary its direction at every instant, without ever allowing it a point of repose. Prose, better than verse, obeys the insinuations of the spirit, obediently allowing itself to be raised, like a feather, sometimes to regions serene and tranquil, and again to be wafted through places intricate and obscure.

It is not ours to realize in all fulness the harmonies of a language which has ceased to be a living medium. That the harmonies were there, and that they were assiduously and lovingly cultivated, there is no doubt. We know it from Cicero's own references to choice of words, and, still more, from his employment of ample and sonorous expression.

Who has failed to be struck with the abundance of superlatives in the *Orations*? A great man may be referred to in a single clause as *optimus et sapientissimus et fortissimus*. A people is *potentissimus*, kings are *clarissimi*, lands are *disiunctissimae*, in one sentence.

The superlative is resonant as well as emphatic, and its frequency is probably due as much to the former quality as to the latter.

The gerund and gerundive constructions, too, with what evident fondness the orator employs them, for the same reason. *Excitanda, constituenda, revocanda, comprimendae, propaganda, vincienda*—all six occur in one sentence of thirty-six words.

But there is another harmony than that of the sonorous word. There is rhythm. In spite of Zielinski, Laurand, and others, we are not yet convinced that a prose rhythm with definite laws occurs in Cicero. It is certain, however, that his ear was sensitive to the rhythm of sentence endings, and that he was conscious of the art of rhythm, and, both consciously and unconsciously, used it. When he finds fault with Demosthenes, who for him excels in every kind of eloquence, it is in terms which strongly suggest how his judgment of oratory is based in great part on its appeal to the ear: "Who, although he outranks all in every kind of eloquences, nevertheless does not always fully satisfy my ears; so exacting are they, so sensitive, and always craving something without measure and without bounds." It is not improbable that a study of the style of our best modern speakers and writers would reveal the same sensitiveness of ear, and even the same avoidance of certain unrhythmical combinations—though in a less degree, because the conscious element in Cicero is large.

For, in spite of the natural gift which is manifest on every page, we must not think of Cicero as unstudied. No one is farther than Cicero from the appearance of being labored. We naturally think of his work as effortless. Yet some of the best prose in the world has been the product of as much pains as verse itself, and prose successes have been hardly more frequent than successes in poetry. Pitfalls beset the ready writer.

> You write with ease to show your breeding,
> But easy writing's curst hard reading,

wrote Sheridan. When we remember the severe training to which Cicero subjected himself, the translation and retranslation of Greek and Latin authors during his practice in composition and declamation, and his emphatic assertion that the stilus is the *effector ac magister dicendi*, "the author and master of eloquence," and the fact that the style of his letters ranges from the familiar conversational to the polite and literary, we shall not be too quick to conclude that he wrote without effort. However great his instinct for language, writing and speaking were with him an art. He would have agreed with Horace that talent and cultivation should go hand in hand, just as he agrees with Horace that wisdom is the source of all good writing: "The faculty of eloquence flows from the innermost fountains of wisdom."

The essential characteristic of Ciceronianism, then, is fluency—

fluency of mental process, and fluency of expression secured by fulness of vocabulary, grace of transition, resonance, and rhythmical movement. The style of Cicero is an easily gliding stream, calm and noiseless, but sweeping and powerful.

Yet easily gliding streams are sometimes monotonous. The Ciceronian stream is not. Here and there the smooth and sweeping current narrows and deepens, and surges between the rocks in the noisy rapids of the passionate invective or the still more passionate appeal to patriotism. Here, it expands again into the broad and placid pools of the *loci communes*. Here, the surface breaks in the ripples of vivacity and wit. Even its broadest reaches are dimpled with the eddies of variety. It is neither Asian nor Attic, but each in turn, and both together—or, rather, neither of them; for perfect oratory belongs consistently to itself. Cicero's oratory, like his philosophy, is eclectic. His style belongs to no school; it represents the selection and assimilation of the best qualities in both schools by a nature well tuned to the harmonies of thought and sound. As the philosophy which he formed for himself out of his wide study of the Greek systems was an individual philosophy of action, so the result of his enthusiastic study of Greek oratory was a living product belonging all to himself. He is a Phidias or a Raphael of style—facile, abundant, inspired; not without fault, but summing up as no one else the excellences of the times that begot him.

But there were other writers of prose in Cicero's time, just as in the times of Raphael and Phidias there were other painters and sculptors. When we read the solid, well ordered, and masterful Latin of Servius Sulpicius, or Julius Cæsar, or others whose letters have come down to us mingled with the correspondence of Cicero, we sometimes wonder whether the great orator and essayist and letter-writer was so far above them as to deserve the credit he receives.

The fact is that the world's geniuses, whether in art, science, or invention, are not the sudden apparitions they are sometimes conceived to be. The genius must create from material at hand. His is the hand or the brush or the pen which applies itself to the mechanical or pictorial or literary art already on the road to culmination, and brings it to the highest perfection possible to human powers.

But let criticism in the field of another art contribute to our understanding.

Writes Daniel Gregory Mason in *Beethoven and His Fore-runners:*

The artist who is to attain supreme greatness must in the first place have at his command a type of artistic technique that has already been developed to the verge of maturity, but that still awaits its efflorescence.... If the technique is primitive, no ardor of artistic enthusiasm can reach through it a full utterance; if all its potencies have been actualized, no inspiration can reanimate it. In the second place, the artist so happy as to inherit a technique ripe but not over-ripe, must also, if he is to attain supreme greatness, be in unison with the thought and feeling of his age, echo from the common mind of his fellows a deep, broad, and universal eloquence, as though all mankind spoke through him as mouthpiece.

Mr. Mason applies this to Beethoven: "He had at his command an inherited technique, just brought to the verge of maturity. And he had furthermore, behind and below him, as a rich nourishing soil for his genius, a great, new, common enthusiasm for humanity."

That Cicero had at hand the inherited, ripened technique awaiting the master tongue and pen is clear from the prose of his contemporaries. If we look for the rich, nourishing soil for his genius, we shall find it in two enthusiasms: the one, the matchless devotion to the Roman Republic which possessed him throughout his career and to his very end; the other, his intense enthusiasm for the intellectual life and the art of expression. In the first, he was in unison with the thought and feeling of the greatest representative body of the age, the Senate, whose common mind and the mind of all its followers he indeed echoed in a "deep, broad, and universal eloquence." In the second place, he was in unison with the fewer but elect who were possessed by intellectual curiosity and sensitiveness to the art of letters; and the elect minority caught up in a passion for excellence may represent the thought and feeling of the age because they only of the age have reached the real depths of thought and feeling that count in the advance of the race.

But here a question may be asked. If the prose of Cicero represents the perfect style, why did not the ancients universally cultivate it, and why are we not all today Ciceronians?

The first comment that suggests itself in answer to this question is that the prose of oration and essay in Cicero's own day was already Ciceronian, and Ciceronian by nature, in so far as the orators and essayists contemporary with Cicero were with him the founders of the Ciceronian; and that the literary world of today, in so far as it attempts to write at the same time fluently, graciously, amply, and with perspicuity, is also Ciceronian.

Still, not every stylist of Cicero's lifetime, or of later Latin times, was a Ciceronian, and the number of writers today who ignorantly neglect or arrogantly flout the virtues of fluency, grace, amplitude, and even perspicuity, is not inconsiderable. Let us hear of their views, though the fact is that neither in ancient times nor modern have the fountains been wholly pure from which the words of Cicero's adverse critics flow.

The motives of the ancient critic may be estimated from what is told us by Quintilian and Tacitus. The former says, referring to Cicero:

Whom, nevertheless, men of his own time dared to assail with the charge of being tumid, Asiatic, redundant, too fond of repetition, sometimes frigid in his wit, and in composition scrappy, jingling, and —far be it from the truth—almost too soft for real vigor.... Especially did those press upon him who were eager to seem imitators of the Attic orators. This clique, as though initiated into certain religious mysteries, assailed him as an alien-born, so to speak, who would not bow down in awe before their precepts, and refused to be bound by them.

Again, in the *Dialogue* of Tacitus, of the same generation and by the pupil of Quintilian, we read:

Of course you have read the letters of Calvus and Brutus to Cicero. From them it is easy to understand that to Cicero, Calvus seemed bloodless and arid, and to Brutus, leisurely and disjointed; and, in turn, that Calvus gave Cicero a bad name for being loose and sinew-

— /8/d

less, and that Brutus, to use his own words, charged him with being, so to speak, broken and limping.

The criticisms of the second-century New Speech enthusiasts, who, with a freakish desire for originality, and with freakish devotion to a freakish theory of style, sought the golden days of style in the time long before Cicero, we may pass over without comment.

It is clear that this ancient criticism is for the most part the detraction of the Atticists, a school of the plain style, and that they are employing the stock objections of the Atticists to Asianism, which represented the florid or ornamental style. With the narrow partisanship of the school, they take no account of the fact that Cicero is no mere Asiatic, but an eclectic whose style is compounded of the best elements of more than one school, and put upon him all the faults with which their enemy, Asianism, is commonly charged. Just how much of their criticism is due to rhetorical allegiance, and how much to actual and sincere taste, we cannot determine.

With modern criticism the case is somewhat different. The modern finds it easier to criticize Cicero, for the reason that our times attribute less importance than the ancients to the spoken word, and even to the written word. Even the Frenchman sympathizes with the spirit of an age which, through long suffering from the abuse of words, has come to despise the art of speech, and is impatient with the mere idea of it. Said Fénélon: *L'homme digne d'être écouté est celui qui ne se sert de la parole que pour la pensée*—"The man worthy of being listened to is he who uses words only for their thought." The very names of rhetoric, oratory, elocution, and declamation are in bad repute. Our college courses now are in English and Speech instead of in Rhetoric and Elocution.

That the reaction against the rhetorical has an element of health, no one would think of denying. It is equally clear, however, that the modern ear is dull to the art of the spoken word, that the modern eye is unresponsive to the niceties of the written word, and that the modern tongue disparages an art to which it cannot attain. Those who settle the business of writing and speech by asserting that "when one makes himself understood he is always a good speaker," have no very fine perception of the possibilities of language as the instrument of either pleasure or persuasion.

One further remark should be made in regard to the place of Ciceronian art in the history of prose style. It is in the nature of the literary art, as it is of other arts and of science, to change. So long as an art or a science has not attained to full development, change will consist in advance, and will be in the way of nature and health. When perfection has been attained and advance is no longer possible, the artist, to adopt Rhys Carpenter's words on sculptor and painter, "must do one of three things— stay where he is, go back, try to break a path in a new direction"; that is, he becomes an imitator, who is usually called an academic, or a revivalist, like the Pre-Raphaelites, or an innovator, like the modernist. Each of these courses has its faults. The revivalist works against nature and sooner or later encounters defeat. The innovator disregards the laws established by experience and finds his work without appeal and ephemeral. The imitator's work is in danger of becoming formal, monotonous, and lifeless.

If we were compelled to choose, the part of imitation would be sanest and safest. The traveller in the trodden path is not likely to go entirely astray. But we are not compelled to exclusive choice. We may be imitators in principle and innovators in detail or on occasion. Ciceronian oratory moved an august body of senators, a prætor, a chosen body of jurors, the assembly of citizens trained by life in the capital to a high degree of competence. Ciceronian letter and essay were addressed to the cultivated minority. Ciceronian prose was aristocratic. Style is by nature aristocratic. To speak in Ciceronian periods before the democratic multitude today, which is predisposed by nature, permitted by slackness of school discipline, and trained by platform, radio, and press to read and listen and think and speak on the plane of the low average, would be as futile as to write with Ciceronian amplitude and balance for the cheap newspaper straining for the largest circulation. Yet we need not surrender to the urge of the practical or renounce allegiance to the ideal of the spoken and written

CASCADES OF THE LIRIS AT ISOLA

PREHISTORIC WALL ABOVE ARPINUM

THE FIBRENUS AT CARNELLO

THE LICEO "TULLIANO" IN ARPINO

word. It would probably surprise political orators and cheap journalists and radio speakers and story writers if they knew how large a number of their listeners or potential listeners and readers resent the debasement and degradation of the English language and the annihilation of style, and if they realized how impressive and how persuasive, even to the uncultivated and ignorant, the use of disciplined and tasteful speech may be. To encourage this use, and to widen the circle of those who can appreciate it, is the interest as well as the duty of the enlightened State. The great means to the end is the school, but only if it keeps alive and before its pupils the ideal of eloquence as exemplified in the world's great stylists, of whom the greatest, as measured by his effect upon the history of prose, is Cicero.

To bring to a close our consideration of Cicero and style, let us say that whether we are enthusiastic admirers of Cicero or not is in part a matter of temperament, and in part a matter of real and familiar acquaintance with him—and, though we have been considering only Cicero the stylist, the same may be said of the man. If we are possessed of a strong sense of art, we shall see in him one of the world's few masters of the written and spoken word. If we are of plain, matter-of-fact temperament, we shall probably not rise to the heights of greatest enthusiasm over his work, or that of any other orator or essayist whose eloquence depends largely upon style; but we should in that case move cautiously, giving heed to the dignified admonition of Quintilian: "In pronouncing judgment on great men like these, we should be modest and circumspect, lest we condemn what we do not understand—a thing which often happens."

. XVI .

THE WISDOM OF THE ANCIENTS

THE wisdom of the ancients..." As the familiar expression sounds in our ears, or, in Homeric phrase, "passes the barrier of our lips," our mind's eye has glimpses of patriarchal Romans with long grey beards, of the Seven Sages of Greece leaning upon their staves in grave deliberation, of the Preacher who was king over Israel in Jerusalem declaring that there is no new thing under the sun, of the recorder of Proverbs assuring us that wisdom is the principal thing and counselling us to forget it not. With all the sophistication of an age which has sought out many inventions and in which there is no end of making many books, we still use the phrase, and we still incline to associate wisdom with reverend figures in the distant past.

Were a critic disposed to correct this inclination of ours to think of the ancients as the people with whom wisdom died, he might argue that the reputation of antiquity for wisdom is at least partly in the nature of accident. He might plead that ancient literature only seems to display greater wisdom than modern because of its being less abundant and more concentrated; that its lesser compass and greater solidity were due to aristocratic intellectual and educational conditions which so limited the number of readers and purchasers that publication unless austerely selective and in compressed form was prohibitively expensive. In the days of papyrus and vellum and wax tablets, of reed and quill pens and the stylus, and of a market in which the best seller was only better than the worst, what was published had to be important and of minimum compass. The times were neither economically nor pedagogically nor socially ripe for the smartnesses of the "column" and "feature," or the diffuseness of longer works.

The plea might go on to point out that this so-to-speak natural selection operating in ancient authorship had found an ally in the sifting process of the decade of dark centuries during which the already slight bulk of ancient literature was even further reduced by accident, neglect, loss, or, as in the case of works in disfavor with the new religion, even by design.

Still further, the assailant of the presumably false reputation of antiquity for wisdom might object on psychological grounds. We credit antiquity with wisdom because of the *omne ignotum pro magnifico,* "everything beyond our ken is wonderful," and also because we have learned to think of old people as wise people; as indeed, other things being equal, they are. The Spartan higher council was composed of the *gerontes,* or old men; the Roman Senate was composed of *senes,* more old men; the Church has always had its presbyters, its older men, its elders; it requires five of the seven ages of man before the age of the justice and his wise saws is reached; and there are our aldermen, who preserve at least the name of age.

And here the assailant might object also on grounds of logic. It may be right enough to presume that a human being is wise because he is old, but to presume that the times of Pericles or Solomon or Cato are wise because they are old is romantic confusion. Pericles never got to be old, and Cato at least was wise long before his death at eighty-five. Logically, the men of today, both individually and collectively, should be wiser than the men of old, because society is older and because both society and individual have had before them through the ages the experience of the ancients to build upon.

Sometimes indeed the critic grows bold and ventures to think that the modern man and modern society *are* wiser. They manage greater empires, they are masters of sea and land and air. They annihilate space, or nearly so, and, if they have not succeeded in getting more than twenty-four hours into the day and more than sixty minutes into the hour, they have accomplished the equivalent by self-development as fast workers. Their inventive cunning surpasses the powers of ordinary imagination. They print more books in a day than the total surviving amount of ancient publication, they all go to school, and most of them possess degrees or diplomas or certificates proving that they are doctors or teachers and therefore possessors of wisdom in the form of Letters, Laws, Philosophy, or Science; or that they are masters and mistresses of the Arts, meaning as in Ciceronian times the various branches of learning suitable to enter into the education of a free man and a gentleman; or that they are bachelors of the Arts and have gone through a courtship with learning, but without getting farther than the companionate stage; or that they have climbed the grades or steps of the long stairway of learning even to the dizzy elevation of the high school.

But it might be in turn objected to this reasoning that wisdom is not something which can be taught, like penmanship, or produced in laboratories, like a serum, or memorized, like the multiplication table; that it cannot be appropriated or taken over from another possessor, as by seizure, purchase, or inheritance, but must be won by conquest of experience if it is to become our own; that a man's wisdom is not measured by the abundance of knowledge he possesses or the number of statistics he compiles. If wisdom were in the nature of tables or graphs, or of compilations, or of mechanical invention, we should long ago have left the ancients far behind in the dust and beyond it, and should now be as superhumanly wise as we are superhumanly mechanical.

But it is hardly the part of wisdom to be debating as to its presence among the ancients without first having attempted to define it. For the present, let us say that wisdom consists in creative thoughtfulness about the problems of life and death and human behavior; by "creative" meaning that the wise man in his thinking comes to conclusions. They may not represent the whole truth; such finality is not in the gift of human thinking in an infinite world; they are only steps toward the more perfect understanding. With this definition as a point of departure, let us inquire whether anything substantial lies behind "the wisdom of the ancients."

"But wisdom is justified of her children," said One whom the people heard gladly. Without further argument, let us look to some of wisdom's great exemplars. Let us examine into the wisdom of the ancients as represented by the Greeks, and let us determine also the relation to it sustained by Cicero.

Measured by our definition of wisdom as "creative thoughtfulness about life and death and human behavior," the Greeks were indeed wise. Of all races, they were the most intellectually curious. The word we use for the study of wisdom is their invention—philosophy, "the love of knowing." They were possessed by the grand passion for inquiry. Philosophy, said Plato, is the child of wonder. It was the healthfulness and persistence of wonder, of intellectual curiosity, that brought forth the wisdom of ancient Greece.

The wonder of the Greeks led them first into speculations as to the nature of the physical universe. Of what was composed the great All, the source of the life that was in and about them? They reasoned with Thales that Water in its various changing forms was the basis of creation; with Anaximenes, that it was not Water, but Air with its condensations and rarefactions; with Anaximander, that it was neither Water nor Air, but First Matter or the Illimitable; with Pythagoras, that in some way Number, Rhythm, Music, was the essence of all things; with Xenophanes, that, whatever their composition, a Divine Unity was at their foundation; with Heraclitus, that the mysterious base was best described by Fire; with Empedocles, that the varied mingling of Water, Air, Fire, and Earth accounted for the All and all its parts; with Democritus, that the basic unit was the Atom; with Aristotle, that the Universe was a Thought in the mind of God. They reasoned that everything was in a state of Being; they reasoned that it was in a state, not of Being, but of Becoming. They reasoned of creative movement and of change—with Heraclitus, that Strife was the father of it all; with Empedocles, that all came from Attraction and Repulsion, Love and Hate; with Anaxagoras, that all came from Mind; with Aristotle that it came from the Moving and Unmoved First Principle. In their wondering search after the great secret of creation they arrived at a surprising degree of scientific enlightenment. Nearly six hundred years before Christ, Thales predicted an eclipse of the sun. Anaxagoras called the sun a mass of molten iron, and said the moon had cooled until habitable. Hipparchus declared the moon 237,500 miles distant, and knew of the precession of the equinoxes. Eratosthenes knew of the obliquity of the ecliptic. Aristarchus taught that the moon was one-thirtieth the earth's size, and that the earth was a satellite of the sun. Democritus taught the atomic theory, and the Epicurean system accounted for the status of man on the basis of evolution. Hippocrates and medicine, Theophrastus and botany, Euclid and mathematics, Archimedes and mechanics, Aristotle and universal knowledge—these names suggest the heights to which Greek learning attained, both pure and applied.

But research and speculation did not stop with the physical. The physical philosophers were succeeded by the moral philosophers, who against the background of knowledge fashioned their theories of living. There came Socrates and Plato with their doctrine of Recollection and theory of Ideas, teaching the divine origin and divine destination of the soul, and establishing the nature of perfection in character and conduct. There followed the systematic philosophers—the Stoics, reasoning of an All which was alive and sentient, and in which right conduct for the part, and virtue for man, consisted in being in harmony with the whole; the Epicureans, arguing for the material basis of all creation, the mortality of body and soul, the foolishness of fearing death, and the *Summum Bonum* of pleasure, but not pleasure intemperate, ill-advised, or productive of unhappiness; the Cyrenaics, finding the highest good in immediate pleasure, the "here and now"; the Cynics, snarling with contempt at civilization and its ideals; the Skeptics, denying the possibility of knowledge; the New Academics, questioning all dogma and all so-called truth, but admitting probability as the basis of speculation and conduct. The accumulated thoughts, oral and published, of the long line of philosophers in Greece, most of them sooner or later identified with Athenian life, made the capital a hive that hummed with the mechanics of thought and buzzed with its formulation and discussion.

"It may be safely asserted," wrote Lowes Dickinson in *The Greek View of Life*, "that in the first half of the fourth century

Athens was a city which diffused throughout the world a wealth of ideas unmatched by any single city at any other period of history." When Aristophanes jests of Socrates and his phrontis-terion, or "thinking-shop," he is characterizing Athens and the Greek race.

THE WISDOM OF CICERO

IT was this wealth of ideas that inspired the mind and heart of the youthful Cicero as he studied at home and in Athens and Greek lands, that enriched his life as with advancing years and accumulation of intellectual experience it matured in his nature, and that in his ripened and mellowed age came flooding forth for the healing of his wounds, for the satisfaction of his urge to expression, and for the edification of the Roman world—which by inheritance, we must not forget, is our own world. The wisdom of the ages—the wisdom not only of Greece but of the wise men of Chaldæa that went before, and of Egypt the cradle of civilization and the birthplace of conscious inquiry—thus sought expression through the pen of one man. If in our inquiry as to the wisdom of the ancients we were to summons but a single witness, none could be found more convincing and more convenient than Cicero.

This is true for several reasons. One is that Cicero, more than any other person since Greek times, is the conserver of the wisdom of the ages preceding him. Another is that, more than any other Roman, he represents the wisdom of his own times. A third is that he may claim in his own right the title of the wise man.

Let us look more closely. First, let us note that the studies of Cicero's enthusiastic youth in preparation for the orator and public man's career, his mature half year in Athens and his year of travel and study with professors of philosophy and eloquence in other famous Greek cities, and his continued, lifelong devotion to Greek letters and association with Greek intellectuals, all prepared him for one of the greatest cultural services ever rendered the world by one man. During the sixty-first and sixty-second years of his life, when the Roman State had passed quite definitely

RAPHAEL'S "THE SCHOOL OF ATHENS"; PLATO AND ARISTOTLE UNDER THE VAULT

THE CAMPAGNA AND ALBAN MOUNT, WITH THE HEIGHTS OF TUSCULUM TO THE LEFT

into the hands of Cæsar, and the breaking of the senatorial power had left Cicero a private citizen without a party to lead and almost without an occupation, the orator, true to his enthusiastic conviction of earlier years that "letters are the charm of age, in adversity a refuge and a solace," sought in study and writing his consolation for the death of the Republic, for the ruin of his household by divorce, and for the loss of his beloved daughter Tullia, whose decease in February, 45 B.C., had crushed him almost beyond recovery.

So long as ambition, offices, cases at law, and not only an interest in but a certain participation in public affairs kept me entangled in and bound by a multitude of duties, I used to keep these studies within limits, and, to guard against their dying out, I would as opportunity offered renew them by reading; but now that I have been smitten by a most grievous wound of fortune and besides am left free from administration of the State, I am looking to philosophy as a cure for my grief, and judge this to be the most honorable diversion for my leisure . . . Also nothing is more useful for the education of our citizenry.

He went once more to the Greeks. He wrote the essays entitled *Academics, Theories of the Chief Good and Evil, On the Nature of the Gods, On Divination, The Tusculan Discussions, On Ethics, On Old Age, On Friendship.* Add to these the previously written essays *On the State, On the Laws, On the Orator, Brutus,* and *The Orator,* and we have a great body of knowledge and criticism taken from or inspired by Greek sources and made available to Cicero's countrymen and ourselves. In his own words, he does indeed "deserve well of his fellow-citizens by introducing to their acquaintance those divine intellects." His work, writes Mr. Rackham, "was designed as a sort of encyclopedia of philosophy for Roman readers."

It proved to be more than that. It served not only the pagan generations of Cicero's and succeeding centuries, but the Christian generations from the times of the Latin Fathers of the Church, who admired and utilized it. To modern generations it has been not only useful, but indispensable; for, whereas in ancient Roman times the Greek authors forming its basis were still available to those who were masters of the Greek tongue, to all the centuries since, with only Plato, Aristotle, and Theophrastus of the philosophers surviving in anything like satisfactory completeness the neglect, decay, and violence of barbaric times, nothing like a full appreciation of Greek philosophy would have been possible without the intervention of Cicero. It is not exaggeration to say that, next to Plato and Aristotle the creators and inspirers, the most important figure in the history of philosophy is Cicero the translator, preserver, interpreter, and critic. When we have risen from the study of Plato, Aristotle, and Theophrastus, and of the fragmentary remains of the schoolmen, it is to Cicero we must go if we would have a fuller knowledge—knowledge of the masters themselves, their themes, their methods; knowledge of the systems, Academic, Peripatetic, Stoic, Cyrenaic, Epicurean, Skeptic, New Academic; knowledge of a host of teachers and followers, Roman and Greek, of Cicero's own time and earlier, many of them interesting and attractive personalities whose acquaintance we should otherwise not possess; knowledge of how the themes, systems, works, and persons appealed to a Roman, a broadly educated and deeply cultivated man, a statesman, patriot, and moralist, an orator, essayist, and stylist, a man in the last decade of the three score years and ten who had mingled in public and private affairs and lived intensely and dangerously.

Cicero not only preserves thus the wisdom of the ancients, but criticizes, interprets, and evaluates it as a working factor in life. We should beware of those who take him at his word when he says his essays "are mere transcripts, and cost comparatively little labor"; and who do not recognize as understatement his "supposing that for our part we do not fill the office of a mere translator, but, while preserving the doctrines of our chosen authorities, add thereto our own criticism and our own arrangement." It is true that no ordinary person in the space of two years would be capable of reading, studying, appropriating, assimilating, and putting into precise and artistic form so vast a body of learning as all Greek philosophy. But Cicero was no ordinary person.

In the first place, Cicero was not a professor, and it was not his purpose to write research treatises for specialists in philosophy;

his intent was to make accessible to cultivated Romans the field
of thought which had so fructified his own life. In the second
place, he was uniquely prepared for the task he set himself—in
all likelihood better prepared than any professor who ever lived.
As we have noted, he had had in youth an ideally broad education, and in maturer years in the midst of professional activities
had built upon this foundation by reading, writing, and contact
with intellectual men. His knowledge of Greek language and
literature likewise was ideal. He had an alert and eager mind;
few men have the mental quickness and the insatiable intellectual
curiosity that manifest themselves in every paragraph of Cicero's
writings. He had a legal mind, by long exercise trained to think
precisely and with subtlety. He had a quick and sure feeling for
word values; he used with such discrimination the full resources
of the Latin vocabulary, which it was the fashion to reproach
with poverty and rigidity, that it hardly seems exaggeration when
he declares, "In my opinion, as I have often argued, the Latin
language, so far from having a poor vocabulary, as is commonly
supposed, is actually richer than the Greek." He not only utilized
to its fullest extent the Latin vocabulary as it stood, but with
marvelous inventiveness in term and phrase made up for its de-
ficiencies in the field of philosophy to which it was not bred.
Says Mr. Rackham, "He created a philosophical terminology in
Latin which has passed into the languages of modern Europe."
His mastery of words was equalled by a mastery of clear and fluent
presentation; his feeling for style was unerring and always present.
Because he had a sensitiveness to words and style, and because
as he wrote he was conscious of success, he wrote with the glow
of inspiration. He wrote with ease. He wrote with delight. He was
at the maximum of his intellectual powers, he had behind him a
lifetime of mingling with men and affairs, and he was in the later
and culminating years of the philosophic age. The haste and
repetition charged against him are of trifling importance in the
sum total of his contribution.

Given these qualifications, all that was wanting their possessor
was the creation of opportunity for their use. When to the tragedy
of his political life was added the tragedy of a broken home in-

vaded by death, with the imperative need of distraction from grief, it was as if all the lines of Cicero's career had finally converged upon the one task of setting in order for his own and coming generations the house of Greek philosophy.

So much for Cicero as representing the wisdom of his own and of preceding times. But perhaps we are not quite sure that what Cicero set in order is to be described as wisdom. Greek philosophy was a vast field of intellectual endeavor including not only what we call philosophy, but scientific subjects. Its province was practically the sum of knowledge. Is it the wisdom of the ages which Cicero transmits, or only their learning? And was Cicero a mere mouthpiece and recorder, or was he also wise in his own right?

The answer to the first of these queries need not detain us. Cicero in his essays concerns himself little with the scientific aspects of Greek culture; his purpose is to present Greek philosophy, and, while he does give many pages to the minutiae and the quibblings of schoolmen defending their systems in lecture hall or treatise, he is even there engaged in the effort to reach conclusions affecting conduct in this life and faith as to the life to come.

The best answer to the question as to Cicero's own wisdom may also be returned without hesitation. Cicero not only presents the various systems of Greek philosophy, but interprets, criticizes, and draws from them their lessons of life. This needs no documentation. No reader of any philosophical essay of Cicero's is left without certainty as to where the essayist stands, and no reader finds him standing unreservedly with any one school or system. With the impartiality of the Roman prætor on the bench, he allows each of the sects through its dramatic mouthpiece to set forth its tenets, and with the expertness of the legal mind points out its inconsistencies and errors. Stoicism appeals to him with its moral austerity, but its doctrine of the equality of all offenses, and its unattainable ideal of the wise and happy man, rule it out of our world of actualities. He stands for Virtue as the *Summum Bonum,* but admits to minor partnership with it the advantages of health and possession. The Epicurean doctrine of pleasure will not breed serious and heroic men in any case, and its inclusion of "freedom from pain" in the definition of pleasure is a destructive inconsistency. The Cyrenaics, with their choice of pleasure defined as agreeable excitement of the five senses, are contemptible. The Cynics are narrow and egotistic, the Skeptics are unreasonable in a world where action is not to be avoided. Even the New Academy, to which Cicero gives formal allegiance, wins him not because of system but because its chief distinction is the denial of system. Cicero is best described as an eclectic, and an eclectic on grounds of pragmatism. He chose according to his need from the schools, when indeed he did not go direct to Plato, and his philosophy was above all a philosophy of life.

A statement of that philosophy of life is in itself the best demonstration of the wisdom of Cicero. As might be expected of one so thoroughly Roman, it was a philosophy of strict morality, and in its essence was Stoic. Its Highest Good was Virtue, or Moral Goodness. "For he who posits the supreme good as having no connection with virtue and measures it not by a moral standard but by his own interests—if he should be consistent and not rather at times over-ruled by his better nature, he could value neither friendship nor justice nor generosity; and brave he surely cannot possibly be that counts pain the supreme evil, nor temperate he that holds pleasure to be the supreme good. These truths are so self-evident that the subject does not call for discussion." If we inquire as to the content of Moral Goodness, we find that "it is concerned either (1) with the full perception and intelligent development of the true; or (2) with the conservation of organized society, with rendering to every man his due, and with the faithful discharge of obligations assumed; or (3) with the greatness and strength of a noble and invincible spirit; or (4) with the orderliness and moderation of everything that is said and done, wherein consist temperance and self-control." These are the familiar four Platonic virtues of Wisdom, Justice, Courage, Temperance.

And the *Summum Bonum* is not only Virtue, but Virtue in action; "for, after all is done, it is action only that gives a true value and commendation to virtue." "Service is better than mere theoretical knowledge, for the study and knowledge of the universe would somehow be lame and defective, were no practical results to follow." It need not surprise us that Cicero's more than once repeated definition makes wisdom "the art of living." Wisdom, justice, courage, and temperance do not end in themselves, and cannot exist in themselves alone. They are social virtues, and therefore virtues to find their end in practice. "The normal sphere for virtuous action is human society," as Dr. Margaret Henry summarizes in her illuminating *Dogmatism and Scepticism in Cicero's Philosophy*. No one more than Cicero has realized that "we are not born for ourselves alone." His philosophy of life never loses consciousness of the fact that mankind is a society, a world brotherhood, that the great instrument for the promotion of human welfare is the State, that nothing so meets divine approval as devoted citizenship, and that nothing which does not work out to serve the State is to be ranked as virtuous.

There is nothing more glorious nor of wider range than the solidarity of mankind, that species of alliance and partnership of interests and that actual affection which exists between man and man, which, coming into existence immediately upon our birth, owing to the fact that children are loved by their parents and the family as a whole, is bound together by the ties of marriage and parenthood, gradually spreads its influence beyond the home, first by blood relationships, then by connections through marriage, later by friendships, afterwards by the bonds of neighborhood, then to fellow-citizens and political allies and friends, and lastly by embracing the whole of the human race.

And Virtue is not without warrant from an authority higher than human. That authority is Nature herself. Right and wrong are not relative and changeable, and dependent on human judgment; they are eternal verities founded in nature. Virtue is innate, is not only human but divine, and is the same whether in man or God. The virtuous man and the wise is he who "applies to the conduct of life a knowledge of the working of natural causes, choosing what is in accordance with nature and rejecting what is contrary to it." Nor does Virtue, thus constituted and thus operative to the good of individual and collective men, leave its exemplars unrewarded. The virtuous man only is wise, and the wise man alone is happy. His reward also is not for this life only.

With Cicero, life is eternal. We have come from afar, and for those who serve their country well there is open "something like a path to the gate of heaven," where, "escaped from the fetters of the body like prisoners released," they truly live; for "what you call life in the world below is really death."

This is but the skeleton of Cicero's philosophy of life, and with perhaps less than due lingering upon its connection with the other world. That we shall consider at greater length in the next chapter.

But here let us pause for a remark. To those who are disposed to object that most of Cicero's utterances are transfers from the writings of the Greek masters and therefore do not beyond a doubt represent his own thought and feeling, it is enough to say that his philosophy of life, as a whole and in detail as we have given it and shall hereafter give it, is in conformity with the convictions as to his character left in us as we rise from the reading of his works and the contemplation of his life through enthusiastic youth, active manhood, settled age, and the supreme trials of its tragic end. We must not forget that the chief reason why we have these opinions at all is that they represent his enthusiasm.

It would be easy, were there space and the need of so doing, to clothe this skeleton of Cicero's philosophy of life in flesh and blood and give it finished human form. We should find Cicero a man of lively mind and many ideas, a person of consideration and taste, an idealist sensitive to the fine distinctions of enlightened morality.

He knows the cheapness of compulsory virtue. "For an action, though honest, is not therefore truly virtuous, unless it be done out of choice and with a good will."

He knows that mankind must be taken as it is. "The men we live with are not perfect and ideally wise, but men who do very well if there be found in them but the semblance of virtue."

He is a man of peace, but realizes that there may be things worse than war. "Since there are two ways of settling a dispute—first, by discussion; second, by physical force; and since the former is characteristic of man, the latter of the brute, we must resort to force only in case we may not avail ourselves of discussion. The only excuse, therefore, for going to war, is that we may live in peace unharmed; and when the victory is won, we should spare those who have not been blood-thirsty and barbarous in their warfare."

He knows the dangers of coveting riches and glory. "There is nothing so characteristic of narrowness and littleness of soul as the love of riches; and there is nothing more honorable and noble than to be indifferent to money, if one does not possess it, and to devote it to beneficence and liberality, if one does possess it. We must also beware of ambition for glory; for it robs us of liberty, and in defense of liberty a high-souled man should stake everything."

With him, a public office is a public trust. We remember his own just and humane governorship in Cilicia as we read: "For the administration of the government, like the office of a trustee, must be conducted for the benefit of those entrusted to one's care, not of those to whom it is entrusted." "It is, then, peculiarly the place of a magistrate to bear in mind that he represents the State and that it is his duty to uphold its honor and its dignity, to enforce the law, to dispense to all their constitutional rights, and to remember that all this has been committed to him as a sacred trust."

He has ideas about democracy. "Liberty has no dwelling-place in any State except that in which the people's will is the greatest, and surely nothing can be sweeter than liberty; but if it is not the same for all, it does not deserve the name of liberty." But he has no delusions regarding equality. "For if we cannot agree to equalize men's wealth, and equality of innate ability is impossible, the legal rights at least of those who are citizens of the same commonwealth ought to be equal. For what is a State except an association or partnership in justice?" "When equal honor is given to the highest and the lowest—for men of both types must exist in every nation—then this very 'fairness' is most unfair." He does not believe in unrestricted democracy. Liberty without restriction is sure to bring tyranny. "For just as an excess of power in the hands of the aristocrats results in the overthrow of democracy, so liberty itself reduces a people who possess it in too great degree to servitude." He has Scipio paraphrase with approval which means Cicero's unreserved approval as well, the famous passage from Plato:

Scipio. We have a condition which is splendidly described by Plato, if only I can reproduce his description in Latin; it is difficult, but I will attempt it. He says: "When the insatiable throats of the people have become dry with the thirst for liberty, and, served by evil ministers, they have drained in their thirst a draught of liberty which, instead of being moderately tempered, is too strong for them, then, unless the magistrates and men of high rank are very mild and indulgent, serving them with liberty in generous quantities, the people persecute them, charge them with crime and impeach them, calling them despots, kings, and tyrants." I think you are acquainted with this passage.

Lælius. It is very familiar to me.

Scipio. He continues thus: "Those who follow the lead of prominent citizens are persecuted by such a people and called willing slaves; but those who, though in office, try to act like private citizens, and those private citizens who try to destroy all distinction between a private citizen and a magistrate, are praised to the skies and loaded with honors. It necessarily follows in such a State that liberty prevails everywhere, to such an extent that not only are homes one and all without a master, but the vice of anarchy extends even to the domestic animals, until finally the father fears his son, the son flouts his father, all sense of shame disappears, and all is so absolutely free that there is no distinction between citizen and alien; the schoolmaster fears and flatters his pupils, and pupils despise their masters; youths take on the gravity of age, and old men stoop to the games of youth, for fear they may be disliked by their juniors and seem to them too serious. Under such conditions even the slaves come to behave with unseemly freedom, wives have the same rights as their husbands, and in the abundance of liberty even the dogs, the horses, and the asses are so free in their running about that men must make way for them in the streets. Therefore," he concludes, "the final result of this boundless license is that the minds of the citizens become so squeamish and sensitive that, if the authority of government is exercised in the smallest degree, they become angry and cannot bear it. On this account they begin to neglect the laws as well, and so finally are utterly without a master of any kind."

He knows the fitness of humility. "When fortune smiles and the stream of life flows according to our wishes, let us diligently avoid all arrogance, haughtiness, and pride. For it is as much a sign of weakness to give way to one's feelings in success as it is in adversity.... There seems to be sound advice, therefore, in this word of warning: 'The higher we are placed, the more humbly we should walk.' "

He is not content with obeying the letter of the law. "There is, too, a difference between justice and considerateness in one's relation to one's fellow-men. It is the function of justice not to do wrong to one's fellow-men; of considerateness, not to wound their feelings."

He stands for decency, and on the only and sufficient ground that the indecencies are ugly and offensive *in nature* and therefore to be avoided.

Nature seems to have had a wonderful plan in the construction of our bodies. Our face and our figure generally, in so far as it has a comely appearance, she has placed in sight; but the parts of the body that are given us only to serve the needs of nature and that would present an unsightly and unpleasant appearance she has covered up and concealed from view. Man's modesty has followed this careful contrivance of nature's; all right-minded people keep out of sight what nature has hidden and take pains to respond to nature's demands as privately as possible; and in the case of those parts of the body which only serve nature's needs, neither the parts nor the functions are called by their real names. To perform these functions—if only it be done in private—is nothing immoral; but to speak of them is indecent. And so neither public performance of those acts nor vulgar mention of them is free from indecency.

He knows how to reply to the Stoics and Cynics, who were "advanced" in their ideas as to frank speech.

But we must give no heed to the Cynics (or to some Stoics who are practically Cynics) who censure and ridicule us for holding that the mere mention of some actions that are not immoral is shameful, while other things that are immoral we call by their real names. Robbery, fraud, and adultery, for example, are immoral indeed, but it is not indecent to name them. To beget children in wedlock is indeed morally right; to speak of it indecent. And they assail modesty with a great many other arguments to the same purport. But as for us, let us follow nature and shun everything that is offensive to our eyes or our ears.

He tells us that the manner of jesting itself ought not to be extravagant or immoderate, but refined and witty.

The distinction between the elegant and the vulgar jest is an easy matter: the one kind, if well timed (for instance, in hours of mental relaxation), is becoming to the most dignified person; the other is unfit for any gentleman, if the subject is indecent and the words obscene.

He has the gentleman's ideas of taste in conversation.

And above all, he should be on the watch that his conversation shall not betray some defect in his character. This is most likely to occur when people in jest or in earnest take delight in making malicious and slanderous statements about the absent, on purpose to injure their reputations.

He is equally tasteful in his ideas about giving.

Kindness is shown to the needy either by personal service, or by gifts of money. The latter way is the easier, especially for a rich man; but the former is nobler and more dignified and more becoming to a strong and eminent man. For although both ways alike betray a generous wish to oblige, still in the one case the favor makes a draft upon one's bank account, in the other upon one's personal energy; and the bounty which is drawn from one's material substance tends to exhaust the very fountain of liberality.

He has the highest ideal of truthfulness.

But when the judge comes to pronounce the verdict under oath, he should remember that he has God as his witness—that is, as I understand it, his own conscience, than which God himself has bestowed upon man nothing more divine.

His conception of the lawyer's duty is of as much interest today as it was in his own time.

While we should never prosecute the innocent, we need not have our scruples against undertaking on occasion the defense of a guilty person, provided he be not infamously depraved and wicked. For people expect it; custom sanctions it; humanity also accepts it.

Finally, he has enlightened ideas as to the care of the body.

We must fight against old age exactly as we fight against disease. We must have regard to health; we must engage in regulated exercise, we must take only so much food and drink as will restore our strength, not weigh it down. Nor indeed must we minister only to the body, but to the mind and soul much more; for these too, unless you pour oil, as it were, into the lamp, are extinguished by old age.

But we have gone far enough in our appreciation of Cicero's ideas on the "art of living"—*sapientia, quae ars vivendi putanda est.* It is clear not only that he was an earnest student of the ancient wise men, but that he had assimilated their wisdom and was saturated with it. Let us hear a conclusion of the matter. A thousand years before Cicero there was no new thing under the sun. Wisdom really *is* a thing of the ancients. It grew, it was an accumulation, and perhaps it is growing still, but we need not hope to add greatly to its sum. And yet, though we may be denied the power of creation, we are not denied the privilege of making our own by adaptation or assimilation what already exists.

> *Was du ererbt von deinen Vätern hast,*
> *Erwirb es, um es zu besitzen.*

> What from our sires is handed down,
> By conquest we must make our own.

. XVIII .

ROME'S LEAST MORTAL MIND

I T is the privilege of the poet, and his great service as well, to
flash forth the truth without argument or annotation. His
inspired phrase need not be the whole truth, but it must be
essentially the truth. When Byron calls Cicero's contemporary,
the jurist Servius Sulpicius,

> The Roman friend of Rome's least mortal mind,

the impression left upon our minds is of an intimate and ideal
friendship between ideal characters. The scholar's annotations
might demonstrate to the studious that neither the characters nor
the friendship were without imperfection, but so long as they do
not disprove the more than usual virtue of Cicero and the more
than usual sympathy of Servius we accept the verse as a convenient
statement of truth.

The poet helps us to see the real and the significant. The statement of the essential in apt and beautiful phrase causes the accidental to recede into the background, there to remain except as
it is needed as a corrective to the excessive and harmful enthusiasm of the idealizer. The truth thus simplified and relieved of
baggage is ready for action and becomes inspirational. If we had
not the poetic to teach us the meaning of the scholastic, we should
be in a poor way to profit by what we learn of the past.

"Rome's least mortal mind" is a poet's phrase. When the
scholar, with the scholar's distrust of easy phrase, attempts to
make it safe by annotation, he is confronted by more than one
act of Cicero that seems to mar the orator's career, and more than
one trait that seems a blemish on his character. He finds that
Cicero was not far-seeing in the train of events beginning with
the execution of the conspirators in 63 B.C. and leading to the
exile in 58, that he allowed banishment to unman him, that he

was suspicious and censorious of those who had accomplished his recall; that in the *Oration on the Consular Provinces* in 56 B.C. he seemingly renounced principle and went over to Cæsar, that because of the new allegiance he befriended men whom he had hitherto despised, that thereafter he was wavering and inconstant until finally siding with Pompey, and that he was reconciled with Cæsar after Pompey's death; that in court he defended men he did not approve, that on occasion he was abusive of his opponents before prætor and jury, and that in ordinary relations he too often indulged an unkind tongue; that he had a long and bitter quarrel with his brother Quintus, that he divorced Terentia after thirty years, that he married Publilia for her money, and that on Tullia's death he put no restraint upon his grief; that he was not a statesman and did not appreciate the inevitability of change and the hopelessness of the senatorial cause; and that he was a vain man.

The scholar does not stop with all these annotations as positive conclusions. That would be to leave Cicero under condemnation as Rome's *most* mortal mind, and his inner impulse on the reading of Cicero, if he is the average scholar, has always been to accept him, with the poet, as indeed Rome's least mortal mind.

Having obeyed conscience by annotating the poet's phrase, the scholar obeys conscience again by annotating the annotations. He reminds himself, and us, that Cicero as consul was a fearless and energetic guardian of the peace, that during the years that led to the banishment he was a conscientious, public-spirited, and independent citizen if not always a prudent guardian of his own interests, and that his lack of prudence was in fact a proof of courage and civic devotion. He reminds himself further that the exile was a tragic reversal of fortune, and that its disgrace and danger were the more overwhelming to a man of sensitive nature who had not had the soldier's hardening, and whose allies, political rather than personal, for he was a provincial and a "new man," stood by inert while his enemies acted. He reflects that Cicero's mobility in politics was due to his rôle as mediator between factions in the hope of forming the ideal alliance of the senatorial and equestrian classes; that it is the lawyer's right and sometimes his duty to defend the client whose guilt he knows,

and that law and politics are full of complex situations of whose
right and wrong it is difficult to judge. He reflects that not Cicero
alone was unable to see on which side the right preponderated in
the civil war, or even the expedient, but that his final decision
was consistent with his career as a man of character and a loyal
citizen; and that it is no easy task, even after the event, to determine the measure of right and wrong in the great turmoil that
ended the old régime. He reflects that it takes two to make a
quarrel, that Quintus and Terentia were not free from responsibility, and that the misunderstanding between the brothers was
not lasting. Finally, perhaps he reproves himself and others who
find fault with a man of sixty-three, a man who has lost home and
State and seen the circle of his friends lessen and all the world
begin to totter, for giving way to grief when the daughter of his
heart is taken from him.

Closer examination thus reduces to comparative insignificance
one charge after another against Cicero's character and conduct.
One charge alone persists in maintaining its ground. There is no
doubt that Cicero did not resist the temptation to tell of his
achievements. The *Orations against Catiline* are full of self-asser-
tion, and the Catiline episode is too much on his lips for the
remainder of his life. Yet even here something may be said in
explanation, if not in excuse.

In the first place, neither in antiquity nor today has Italy had
the same sensitiveness to the use of the first person as characterizes
the Anglo-Saxon. In the second place, we should remember that
with the end of the consulship Cicero had passed the highest
point in his career, and that at the same moment the uncertainties
of senatorial control were becoming acute. The conservative ex-
consul felt himself, together with his party, slipping from fame
and security and threatened with unimportance and neglect. As
a usual thing, the ex-consuls made good soldiers or governors; but
Cicero had neither military nor provincial ambitions, and accepted the governorship of Cilicia only under protest a decade
later. It is not strange that when he felt circumstances and men
conspiring to relegate him to uselessness, helplessness, and danger,
he yielded somewhat too often to the impulse to remind a forget-

ful world of the courage and devotion he had displayed in its time of danger. It should be remembered, too, that the desire to be well thought of is not a mean fault, but "that last infirmity of noble mind." And, finally, it is to be noted that it is only in connection with his services to the State that Cicero's insistence upon recognition and credit becomes offensive. We do not think of it as immodesty or impropriety when in the rhetorical essays he writes of his intellectual qualifications, of his style, of his mastery of Greek philosophy, of his success in oratory. It is as if his attainment to the consulship and his getting through its duties with credit had seemed to him so great an honor to strive for, and so difficult a task to carry through, that the accomplishment of his ambition never ceased to be a surprise and a wonder.

Having thus appeased his conscience by the presentation and appraisal of Cicero's negative qualities, the scholar continues his study by inquiring what positive qualities justify the poet's phrase. Let us participate in the inquiry.

We are struck first by Cicero's enthusiasm as a student. Nothing less than the ideal preparation for the orator in the public career satisfied him. He studied under Latin masters and Greek masters, in both languages. He studied a year and a half abroad under the most famous teachers in Greek centers. Night and day he submitted himself to his masters, or.was master to himself. We are next impressed by the vigor of his ambition to hold all the posts of honor in the service of the State, and by his courage. We are impressed by his courage in undertaking the case for Roscius of Ameria, which brought him onto dangerous ground occupied by a favorite of Sulla the dictator. We notice the same fearlessness in the consulship when the conspirators are to be put down. We witness its supreme manifestation during the struggle of the twenty-one months following the death of Cæsar and ending in the murder of Cicero himself, his brother, and his brother's son. In the third place, we note his uprightness in the administration of his quæstorship in Sicily and his prosecution of Verres, in the successful ædileship and prætorship, in the just and patriotic consulship, and in the scrupulously honest and merciful governorship of Cilicia.

CICERO

THE MONASTERY OF CASAMARI, NEAR ARPINO

THE CHURCH OF SAINT AMBROSE IN MILAN

We have been considering thus far Cicero in action. The scrutiny of his life reveals the man of principle worthily comporting himself in ordinary times, and worthily acquitting himself in times of perplexity and stress; not the perfect man, but the virtuous man with the defects of his qualities. To deny him the title of the virtuous would be to agree with the Stoics in their extreme doctrine that the presence of a single fault was fatal to the claim of goodness.

The phrase "Rome's least mortal mind" is thus justified by the life resulting from that mind in action. Let us consider now the mind of Cicero in contemplation. What was the nature of his inner life?

The less our mortality, the more the permanence of that for which we strive. The least mortal mind is that which occupies itself most with the solid and enduring goods of existence.

Cicero was an idealist. We have seen the infinite pains he took to prepare himself for the public career. In his writings on orators and oratory, it is evident that he views everything relating to eloquence and eloquent men against the background of perfection. In matters of State the same is true: he is looking for the ideal party with the ideal leader and the ideal devotion to the public good as represented by the State. He has the idealist's way of measuring by eternity rather than by time. He is concerned with what future generations will think of him, and of what the State will be tomorrow as well as today. He assumes a future life after the life on earth, in which the virtues of the earthly man shall be crowned with approval, and in which we shall meet our friends again. The conviction of men that this life to come is the cause of ideal patriotism and of ideal courage in the face of death, and of constancy in the performance of duty. We are soldiers in the warfare of the good life. No one must leave his post unless ordered by God, who is the great commander-in-chief of the armies of virtue.

It is in Cicero's credo of a divinely directed universe in which an all-seeing power cares for humanity, of the human soul as related to and partaking of the divine nature, and of happy immortality in another world as virtue's ultimate reward, that we find the central reason for our thought of him as Rome's least mortal mind. "When God Himself has given a valid reason as He did in the past to Socrates, and in our day to Cato, and often to many others, then of a surety your true wise man will joyfully pass forthwith from the darkness here into the light beyond. All the same he will not break the bonds of his prison-house—the laws forbid it—but as if in obedience to a magistrate or some lawful authority, he will pass out at the summons and release of God." "The beauty of the universe and the order of nature in the heavens compels us to confess that there does exist some excelling force to be looked up to and admired by the race of man." Thus does Cicero see in creation a unity and a purpose.

With this credo is bound up the whole galaxy of virtues as we know them today—truthfulness, honor, loyalty, courage, constancy, patriotism, self-control, and faith in their ultimate triumph. These are Christian virtues, and it is not strange that Cicero was beloved of the Christian Fathers, and that Ambrose in his *Ethics of the Ministry* made use of the *De Officiis* of his pagan predecessor. "You could fancy sometimes it is not a pagan philosopher, but a Christian apostle who is speaking," says Petrarch.

Cicero lacks the Savior, the doctrine of the forgiveness of sins, and the self-examination, repentance, and self-abasement of the Christian, but in the sentiments regarding the after-life and in faith in an almost personal God of wisdom and justice, he is remarkably at one with the Christian philosophy. It is the God of Plato rather than the God of the New Testament, or even of the Old, yet we need make only a slight change of wording in Cicero's references to Him, and He becomes the God of Ambrose and Augustine. Parts of *De Senectute* indeed might be uttered as they stand by any Christian.

I withdraw from life not as one who leaves his home, but as if from a hospice. For nature provided us, not with a place in which we might dwell, but with a shelter at which we might tarry. O brightest of all days when I shall set out for yonder divine council and gathering of spirits, and when I shall depart from the confusion and impurities of this world! For I shall be setting forth not only to those men of whom I spoke before but also to my own Cato, than whom no better man ever was born, no one excelling him in devotion; whose body was burned by me, whereas on the contrary mine should have been burned by him—but whose soul, not indeed leaving me forever, but looking back upon me, set out for places whither it perceived that I too was to come. If I seemed to support this calamity with fortitude, it was not that I bore it with a composed spirit, but that I consoled myself with the thought that the parting and separation between us would not be for long. . . . But if in this I am mistaken, that I believe men's souls are immortal, I am glad to be mistaken, and as long as I live I do not wish to be relieved of an error that gives me pleasure.

It was not only Cicero's golden style and the abundance of knowledge preserved in his works that commended him to his own and succeeding times. It was also the moral earnestness of both his written words and his life.

Says Professor Rolfe in *Cicero and His Influence:*

Cicero offers an example of one who possessed to an eminent degree the moral virtues of honesty, chastity, and temperance in an age when those virtues were not common in the men whose names appear on the pages of history. . . . Cicero's influence continued potent even after his death, and has endured down to our own day, varying in intensity at different periods, sometimes almost extinct and apparently exhausted, but as constantly reviving and dominating human thought. . . . In the history of the early Church Cicero played an important part, purifying and elevating the style of the Christian writers and influencing their thought, warring against superstition and the belief in prodigies and magic, furnishing a code of ethics which required but slight modification to adapt it to a Christian community and to the conditions of modern life.

We may conclude with De Quincey's estimate of Cicero's character. He is speaking of the revolution that brought about the new régime.

For the age, it was fruitful in great men; but, amongst them all, if we except the sublime Julian leader, none as regards splendor of endowments stood upon the same level with Cicero. For the revolution, it was that unique event which brought ancient civilization into contact and commerce with modern; since, if we figure the two worlds of Paganism and Christianity under the idea of two great continents, it is through the isthmus of Rome imperialized that the one was able virtually to communicate with the other. . . . Yet, in a revolution thus unexampled for grandeur of results, the only great actor who stood upon the authority of his character was Cicero. All others, from Pompey, Curio, Domitius, Cato, down to the final partisans at Actium, moved by the authority of arms: *tantum auctoritate valebant quantum milite;* and they could have moved by no other.

. XIX .

THE LIFE IN HARMONY WITH NATURE

CICERO pondered much on the problems of life. A great proof of this is to be seen in the fact that he subscribes to no single system of philosophy. If he had been exclusively either Epicurean or Stoic, he would have been by so much the less thoughtful as he allowed system to constitute authority and determine what he was to believe. It is in the nature of the machine, whether in philosophy, politics, religion, industry, or education, to save labor by making conclusions easy.

Cicero was neither Stoic nor Epicurean. He could follow either of the schools in part of its teaching, and did so, but when either failed to be practical in its meeting of the conditions of life he refused further allegiance. He will agree with the Epicureans that the will of man is free, and that virtue is man's own responsibility and not the gift of the gods, but when they make of pleasure the *Summum Bonum* he will have nothing to do with them. He agrees with the Stoics that right and wrong are realities, but is outraged by their dogma that all sins represent equal guilt, that to steal one bean or a bushel calls for equal condemnation. His allegiance is to the New Academy, and the allegiance of the New Academy is to no school. Cicero therefore may be called a skeptic in philosophy; or, better, inasmuch as doubt is negative and associated with failure to act, and inasmuch as Cicero was above all the philosopher in action, he is, as we have already seen, best called an eclectic.

In his essay on the New Academics, and elsewhere in less detail, Cicero examines the school theories as to what for him were the two great matters of moment in the life of man and of the State: the Highest Good, and the nature of the Divine. Let it be enough here to say that for him the Highest Good was Virtue—not the virtue as an end which the Stoics professed, but virtue clothed in human circumstance, virtue in action, especially in the form of the good citizen; and that the Divine was a reality in God— not the God of the Stoics who was the fiery essence of and identical with the universe, but a God in vital connection with, and concerned about, human life, a God personally responsible.

It is apparent to even the chance reader of Cicero that he misses no opportunity of expressing his contempt for Epicureanism as a philosophy which deprives man of the divine sanction and encourages him in the gross practices of the materialist. It is also clear that, while he regards the Stoics as too far removed from the goods of the flesh and the realities of this world of actual living, he is by nature of the Stoic persuasion.

Among the Stoic tenets nothing is more prominent than the principle of living in harmony with nature. Given the active and challenging age in which Cicero and his contemporaries lived, it was natural that men, and especially men for whom the gods of Mount Olympus and Homer had become little more than the figures of poetic story-telling, should look to a philosophy of life containing something basic. How were they to live, and who was to be their authority? The Stoic answer to this was that God and His World were identical, that the Universe was an entity and a unity, that man was in it and should be of it, and that the way to fulfilment of the divine purpose, and consequently to peace, was to submerge his will in the will of the universe, to live in harmony with nature.

Let us look into the meaning of this tenet. It will help us to understand the mind of Cicero and the Romans, and may help us to understand our own.

"You marvel at my wisdom," says Cato at eighty-four to his young friends Lælius and Scipio, who have noticed that to him old age, so hateful to most men that they say it weighs heavier than Ætna, is never burdensome.

"I wish I deserved it. As a matter of fact, my wisdom consists only in this, that I regard nature as the best guide of life, and follow and obey her as I would one divine. It is not likely that, having composed all the other parts of life's drama well, she has been like an unskilful poet and neglected the last act. There must of necessity be something to conclude with, just as in the case of the fruits of the trees and the increase of the soil there comes in the fulness of time a ripening and a falling to earth. The wise man will submit to this with patience.... He will grieve at old age no more than the husbandman grieves at the passing of the pleasant springtime and the coming on of autumn. For spring, so to speak, is an image of youth, and gives an earnest of fruits that are to be, while the remaining seasons are suited to the reaping and garnering of the harvest.... All that comes to pass in harmony with nature is to be regarded as among good things. And what is so much in harmony with nature as for the aged to die?"

"Living in harmony with nature" is a phrase which appeals to our ears as modern, but it was as familiar to ancient ears as it is to our own. It was probably familiar to Epicurean as well as to Stoic. The Epicurean existence, too, was in harmony with nature, but more exclusively in the physical and mechanical sense. Body, senses, and soul, like all other things animate and inanimate, were material in their birth, life, death, and ultimate dissipation. To live in harmony with nature was to run the course of life according to the law of atoms; the Epicurean was distinguished from the Stoic by his seeing in sensation rather than in virtue the great object of existence.

It was the Stoic, however, to whom the phrase was really consecrated. Life in harmony with nature was the keystone of the Stoic philosophy. Yet, though modern times are more in sympathy with Stoicism because of its glorification of reason and virtue rather than sensation and pleasure, "to live in harmony with nature" calls up in the minds of most men today ideas far from identical with those entertained by the Stoic, whether the Stoic by profession, like the Greek schoolman, or the Stoic by nature, *anima naturaliter Stoica*, like Cato and Cicero and the serious Roman world in general. There are no doubt today philosophic individuals who reason below the surface, but even the average cultivated mind entertains in its thought of nature only a comparatively shallow and unsystematic conception of mere externals. It thinks of life in the woods and fields, for example, as opposed to life in the town. It is the prevailing conception of romantic literature, which is for the most part responsible for its presence in the general mind.

With the ancients, too, the thought of the general mind was largely crystallized by the art of literature, and the Stoic mode of thinking, as far as nature was concerned, was as prevalent in letters then as the romantic is today. What the ancients were thinking of when they spoke of life in harmony with nature was systematic, reasoned, entire conformity with total, universal nature.

To the ancient, however, nature did not mean sentiment; it meant law. To live in harmony with nature was to live in conformity with law: with the law of one's own being, with the law of human relations, or society, and with the law of the universe. Let Marcus Aurelius, in whom the Stoicism of the Romans found its greatest example in life as well as in letters, make clear what this means.

Look straight to this, to what nature leads thee, both the universal nature through the things which happen to thee, and thy own nature through the acts which must be done by thee. Every being ought to do that which is according to its constitution. . . . For we are made for coöperation, like feet, like hands, like eyelids, like the rows of the upper and lower teeth. To act against one another then is contrary to nature; and it is acting against one another to be vexed and then turn away. . . . Now the good for the reasonable animal is society; for that we are made for society has been shown above. . . . The world is in a manner a State. . . . No longer let thy breathing only act in concert with the air which surrounds thee, but let thy intelligence also now be in harmony with the intelligence which embraces all things. For the intelligent power is no less diffused in all parts and pervades all things for him who is willing to draw it to him than the aerial power for him who is able to respire it.

As for identifying spasmodic retirement into wild solitude, or a return to the life of primitive man, with living according to the law of nature, nothing was farther from the ancient mind. The Golden Age, to be sure, was the era of effortless living in the lap of primordial nature; but this was the stuff of poetry, and not even a Virgil in the *Pollio* seriously expected such an age to return. For the ancients, the Golden Age was forever in the past. The individual found himself alive, in the midst of men, in the presence of universal purpose. To ascertain in terms of law what this purpose was, to establish in terms of law what his conduct was to be, was the problem of existence. To live in harmony with nature was reasoned conformity with law.

The great purpose of conformity with nature, however, was not, as is usual with the modern soul, sympathy, communion, and enjoyment, but acquiescence and consolation. Man was born unto trouble, as the sparks fly upward; he was of few days, and the end of his little existence was not to be escaped or even deferred. To penetrate the secret of the inevitable, to be able to recognize such of the lesser ills of life as were fixed by the constitution of nature, as well as to realize that death, the greatest evil of all, was implacable and impartial, was to lessen the unhappiness that came of fruitless struggle against law, and to reduce the waste of striving for what was not in the province of law and for that very reason not virtue and not a good. To realize that death itself was in the category of the good because it was in accord with universal law was to transform the greatest misery of the soul into a blessed, if not a happy, event. The life in harmony with nature was the life of intelligent submission and calm acquiescence.

Pass through this little space of time conformably with nature, and end thy journey in content, just as an olive falls off when it is ripe, blessing nature who produced it, and thanking the tree on which it grew.... Waiting for death with a cheerful mind, as being nothing else than a dissolution of the elements of which every living thing is compounded. For it is according to nature, and nothing is evil which is according to nature.

It was a life not without struggle, but its struggles were against only the incidental and unessential, always against only that which could be overcome, never against the eternal decrees of universal law; and their end was peace. It is not justice to call this a philosophy of life which was only negative and resulted only in resignation; it could summon the soul to action as well as fortify it for endurance. Neither for Cicero nor for Marcus Aurelius was life to be lived apart from the affairs of men and citizens.

Whatever the occasional extravagances of Stoicism in the mouths of professional philosophers, this reasoned contemplation of life which gave it character possesses the attractiveness of sanity and self-control. So far is it from placing an emphasis upon fanciful or whimsical details of the life in conformity with nature that it leaves us less enlightened than we could wish regarding the particulars of conduct, and contains almost nothing that indicates what we call today communion with nature. Its concern is with human existence, contemplated as a whole against the universal existence. It does not, as the result of a contemplation showing the brevity and futility of life, revel in romantic self-compassion. It does not weep itself into pessimism and despair, or stage its melancholy after the fashion of an Omar. The spirit of Stoicism in action, as seen especially in the discourse of Cato on old age, is calm, self-contained, and full of health. Whether we consider the Stoic here as Cato the *dramatis persona* or as Cicero the author, throughout and permeating the celebrated essay there is a well-tempered purity of feeling and expression that well becomes the old man of much experience who faces calmly the facts of existence.

The similes employed in this golden piece of literature are a proof of this. Life is a stream. Life is a drama written by the hand of nature, the composer who never grows careless in the last act. Life is like the fruit on the tree, which has its blossoming, its greenness and growth, its ripening, mellowing, and falling stages. It is like a fire, which rises, burns fiercely, spends itself, and turns to ash of its own accord. It is a lamp, which flickers and goes out in old age unless constantly fed with oil. It is picket duty, whence to withdraw is forbidden, unless by order of the Great Imperator, that is, God. It is a voyage in which everyone has his appointed duty, and the final sight of land and the sailing into the long-expected harbor bring with them joy; or it is a race, at the finish of which no man wishes to be called back to the starting line; or it is a brief sojourn at an inn before continuing an eternal journey; or a year with its natural seasons, each with its own peculiar richness; or, best of all, it is the playing of a drama in which the actor is privileged, if he is of the proper stuff, to make a reputation for all the play in the very first act: "Nor need the actor play the play to the end in order to please; let him only prove himself in whatever act he does appear. A brief space of time suffices for the living of life honorably and well. The wise man need not keep on to the *Plaudite*." These similes are all of the same sane quality. Not one of them bears the least mark of triviality or unhealth.

To the modern mind, life in harmony with nature has a different meaning. There are a few, but only a few, who conceive of it in the calm and reasoned manner of antiquity; and these, when they do so, are for the most part consciously influenced by the literature of antiquity. The usual conception is superficial and incomplete, or even false. The romantic idea of man and nature has taken the place of the reasoned conception. Time and the participation of the North have brought about a reversal. There is probably as little reasoned conformity with nature today as there was romantic conformity in the days of Marcus Aurelius or Cicero.

What the average man today considers living in harmony with nature is not a reasoned, but a sentimental, conformity. He thinks of it as sleeping rough rather than in a bed, of living in a tent in the woods or a cave in the rocks rather than in a residence in town, of dressing in skins and eating uncooked foods and drinking of the mountain stream, of sleeping with the setting of the sun and waking with its rising; in a word, of doing violence to the customs of civilized man in general and to his own habits in particular. Or, for the less vigorous, there is the more poetic and more easily practised Wordsworthian contemplation, or the passionate Byronic "interview," or the Shelleyan communion. In any case, it is not so much acquiescence with nature as disagreement with man. It is not so much the law of the universe the would-be child of nature is keeping as it is the law of human custom he is breaking. It is not submission to the inevitable so much as rebellion against routine. It is not a consolation for the hardships of trouble and death, but a vacation from civilization. It is not really a philosophy of life he is seeking, but an indulgence of self.

> There is a pleasure in the pathless woods,
> There is a rapture on the lonely shore,
> There is society, where none intrudes,
> By the deep Sea and music in its roar:

> I love not Man the less, but Nature more,
> For these our interviews, in which I steal
> From all I may be, or have been before,
> To mingle with the Universe, and feel
> What I can ne'er express, yet cannot all conceal.

This is not really an interview with nature, but a novel and enjoyable meeting with one's self. It is not really a stealing away from all one has been before; it is keeping a clandestine appointment with an ego. It is not so much a mingling with the universe as a demand upon the universe for approval. It is not so much sympathy with nature as the identification of solitude and the sweep of wind and wave and the pour of the rain with the Byronic passions. As is usual with those who in the love of nature hold communion with her various forms, the various language she speaks is in fact only the dialects of her interlocutor echoed back to his expectant ear.

> Rough wind, that moanest loud
>   Grief too sad for song;
> Wild wind, when sullen cloud
>   Knells all the night long;
> Sad storm whose tears are vain,
>   Bare woods whose branches stain,
> Deep caves and dreary main—
>   Wail for the world's wrong!

This is not the communion of man with nature, but the compulsory communion of nature with Shelleyan man. And as for *Love's Philosophy*—

> See the mountains kiss high heaven,
>   And the waves clasp one another;
> No sister-flower would be forgiven
>   If it disdained its brother:
> And the sunlight clasps the earth,
>   And the moonbeams kiss the sea:
> What is all this sweet work worth
>   If thou kiss not me?—

this again is but the pretense to conformity of life with nature. What it is actually, as is usual with romantic poetry of the kind, is the investiture of nature with the moods and actions of wilful humanity.

In a word, life in conformity with nature in the usual modern sense is not a reasoned penetration into the constitution of universal nature, but a fleeting, light-hearted incursion into novel places. It is not a serious wooing of nature, but a light, sentimental coquetry. It does not belong to serious philosophy in any age, and does not perceptibly belong even to poetry in Greek and Roman times. Its result is not a deep and fruitful pleasure, but a titillation; not a philosophically earnest attempt, but an irresponsible diversion; not communion, but intrusion; not edification, but intoxication.

To say this is not necessarily to disapprove the fact. To spend lonely weeks in the woods and by the water or among the mountains, to contemplate, to enter strenuously into so-called communion with nature, is not in contravention of the law, is pleasant and stimulating, and may be for a time even salutary and beautiful. The question is not one of approval or disapproval, but of the use of terms. It is not the thing itself that is culpable, but the description and acceptation of it as the life in harmony with nature. The extended living of life in harmony with nature in this manner would result in the surrender of invention, the overthrow of custom, and the wreck of civilization.

Happily, to live thus to any considerable extent is less possible than at first sight seems. To go to bed with the shades of night and to rise "when the first cock his matin rings," is a course which, pursued the year around in the temperate zones, would be a serious undertaking, to say nothing of attempting to live in harmony with solar nature in less convenient latitudes; as

> In climes beyond the solar road,
> Where shaggy forms o'er ice-built mountains
>   roam.

To go still farther, and to live in accord with the seasons after the manner of tree or flower or hibernating animal, is an ideal perhaps as justifiable, when viewed as an attempt to live in harmony with nature, as to live like the American Indian. Civilized men, however, have not found this possible. According to such an ideal, the spring should be the time of love and frolic and the impulse to action, the summer a season of the steady putting forth of energy, the autumn a period of realization and enjoyment, and the winter a barren interval of dormant inactivity.

Men still uncivilized do live more or less in this very manner. The American savage did. The vagrant does, as far as he is able. The less advanced of the rural and mountain classes in America do, and the majority of them in older lands. The life of the people in *Daphnis and Chloe* was of this sort. "As every one was of necessity confined within-doors, most of the laborers and shepherds were glad at having an interval of release from their wonted labors, and immediately after their morning meal lay down, and enjoyed a lengthy sleep, winter appearing to them more pleasant than the summer, the autumn, or even the spring."

But persons like these do not represent the highest form of civilization. The intellectual, the ruling, the more creative classes contravene the law of the seasons. It is in autumn, not in spring, that the enterprise of men flowers into fresh vigor. The season that naturally invites to repose, "season of mists and mellow fruitfulness," witnesses the most strenuous outbursts of energy on the part of church and college and of industry, energy that rises to its height in the winter, season of natural inertness and death. In spring, the season of the rebound into life and creative action, man is exhausted, and driven to tonics. In summer, when every cell of nature is swelling and every fibre quivering with the irresistible energy of growth, man must have his vacation. The higher the life of man, the less conformity with nature in the ordinary modern meaning of the phrase. Only the remote rustic, the savage, and the beast are in any measure in accord with her.

A kingfisher, with a sudden descent from his arboreal watchtower, comes up from the plunge and darts away with a minnow in his beak. A dragon-fly meets fate in the air as a jay with neat manœuvres arrests his flight forever. Cries of distress in the night from the darkness of the forest suggest the cruelties of the strong and the tragedy of the weak. To live by the law of the bloody fang is to live in harmony with nature. Yet no civilized man can so live without destruction to his own nature as civilized man. Whenever a whole people has abandoned itself to such a conception of life in harmony with nature, all civilization has been perturbed, and the deluded offenders have found themselves swiftly overtaken by Nemesis.

The fact is, civilization is a contradiction of nature. Civilization is a war against things as they are. Man does not accept nature as she is; she must be improved. What Mr. Woodberry says of life and art we may say of nature and civilization: "Nature is a chance medley; civilization an arrangement." Civilization is the great art. Man is a rebel against his environment. The liberty of bird and beast and the lilies of the field is not the liberty he craves. That liberty he wills to sacrifice for the liberty of civilized man. He violates the so-called laws of nature, and gladly for the sake of freedom submits to the penalty. He enters into the slaveries of civilization in order to possess its freedoms. He tills the surface of the earth and digs into its depths. He navigates the sea and the air, he turns night into day and winter into summer, he annihilates time and space, he perverts the processes of nature in general. All this means the myriad restraints of ordered existence, with the great slavery, labor.

Man perverts the processes of nature—save in one respect. The one thing in nature which man does not pervert is his own nature, which is as much a part of the universe of nature as blossom or crystal. All other perversions are necessary because the soul of man demands them in order to fulfil the law of its own being. For man to interfere with external nature at the bidding of his own nature is itself to act in harmony with nature. We hardly need Anatole France to remind us that from all other animals, to say nothing of the remainder of creation, man is distinguished by two things, *le rêve* and *le rire*. He can laugh and he can dream, he can reflect. He is of imagination all compact. He is never satisfied with mere living to himself or for the moment or in the actual. He is never free from the inner urge to bend the world to his purposes. Effort against material obstruction is the law of his being.

Thus the ancient emphasis upon the nature of man, and the

ancient neglect of sentimental contact with external nature, are sane and true. To search for the laws of being—the laws of one's own nature, the law of society, the laws of the universe—is the only real way of striving to live in harmony with nature. The principal thing in nature is not rock or tree or flower, or bird or beast, but man. In studying the law of man's individual nature, the ancient was probing for the secrets of the most potent force in nature. In attempting to realize the limitations imposed upon himself by the law of the universe as expressed in external nature and in other men, in order that he might resist such impulses as were in contravention of social and universal law, he was really but studying afresh the law of his own nature.

The proper study of mankind is man. The proper study of nature will make its center the nature of man. The proper life in harmony with nature will make its first object conformity with the nature of man. To know what man has willed to do and what he has succeeded in doing or failed to do is the proper basis for expectation as to future failure or success. The habit of reasoned conformity will rob the romantic of many of his cherished excitements, but it will also protect him and his fellows from the falsely grounded enthusiasms of the restless visionary, and leave more time for actual living.

VIRGIL THROUGH TWO THOUSAND YEARS

P UBLIUS VERGILIUS MARO, whose name in its ancient
form was spelled in his own times with an *e* and in later
Roman times with an *i*, and whose name in English and
other modern tongues has been spelled with an *i* for so many centuries that it is an offense against long established usage to write
it any other way, was born on October 15, 70 B.C., year 683 from
the founding of Rome, not far from Mantua in or on the lands
of the little north Italian village at that time called Andes.

Mantua, and very likely the village of Andes itself, stood beside
Milton's

Smooth-sliding Mincius, crowned with vocal reeds;

in the poet's own verse,

Propter aquam tardis ingens ubi flexibus errat
Mincius et tenera praetexit harundine ripas—

beside the waters where great Mincius wanders in tardy windings and
embroiders his banks with the tender reed.

It is a Shakespearean as well as a Miltonic neighborhood. The
Two Gentlemen of Verona got as far as the frontiers of Mantua,
where Valentine communed with himself in the forest:

How use doth breed a habit in a man!
This shadowy desert, unfrequented woods,
I better brook than flourishing peopled towns:
Here can I sit alone, unseen of any,
And to the nightingale's complaining notes
Tune my distresses and record my woes.

It was to Mantua that Romeo fled in banishment from Verona,
twenty miles away, and in Mantua that he had of the apothecary

In tattered weeds, with overwhelming brow,
the dram of poison.

Virgil, the Mincius, Mantua, Milton, Shakespeare. That there is a meaning of Virgil and Italian lands to the lover of English letters is manifest at the first step of our approach.

At the age of twelve, according to Saint Jerome and Donatus his grammarian teacher, who lived four centuries after the poet and derived their facts from Suetonius two centuries less removed, Virgil was sent or taken by his prosperous farmer or potter father, who now perhaps changed his residence, to school in Cremona, forty miles away, the capital of Cisalpine Gaul and for a hundred and sixty years at that time a Roman colony and the center of Romanization. Not only was Virgil not Roman born, but the Roman citizenship ostensibly conferred upon the north Italian allies of Rome in 89 B.C. was not fully confirmed until Virgil was twenty-eight and entering on his career as a poet. This was after the victory of Augustus and Antony at Philippi in 42 B.C. In the year 53 B.C., at the age of seventeen, according to the same witness, he assumed the *toga virilis,* receiving what may be called his civic confirmation, and left Cremona for further education in Milan, whence he soon departed, for the same purpose, to Rome.

In the capital, at that time in the confusion and uncertainties of the approaching conflict between the two great figures and tendencies of the past fifteen years—Cæsar and the restless champions of change, Pompey and the conservative defenders of senatorial tradition—Virgil entered upon the course of training usual to young men destined for the Roman career. It consisted largely in the study of the spoken and written word called rhetoric, with letters and philosophy as its handmaidens, and was to have led to the court room and perhaps to the prætor's bench and the consulship, as it did lead many of his fellow-students, among whom perhaps were Antony and Augustus themselves. We are told that he made but one appearance at the bar, and are left to conclude that his sensitive and shy nature rebelled at the prospect of the public career.

After a period of four or five years in Rome beginning about 52 B.C. and including the excitement of the war between Pompey

THE MINCIO AT PIETOLE; ANITA AND JOHN SHOWERMAN, 1930

THE MINCIO AT PIETOLE, LOOKING DOWNSTREAM

THE VIRGIL MONUMENT AT PIETOLE

THE VIRGIL MONUMENT AT MANTUA

and Cæsar, whose governorship in Virgil's native country had
made of the north Italians and no doubt of Virgil himself his
ardent friends, he left the capital and the rhetoric, mathematics,
medicine, and philosophy of the school and betook himself to
Naples and Mistress Philosophy alone. There, in the garden of
Philodemus and Siro the Epicurean masters, he studied in company with the friends-to-be of the rest of his life or theirs.

Most prominent among these friends were three men whose names
have been made famous by association with Virgil and Horace.
One was Quintilius Varus the critic, mourned by Horace at his
death in 24 B.C. as the modest, the just, the faithful and unspoiled,
the sincere and the truthful, "bringing tears to many good men,
but to no one, Virgil, more than to thee." Another was Varius
Rufus, epic poet and writer of tragedies, who lived five years
longer than Virgil and set the *Æneid* in order for publication.
The third was Plotius Tucca, the associate of Varius in the task.
We meet two of them, with Virgil and Horace, on the famous
diplomatic journey to Brundisium in 37 B.C., when Horace is
twenty-eight, Varius thirty-seven, and Virgil thirty-three. They join
the party at Sinuessa near Capua, to the great joy of all. Writes
Horace:

The light of the following day is much the most pleasing of all; for
Plotius and Varius and Virgil meet us at Sinuessa, souls fairer than
whom the earth has never brought forth, and to whom no one is more
closely knit than I. O what embracings and what boundless delight!
Nothing, in my senses, would I compare with a pleasant friend.

Mæcenas also, the adviser of Augustus, is with them, the chief of
the expedition. When Mæcenas goes to exercise, Horace and
Virgil go to nap, fellow-sufferers, the one from eyes, the other
from indigestion. At Canusium, six days afterward and one hundred and thirty-two miles farther on the way, they lose the companionship of Varius, with many tears.

The philosophy whose teaching bound these friends together during the period of years at Naples was already more than two centuries old in Greek-speaking lands, and had been given currency
in Italy by the great poem of Lucretius as well as by Greek lecturers. Epicureanism demonstrated the atomic basis of all crea-

tion, including the soul, and the perfect mortality of man. It set forth with fervor the error and fraud of religion, the needlessness of the fear of death and a beyond, and the duty as well as the privilege of seizing the here and now of happiness. It was, like Stoicism, a philosophy, the guide of life that in some sort took the place of religion. At its best, it was a philosophy of the inquiring mind, the mind in rebellion against, or in despair of, the faith handed down by the brave days of old. At its worst, it was the philosophy of the luxurious and indolent who welcomed an excuse for self-indulgence and renunciation of the old-time civic and moral responsibilities. It inspired the contempt of Cicero, whose impatience with it kept him from being fair. Whatever effect it had upon the intellectual and spiritual life of Virgil and his friends, it is hardly taken at its own valuation by Horace, and no one reading Virgil would without taking thought call him Epicurean.

The garden of Philodemus did not make of Virgil a professor of philosophy, as the schools of rhetoric in Rome had not made of him an advocate or senator. By the time Antony and Young Octavius were back from the field of Philippi, when Virgil was approaching thirty and had left the garden, he found that nature and education had made him a poet instead of professor or public man. The first of the *Eclogues* were the sign.

Virgil was not the inspired young singer gushing forth abundantly. He was probably in the twenty-eighth or twenty-ninth year when the first Eclogue declared his renunciation of the youthful epic ambition and his dedication to the pastoral Muse:

Agrestem tenui meditabor harundine Musam.

As might be supposed, he had written verses before. Verse has always been a natural thing in Italy. A generation ago there were said to be sixty poets in modern Verona, and the number in the Verona of Catullus, or in Virgil's Cremona, Rome, or Naples, was perhaps no smaller in proportion. There is no great certainty, however, as to what Virgil wrote before the *Eclogues*. During the years from 48 to 42 B.C., the outside limits of the garden

days, he may or may not have written all or part of the twenty
or more poems of varied length which are usually printed as the
Virgilian Appendix. Scholars are still much at variance regarding
the authorship of these poems. Tenney Frank and Norman DeWitt
find nearly all of them Virgil's, A. E. Housman almost none.

Virgil's life was a little less than fifty-one years; his productive
years were twenty-three. The *Bucolics*, or *Eclogues*, ten pastorals
reminiscent of Theocritus, were the work of the three years
ending in 40 or 39 B.C. with the poet's thirtieth or thirty-first.
During these years the youthful Emperor was finding himself in
the task of planning the reconstruction of the Roman State. The
Georgics, reminiscent of Hesiod's *Works and Days*, were the work
of 37 to 30 B.C., when Virgil was thirty-three to forty. In these
years the Emperor quelled the enemies of the new régime under
Sextus Pompeius on the sea, reduced to naught the menace of
Antony and Cleopatra and a rival empire in the East, and possessed
himself of the undisputed title to lordship. From 30 to 19 B.C.,
when the poet was forty to fifty-one, his energies were given to
the *Æneid*, reminiscent of the great epics of Homer, while the
Emperor consolidated his far-flung realms about and upon the
Mediterranean, by this time a Roman lake, and on the Rhine
and Danube, and justified his ways as the architect of the Roman
Empire. In the year 19 B.C., taken ill in Greece, Virgil travelled
homeward with the Emperor as far as Brundisium, where, on the
twenty-second of September, he died. The *Æneid*, which the poet
could not revise and whose destruction was his dying behest, was
edited with little alteration by Varius and Tucca at the bidding
of Augustus, and given to the world in 17 B.C.

The fame of Virgil was immediate. The *Eclogues* met with such
success that they were even recited by professional singers on the
stage. The wise boy Emperor liked and favored them, and the
people applauded them. Tacitus writes, two generations afterward:

I prefer the secure and restful apartness of Virgil, in which nevertheless he did not fail of the divine Augustus's favor or of the familiarity of the Roman people. Witness the letters of Augustus, and the
testimony of the people themselves, who, on hearing his verses in the

theater, rose unanimously and paid their respects to Virgil, who happened to be present and looking on, as if he were Augustus.

The maturer and more Italian *Georgics* had confirmed the fame of the *Eclogues*. The intensely Roman *Æneid* became instantly the national poem.

Virgil's fame was not only immediate, but enduring. Quintilian, a hundred years later, gives him next place to Homer, and remembers his teacher Domitius Afer as saying that Virgil was second to Homer, yet nearer first than third. "All the rest," says Quintilian, "will follow from afar." In Juvenal's seventh Satire, Virgil and Horace are in the schools, the books lamp-blacked from use in the dark early hours of morning. *Arma virumque* and *conticuere omnes*, scratched on the walls of Pompeii, with pictures of Æneas bearing the old Anchises away from the flames of Troy while little Ascanius, holding to his hand, tries "with steps not equal" to keep up, *non passibus aequis*, and of the regimental surgeon treating the wounded Trojan leader while Ascanius stands by in tears and the goddess mother hovers near, are further testimony that the poet was a popular and a national possession. There have been found in Pompeii about one hundred and fifty reminiscences of Virgil. Silius Italicus and Statius revered his memory, kept the anniversaries of his birth, and went as pilgrims to his tomb.

Nor did Virgil's fame cease with the fall of the Roman State and pagan culture. It accomplished the transit from the pagan to the Christian era. When Jerome in his cell at Bethlehem hears of the Goths putting Rome to the sack on August 24, 410, the grieving Saint in order to express the passion of his sorrow mingles with the Scriptures in which he is saturated the language of his beloved Virgil, and uses the words of Æneas to Dido on the destruction of Troy:

In the night was Moab taken, in the night its walls fell. O God, the heathen are come into thine inheritance. . . . What voice could tell of that night's destruction, what speech unfold its tragedies, what tears equal its travail? The city of old, the queen of the world for many years, is fallen to ruin. The lifeless bodies of men lie thickly scattered throughout its streets and palaces . . . and everywhere is the spectre of death.

> *Quis cladem illius noctis, quis funera fando*
> *Explicet, aut possit lacrimis aequare labores?*
> *Urbs antiqua ruit, multos dominata per annos;*
> *Plurima perque vias sternuntur inertia passim*
> *Corpora perque domos . . . et plurima mortis imago.*

Augustine shows himself equally familiar with the pagan poet when he confesses to

weeping the death of Dido for love to Æneas, but weeping not his own death for want of love to thee, O God. Thou light of my heart, Thou bread of my inmost soul . . . I loved Thee not. . . . And all this I wept not, I who wept for Dido slain and "seeking by the sword a stroke and wound extreme," and myself seeking the while a worse extreme. "The wooden horse lined with armed men," and "the burning of Troy," and "Creusa's shade and sad similitude," were the choice spectacle of my vanity.

Despite the prickings of conscience and the desperate effort to cut itself off from the pagan past, Christian culture clung to pagan letters. Minucius, Lactantius, Jerome, Ambrose, Augustine, and their like, unable to give up their Virgil and Cicero, unable likewise to be happy in their affection for the purely pagan, resorted to the conversion, so to speak, of their favorites. The "least mortal mind" of Cicero was easily seen in his work *On Ethics,* and in parts of *On the Nature of the Gods* and other philosophical essays, to be *anima naturaliter Christiana,* a soul by nature Christian.

If Cicero was Christian on intellectual grounds, Virgil's claim was more of the spirit. The poet's reverence for the virtues, his "majestic sadness at the doubtful doom of human kind"; his sensitiveness to the "spirit that goes through all lands and all reaches of the sea and the depths of heaven, whence the flocks, the herds, the human kind, the races of all the wild, each at birth drawing from the Great Source its tenuous life," each finally to be released for the return to deathless existence among the stars of heaven—these noble sentiments were to the Christian mind a communion with God which would surely have been Christian but for the accident of time that brought the poet into the world a hundred years before the Calvary.

The poet survived not only ancient times both pagan and Christian, but the ignorance and superstition of the darker times that made him a Christian prophet, a necromancer, and a magician, and used his works as a means of casting lots, or as a body of allegory in which to find solutions for the mysteries of heaven and earth. He became the "sage guide" of Dante, his "master and author," from whom alone he took "the beautiful manner that gave him honor,"

Lo bello stile che m' ha fatto onore;

and was his companion through the Inferno and up to the borders of Purgatory. In the Renaissance he became one of the chief inspirations of the new learning and the new culture. He survived the enthusiasms of the facile versifiers who fancied themselves his rivals. Maffeo Vegio, 1406-58, an official in the Roman Chancery under Eugenius IV, won the gratitude and admiration of both the historic and the romantic by adding to the Æneid a Book XIII in Latin, in which he set in order the war and politics of Æneas left at loose ends by Virgil, and confirmed the reader's prayerful expectation that Lavinia's affair would terminate, as feeling demanded it should, in her becoming the bride of Æneas.

Virgil survived even more than the ignorance of the Middle Age and the enthusiasm of the Renaissance. He survived the discovery of the Greek manuscripts, the rebirth of Greek literature, the restoration of Homer to primacy, and the reaction against the art epic as distinguished from the natural. He has survived the scientific movement in the study of literature. He has survived the assaults of the so-called practical educator. He is today better understood and more highly esteemed than at any day since he passed from his own times and his own people into the Middle Ages.

During the year 1930, containing the October 15 which for convenience's sake it was agreed to regard as the two thousandth recurrence of the birthday of Virgil, there were many celebrations in the poet's honor. The American Classical League set twenty-six committees at work, including members from all parts of the United States and representing not only schools and colleges but

DOMENICO DI FRANCESCO'S "DANTE AND HIS POEM"

MEDAL COMMEMORATING THE BIMILLENNIUM OF VIRGIL'S BIRTH

business. It struck a medal, designed by Tom Jones of the American Academy in Rome, it arranged for multitudinous anniversary lectures, and conducted in two sections a Virgilian Cruise following the route of Æneas from the fall of Troy to the conquest of Latium. Phi Beta Kappa, as a part of its own celebration of a one hundred and fiftieth anniversary, placed lectures in honor of Virgil at the disposal of a thousand secondary schools.

Among European countries to celebrate the poet's anniversary, the chief was naturally Virgil's own land. The *Atene e Roma* Society of Italy proclaimed in Latin six years previously the coming event, and invited all the world to participate.

The Italian Government had for several years been excavating and disengaging Augustan monuments to be a feature of the year —the ships at Nemi, the Mausoleum, the Theater of Marcellus, the Forum of Augustus, the Capitoline Hill, and the Grot of the Sibyl at Cumae. The Government also put out a series of Virgilian postage stamps, and struck a medal in bronze, silver, and gold, on one face symbolizing the *Eclogues, Georgics,* and *Æneid,* and on the other portraying the famous meeting of Æneas and Anchises in the lower world. At Mantua in September and October, the celebration plans included the publication, by the Royal Virgilian Academy, of a complete Virgil, a volume of Virgilian studies by eminent scholars in Italy and foreign lands, and a volume of Academy records with minor Virgilian works. They included also the holding of a congress of Virgilian scholars; an agrarian and industrial exposition of the province of Mantua by the Provincial Fascist Federation of Agriculture; the inauguration, by the National Forestry Commission, of a Virgilian Grove, *lucus Vergilianus,* to contain all plants named by the poet; an apicultural exposition by the National Association of Bee-keepers; and a national congress of the Dante Alighieri Society. In the newly created Vatican State, the Vatican Library reproduced in facsimile the famous Codex Palatinus, now some 1600 years old, thus prolonging the life of a manuscript destined one day to fade entirely from view.

There were Virgilian celebrations in many other lands. If we think of the infinity of local, provincial, and state observances by way of lectures, readings, plays, pageants, club papers, studies, congresses, and publications, which took place not only in Latin and Anglo-Latin countries, but in Teutonic and Slavic lands, and wherever occidental culture, which is Roman culture, has lodged, it will not seem an exaggeration to declare that the year of our Lord 1930 was marked by the most widespread of all the literary celebrations in the history of the world.

We are now five years past the Bimillennium, but honor to Virgil is timeless. Mankind at any time is responsive to the exhortation of Dante to "honor the most high Poet":

Onorate l'altissimo poeta.

. XXI .

THE VIRGIL COUNTRY

CÆSAR, the soldier, administrator, and statesman, was a man of the city and the camp. Born and reared in Rome, he had no country childhood home to engage his sentiment; always on the march or in the tent when away from Rome, always active and anxious when in Rome, he had no rural retreats, no little nooks of earth for leisurely retirement. If nature did attract him, if he enjoyed fruitful Italy, or the broad fields, the dark forests, and the shining rivers of France, he has left us in the legacy of his pen no sign of it.

Cicero's life was somewhat less removed from contemplation. In the intervals of a career almost as active as Cæsar's though in a different way, he restored and recreated soul and body in favorite spots away from the city. He writes letters from Tusculum, from Formiae, and his many other villa retreats. He enjoys the estates of his friends. He goes into the heart of the forest for consolation in his times of grief. He visits again and again the homestead at Arpinum, and takes Atticus with him. Though rarely indulging in nature sentiment, the setting of *De Legibus* at the meeting of the waters in the Liris valley, and the passage in *De Senectute* on the delights of the husbandman in the growth and care of his plants, are enough to show that he enjoyed a meditative walk in the shade of poplars on the banks of a cool, rushing stream, and that at the contemplation of the seed swelling in the warm earth in springtime, of the waving grasses and grains, of the trailing vines and their clusters, and of all the mellow fruitfulness of an Italian autumn, he felt a sympathy with nature which amounted to communion. The peaceful quiet of the country was healing and restoration to his spirit.

I come now to the pleasures of those who till the soil, in which I take incredible delight; which are in no wise hindered by old age, and

which seem to me the nearest approach to the philosophic life. For
they keep an account with the soil, which never refuses a draft and
never pays anybody back his loan without interest, but sometimes with
less, and oftener with greater, increase. And yet, it is indeed not only
the fruits that delight me, but the natural forces of the earth itself.

The speaker here is really the orator Cicero at sixty-two, though
it is old Cato the patriot farmer who is represented as talking.

From Virgil we shall expect different things. Virgil was not a
soldier, and not in the ordinary sense a public man. He was born

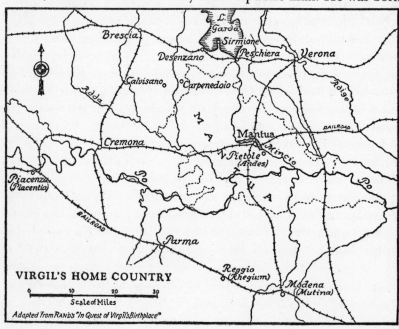

VIRGIL'S HOME COUNTRY

Scale of Miles

Adapted from RAND'S "In Quest of Virgil's Birthplace"

and reared in the country, far from Rome, a northern Italian;
he never belonged to the capital as Cicero and Cæsar and Horace
did; and his earlier contact with the soil was that of the owner
whose home it is and whose livelihood depends upon it.

Yet Virgil is not in the usual sense a nature poet, and he is in
an unusual sense a public man. He mingled little in public affairs,
but much in the public mind; he is the poet of the Empire, just
as Cæsar is the builder of the Empire and Cicero the orator of the
Republic. As a nature poet he does not "describe" or "interpret"
natural phenomena, or otherwise of set purpose sing the out-of-

doors. Of the ten *Pastorals*, few are set in characteristically Italian scenery, and the likeness of the landscape to the Mantuan neighborhood is not so close as to be called reality. In the *Georgics* the great nature passages are accidents. The economics of pasture and harvest field, of hive and orchard and vineyard, yields the exquisite poetic by-product of the well-known passages on the glories of Italy, the joys of the country, the grandeur of the storm, the marvels of bee life, the gallantry of the pastures, the pathetic fate of Orpheus and Eurydice. In the *Æneid* also nature poetry is accidental, and there it is limited to the epithet, the phrase, the line, and the short passage. Just as the purpose of the *Eclogues* was to create Theocritean idyll in Latin, and their setting was Italian or Sicilian or Greek indifferently; just as in the *Georgics* Virgil intended an Italian poem corresponding to the Greek Hesiod's *Works and Days,* and its nature poetry followed on its didacticism; so in the *Æneid* the poet's appreciation of beauty and grandeur in nature is manifest by the way, as with the reader he follows the fortunes of Æneas and the founders of Rome and the Roman people.

Nor should Virgil's appreciation of nature be thought less profound because thus fleetingly expressed. Who that reads can doubt his fondness for the grassy stretches of the pasture, for the cattle on the hills, for the leafiness and shade of thicket and cool grove, for the peaceful silences over broad acres, broken only by the bleating of lambs and the mellow pipings of the shepherd, for golden harvests and heavy-hanging vines and orchards, for the infinite reaches of swinging sea and sky, for the trembling of the moon on heaving glassy waters, for the smoke rising from the cottager's roof as the lengthening shadows descended from the high hills? Virgil saw the great out-of-doors in detail, but he felt it as a whole, and felt himself as a part of it. He was one with the limitless universe—with the night that came up from the depths of ocean and wrapped in mighty shadows the earth and sky, with the dark that brought to weary mortals the sleep that was their greatest boon, with the mood of the storm that gathered in the mountains and hurled itself across the fruitful plain, with the bees in the hive and among the flowers, with the birds in flight before the tempest. If sympathy with creation is to be the measure, Virgil is one of the greatest of nature poets.

Thus it is that everywhere in Italy the presence of Virgil is felt, not less in the hills of Tuscany where mayhap his feet never trod than in the country of his childhood in the Mantuan region and in the lands of his later years in Latium and Campania. Thus it is that Tennyson could address him on the nineteenth centenary of his death:

> Landscape lover, lord of language,
>   more than he that sang the Works and Days,
> All the chosen coin of fancy
>   flashing out from many a golden phrase;
>
> Thou that singest wheat and woodland,
>   tilth and vineyard, hive and horse and herd;
> All the charm of all the Muses
>   often flowering in a lonely word. . . .
>
> Thou that seest Universal
>   Nature moved by Universal Mind;
> Thou majestic in thy sadness
>   at the doubtful doom of human kind.

But lovers of Italy and Virgil will wish to know not only of Virgil's feeling for universal nature but of the actual scenes in Italy which afford the setting for his life and poetry. Of these there are many, and some are very definite.

First of all, there is Mantua, in whose territory or province, according to Probus, commentator on the *Eclogues* in the time of Nero and the Flavian emperors, Virgil was born, in the village of Andes. But there is a difficulty as to the identity of Andes. Probus reads, *vico Andico qui abest a Mantua milia passuum XXX*—"in the village of Andes which is distant from Mantua thirty miles." These are Roman miles and mean about twenty-eight modern miles, a distance which would place Andes farther from Mantua than from Brescia, Cremona, Verona, or Modena, and would make it strange for Virgil to be called a Mantuan rather than a Brescian, a Veronese, a Cremonese, or a Modenese. Besides, the commentator Donatus, two centuries later, and his pupil Saint Jerome, not to mention later witnesses, speak of the poet's birth-

POZZUOLI AND THE PROMONTORY OF MISENO

THE LAKE OF AVERNUS

PANORAMA FROM MISENO TOWARD CUMAE

place as "not far from Mantua," and "near Mantua"; and a popular tradition which is as old as Dante places Andes about three
miles from Mantua at Pietola, now Pietole, where in 1881, nineteen hundred years after his death, a monument to Virgil was
erected. "The gentle shade on whose account Pietola is mentioned more than any other Mantuan village," is Dante's reference to Virgil in *Purgatory* XVIII, 82-3, and it indicates a tradition already old in Dante's time.

There is thus a conflict between the earlier "thirty-mile" tradition of Probus and the "near-by" and popular Pietole traditions
of later commentators and Dante. To reconcile these witnesses,
there have been two methods. One is to search for an Andes
thirty miles from Mantua; the other, to prove the tradition well
founded and the Probus manuscripts mistaken as regards the
distance.

The most recent and the most reasonable of those who stand
for Probus and thirty Roman miles are Professor Braunholtz and
Professor R. S. Conway, of the University of Manchester, who
find ancient Andes in modern Calvisano, approximately thirty
miles to the northwest of Mantua, and hold that the Virgil farm
was somewhere in the country between Calvisano and Carpene-
dolo. Professor Conway, presenting the argument in *The Vergilian
Age*, points out, first, that the distance accords with the thirty miles
of Probus and other commentators. Second, he points out that
the language of the *Eclogues*, especially the First and Ninth, indicates a setting of hilly landscape, a cliff, familiar rivers and
sacred springs, and lengthening shadows descending from the
high mountains or hills, all of which he declares belong in no
wise to the Pietole site, a flat, irrigated region with no hills and
no variety, but do harmonize with the Calvisano country, where
the foothills of the not distant Alps are already beginning to rise.
In the third place, Professor Conway says that inscriptions have
been found in and near Calvisano bearing the names of the poet's
family on either side, Vergilius and Magia. The objection that
Calvisano is not in the Mantuan territory he explains away by
saying that the ancient province was not identical with that of
today.

The most recent defenders of Pietole and tradition are Professor Bruno Nardi of Mantua and Professor E. K. Rand of Harvard. Both call attention to the edition of Virgil by Egnatius published at Venice in 1507, which contains the commentaries of Probus as taken from a very old manuscript since lost, and which prints the testimony of Probus regarding the distance of Andes from Mantua not as thirty miles, but as three. Three Roman miles being the distance of Pietole from Mantua, and three being more in accord than thirty with the "not far from" of Donatus and Jerome, who derive from Suetonius, almost as near to Virgil's time as Probus, Professors Nardi and Rand see in the "thirty," XXX, *triginta*, of the Probus manuscripts a corruption of "three," III, *tria*. Professor Conway, of course, sees the reverse corruption.

Bruno Nardi's argument forms an appendix to his excellent little book, *La Giovinezza di Virgilio*, Mantua, 1927. Professor Rand makes of his findings a plentifully illustrated volume entitled *In Quest of Virgil's Birthplace*, in which with humanistic charm he mingles the grave of scholarship and the gay of exploration in the Mantuan country.

Professor Rand's conclusion is that

Virgil was born in the village of Andes "not far" from Mantua, his mother town. Probus gave the distance correctly as three miles, which a mediæval inadvertence made thirty. Tradition had identified the village with Pietole by Dante's time, nor have we any better guide than that tradition to follow. Virgil did not stay in his birthplace long. . . . There is no proof whatever that he wrote his pastorals while still at Mantua—or Cremona—or Milan. It may well be that some of them were sketched on the banks of the Galæsus, down by Tarentum. The deep well of his mind was filled by that time with the varied splendors of Italy as well as with the varied splendors of Theocritus and others who had sung of grottoes and beech trees and the shadowy hills. From these stored impressions, whether they came from meadow, stream and grove or from no less living poetry, he fashioned, with the vivid force of his genius, a new Arcadia, touched here and there with reminiscences of the dear land of his birth, but unapproachedly transcending any part of it.

Not least among the charms of Italy to the Virgil pilgrim is the recognition of places mentioned only in passing lines. It is a pleas-

ure in Tuscany, for example, to find in the beautiful Clitunno
the ancient Clitumnus:

> There flows Clitumnus through the flowery plain,
> Whose waves, for triumphs after prosperous war,
> The victim ox and snowy sheep prepare.

It delights us to realize that Virgil's eyes, too, looked upon the
lakes of Como and Garda near the Alps:

> Our spacious lakes: thee, Larius, first; and next
> Benacus, with tempestuous billows vexed.

Omitting farther mention of random passages like these, set
like precious stones in the rich brocade of *Æneid* or *Georgics*, let
us pass to the two chief parts of Italy in which the lover of Virgil
feels the presence of his poet. One is Rome and the Campagna;
the other, the region bordering the Bay of Naples on its north.

No more beautiful setting in the whole world, and none more
suited to keep its poem fresh in the memory of men, could be
found than the Virgil country near Naples, the scene of the Sixth
Book of the *Æneid*. A charming region of mingled gardens and
wilderness, a lovely bay with islands near and with leafy shores
that sparkle with white-walled villas and towns, a towering volcano
always active enough to stimulate, two buried cities in its shadow
in the process of resurrection after a sleep of nearly nineteen
hundred years, a great harbor and railroad center in a much
travelled land—all these are Nature's aids in the making and the
keeping of Virgil a poet known to all the world.

About twelve miles west of Naples, at the extreme limit of the
bay, is the Cape of Miseno, the great mound-like promontory whose
name Virgil accounts for by the legend of Misenus the trumpeter.
Five miles to its north, outside the bay and a quarter of a mile from
the seashore, are the hill and grot of Cumae, the scene of Æneas's
landing and visit to the Sibyl. A mile east of Cumae is the Lake
of Avernus. These three, but especially Cumae and the Lake of
Avernus, are the places which must be visited by the reader of
the Sixth Book; but there is much else that is interesting. There
is Baiae, the famous resort of the lordly rich in ancient Roman
society; there is the Lucrine Lake; there is Pozzuoli, the ancient

Puteoli, important in Virgil's time as a seaport; there is the volcanic area of the Solfatara, still sending forth jets of heated sulphurous vapor; there is the Mare Morto at Miseno, the Dead Sea which was once the harbor for the Roman fleet on the west coast, as Ravenna was on the east coast. At the edge of the city of Naples, there is the monument called the Tomb of Virgil, though the actual tomb, we are told, was sunk by geological forces below the waters of the bay.

All these places are easily visited by rail and on foot, or by motor; the slower and harder way, as usual, being the more stimulating. If Miseno is included, it makes a long day; Avernus and Cumae may be seen with great satisfaction in half a day.

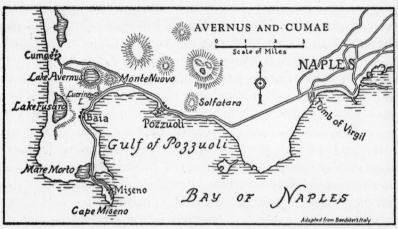

What is called the Tomb of Virgil is at the southwest corner of the city, in a high place not far from the shore and at the end of Posilipo, the long and beautiful leafy ridge on which the poet made his home. All that is certain about the ruin is that it represents an ancient tomb, has for centuries been known as the Tomb of Virgil, and is in a place where the tomb might reasonably be looked for. It may be seen from the Mergellina railway station. What was presumably the authentic tomb was well preserved six hundred years ago, when someone recorded the fact, together with the verses on its frieze referring to the poet's birth, death, entombment at Naples, called Parthenope, and three poetic achievements:

Mantua me genuit, Calabri rapuere, tenet nunc
Parthenope: cecini pascua, rura, duces—

Mantua bore me, Calabria brought my death,
 Parthenope now contains me:
I sang the pastures, the farmfields, the heroes.

The present inscription dates from 1554:

Qui cineres? tumuli haec vestigia: conditur olim
 Ille hic qui cecinit pascua, rura, duces—

What ashes? These are the ruins of a tomb:
Here lies he who once sang the pastures, the farmfields, the heroes.

The convenient train of the Ferrovia Cumana starting from
the Monte Santo station in Naples passes through Pozzuoli, ancient
Puteoli, at seven and a half miles from the city. In the neighborhood are the giant ruins of an amphitheater almost vying in
dimensions with the Colosseum, and columns of a temple to Isis
and Serapis. Cicero had a villa here, and here the Apostle
Paul landed, "where we found brethren, and were desired to
tarry with them seven days: and so we went toward Rome."

At ten miles from Naples is the Lucrine Lake, still with oyster
beds as in Horace's time. Here the Virgilian leaves the train and
walks a half mile north between high vineclad banks to Lake
Avernus. The famous entrance to the lower world is a crater
lake not quite a mile in diameter, two hundred feet deep, and
three and one-half feet above sea level, surrounded almost entirely
by lofty banks with steep slopes covered by gardens, orchards, and
trees. A pleasant walk of less than a mile to the west and north
along the path near the shore leads to the mouth of a great
tunnel through the high western bank. This passage, half a mile
long and absolutely dark except under two lofty light shafts,
opens at its upper or western end onto the shaggy landscape
of vineyard, orchard, and thicket that surrounds the high rock
of Cumae, another half mile distant and looking down on the
near-by coast.

Standing on the cliff of Cumae, looking out to sea and back
over the billowing foliage to the rim of Avernus, the reader of

the Sixth Book may easily imagine the action of the story. Down where the gently rolling waves leave a curling white fringe on the sands, the ships of the Trojans glide in, are beached with prows toward the sea, and embroider the shore with their curved sterns. The men leap ashore and scatter for their various tasks; but Æneas makes for the high places where Apollo has his lofty seat, and for the vast cavern of the dread Sibyl and her secrets.

The ruins on the southernmost crag of the Cumæan heights represent the last form of the ancient temple, and the great fissures and chambers in the west face of the rock below it are the ancient Grot of the Sibyl. "And now they come to the holy groves of Diana, and to the golden temple." The groves and the grot are first in their path, forming a first approach to the temple above, to which they climb by a steep path. There, as eagerly the Trojan hero scans the sculptured stories on the temple doors, faithful Achates, who has been sent on the errand, returns with Deiphobe the Cumæan Sibyl, priestess of Apollo and Diana, who bids the Trojans first to make sacrifice and then to enter into her lofty courts—*in alta templa*. By these are meant the immense grot extending far into the cliff almost under the temple that stands on its crest. The temple remnants were uncovered in 1912; the exploration of the grot began in 1925, and in 1930 the celebrated cavern was open to Virgil pilgrims.

The grot consists of eighty feet of vestibule, now cleared of forty to fifty feet of earth and débris, an antechamber, and the main cavern ninety feet long, twelve wide, and fifteen high. The whole cavern is rangy, irregular, and rugged with natural vaulting of rock. Here and there, to right and left, are rocky chambers mysterious in the darkness. Clefts in the living rock lead off to other parts of the hill, which is filled with galleries due in part to nature's whims and in part to human seekers after shelter. Lightholes and vent-holes pierce the rock above in many directions, even to the temple ruins far overhead. It can hardly be that this is not Virgil's Grot of the Sibyl—"the side of the Eubœan cliff cut out into a huge cave, to which a hundred broad approaches lead, a hundred mouths, whence rush forth as many voices, the responses of the Sibyl," "the words with which Cumae's Sibyl

THE TIBER AT OSTIA, LOOKING SEAWARD

AN ITALIAN LANDSCAPE

THE AMPHITHEATER AT VERONA

from her cell shrills forth awful mysteries and booms again from the cavern, robing her truth in darkness."

For those who have seen the wonder-working sanctuaries of modern times, the shrine at Loreto or the grot and spring at Lourdes, it is not difficult to reconstruct in imagination the one-time splendid and mysterious Grot of Cumae; and, as they walk in the cavernous reaches under the rugged vaulting pierced by uncanny orifices, to hear the tread of the timid feet and the sound of the murmuring voices of pilgrims come from the ends of the earth to receive the Word that shall lift the burden from their souls; and to appreciate the subtle combinations of superstition, faith, sentiment, and politics that made and kept it a chosen sanctuary.

When the frenzied Sibyl has finished giving forth her responses from the mystic recesses of the grot, ending with the veiled news of some comrade's death, Æneas and Achates emerge from the cavern, rejoin their friends, and are told of the fate of the trumpeter Misenus. They set on foot the preparation for his obsequies. As they fell and carry from the boundless forest the great timbers for the pyre of their dead comrade, lo! the doves of Venus flutter past the Trojan leader and settle on the green earth. The doves lead on from flight to flight, until, "when they come to Avernus's noisome jaws, swiftly they soar aloft, and, gliding through the clear sky, settle twain on the same tree, their chosen seat, whence there flashed through the branches the contrasted gleam of gold."

Meanwhile, after due obsequies, the Trojans rear above Misenus a mighty mound at the foot of the promontory still bearing his name, the Capo Miseno. "But good Æneas raises over the dead a monument of massive size, setting up for the hero his own proper arms, the oar and the trumpet, under a skyey mountain, which is now from him called Misenus, and retains from age to age the everlasting name." The cape is five miles from Cumae and the probable landing place of the Trojans, but we must not hold the poet too strictly to account.

This done, he hastens to execute the Sibyl's bidding. A deep cave there was, yawning wide with giant throat, rough and shingly, shadowed by the black pool and the gloom of the forest—a cave, over whose mouth no winged thing could fly unharmed, so poisonous the breath that exhaling from its pitchy jaws steamed up to the sky— whence Greece has given the spot the name *Aornos*.

Here, in his picture of the descent to Avernus, the poet's imagination uses the Cumæan landscape in general: the still and somber waters of the crater lake, the dark green wooded rim reflected from it, the shaggy, half-wild groves and thickets of the surrounding country, the sulphurous jets that issued from cleft and crevice in his day as in our own, the quakings and the rumbling unrest of the Vesuvian neighborhood, and the natural caverns of a rocky region. It would be useless to look for further agreement between reality and the poet.

Returning with the Sibyl from the revelation of "things buried underground, deep and dark," Æneas is dismissed by Anchises through the Gate of Ivory. He "traces his way to the fleet and returns to his comrades; then sails along the shore for Caieta's haven."

Caieta is modern Gaeta. Above the town of Gaeta at the west end of the lovely gulf of Formia, where Cicero wrote many a golden letter, where he met and talked with Cæsar, and where he bent his neck to Antony's murderers, is the moundlike promontory of Gaeta, accounted for, like Miseno, by the story of a burial. "Thou, too, in thy death, Caieta, nurse of Æneas, hast left to our coast the heritage of an ever living fame."

From Caieta, "the fleet spreads sail and leaves the harbor. Nightward the breezes blow, nor does the fair Moon scorn to show the way: her rippling light makes the sea shine again."

"The next land they skirt is Circe's realm," a dangerous place, today seen in the grand mass of Monte Circeo, standing out of lowland and sea apart from the grey mountains where they end at Terracina. "Neptune filled their sails with favoring breezes, sped their flight along, and wafted them past the seething waters." The next morning they will see the Tiber.

What Italian, what Virgilian, standing at the yellow Tiber's mouth today, a mile farther to seaward than in Virgil's day, and commonplace with dykes and shallows and reeds and scanty groves, is not thrilled nevertheless by the magic language transmuting the leaden scene into purest gold?

The sea was just reddening in the dawn, and Aurora was shining down from heaven's height in saffron robe and rosy car, when all at once the winds were laid, and every breath sank in sudden sleep, and the oars pull slowly against the smooth unmoving wave. In the same moment Æneas, looking out from the sea, beholds a mighty forest. Among the trees Tiber, that beauteous river, with his gulfy rapids and the burden of his yellow sand, breaks into the main. Around and above, birds of all plumes, the constant tenants of bank and stream, were lulling the air with their notes and flying among the woods. He bids his comrades turn aside and set their prows landward, and enters with joy the river's shadowed bed.

With the Seventh Book begins the "tale of grisly war, of battle array, and princes in their fury rushing on carnage—of Tyrrhenian ranks, and all Hesperia mustered in arms. Grander is the pile of events that rises on my view, grander the task I essay." It should not be forgotten by the reader of the *Æneid* that to Virgil and the Romans the battlefields of the last six books were home ground, and that the Latins, Rutulians, Etruscans, Trojans, and Greeks who moved on them were their forerunners and forefathers. If he wishes the stimulation of acquaintance with Virgilian scenes, he should not stop with Avernus and Cumae, but should go to Lavinium, modern Prattica di Mare, rising on its rolling hill among the groves twenty miles to the south of Rome and three miles from the sea. He should go to Ardea, six miles farther on, neglected and lonely on its ancient rocky citadel; and know the never ending solitudes of the Campagna, and the hidden windings of the Tiber through its midst, on which the Trojans and their leader came gliding between the banks the whole night long on their way to Rome when it "was but Evander's poor domain." "The rowers give no rest to night or day, as they surmount the long meanders, sweep under the fringe of diverse trees, and cut through the woods that look green in the still expanse."

Above all, he must read the Eighth Book under the ilexes on the Palatine.

The sun had climbed in full blaze the central cope of heaven, when from afar they see walls, and a citadel, and the roofs of straggling habitations—the place which the power of Rome has now made to mate the skies: then it was but Evander's poor domain. At once they turn their prows to land and approach the town.

It happened that on that day the Arcadian monarch was performing a yearly sacrifice to Amphitryon's mighty child and the heavenly brotherhood in a grove before the city. With him his son Pallas, with him all the prime of his warriors and his unambitious senate were offering incense, and the new-shed blood was steaming warm on the altar. Soon as they saw tall ships gliding toward them through the shadowy trees and plying the oar in silence, alarmed by the sudden apparition, each and all start up from the sacrificial board.

Pallas, the king's son, running to meet the strangers, finds them friends. "They advance under the shade of the grove, and leave the river behind." As the Trojans sit at the feast of the friendly king, he tells them of the monster Cacus and the visit of Hercules. When the feast is done and they enter the city at evening, Evander pictures to his guest the nature of the primitive folk on the site of Rome, of Saturn and the golden age, and of his own coming from Greece: "These woodlands were first inhabited by native Fauns and Nymphs, and by a race of men that sprung from trunks of trees and hard oaken core; no rule of life, no culture had they: they never learnt to yoke the ox, nor to hive their stores, nor to husband what they got; the boughs and the chase supplied their savage sustenance."

The King points out the grove of the Asylum, and the cave of the Lupercal, and "leads the way to the Tarpeian temple, even the Capitol, now gay with gold, then rough with untrimmed brushwood." "So talking together they came nigh the palace where Evander dwells in poverty, and saw cattle all about lowing in the Roman Forum and Carinae's luxurious precinct." Finally, "beneath the slope of his narrow roof he ushered in the great Æneas, and laid him to rest on a couch of leaves and the skin of a Libyan bear. Down comes the night, and flaps her sable wings over the earth."

The picture of the old king in early morning is one of the most beautiful in the poem:

Evander is roused from his lowly dwelling by the genial light and the morning songs of birds under the eaves. Up rises the old man, and draws a tunic over his frame, and puts Tyrrhenian sandals round his feet; next he fastens from below to side and shoulder a sword from Tegea, flinging back over him a panther's hide that drooped from the left. Moreover, two guardian dogs go before him from his palace door, and attend their master's steps. So he made his way to the lodging of his guest.

But a greater pleasure even than reading the *Æneid* in Rome is that of climbing the Alban Mount for a survey of Virgil's Latium. Monte Cavo, its most prominent summit, eighteen miles from Rome and 3,200 feet above the sea, is easily reached by electric line or automobile, and from it one looks down on the story of Turnus and Æneas in mighty panorama.

Hither, in the Twelfth Book, came Juno to counsel with Juturna, glory of the rivers, favorite of her heart, regarding the peril of Turnus. "But Juno, from the top of the mount now styled Alban—in those days it had no name, nor glory, nor honor—was looking in prospect on the plain, the two armies, Trojan and Laurentine, and the Latian town."

From where the goddess stood on the crown of the mountain, above the high, steep slopes dark with the foliage of oak and ash and chestnut, the whole Campagna lies spread out to view. Far away and faint appear bits of the sun-lighted silver ribbon of winding Tiber, whose mouth at Ostia is still more faintly seen. Lavinium and Ardea are lost in haze and forest. Down yonder among the dark patches of woodland is the scene of the gathering of the clans, and of the tragic story of Nisus and Euryalus.

Volscens shouts from his band: "Halt, gallants; tell your errand, who you are thus armed, and whither you are going." They venture no reply, but hasten the faster to woods, and make the night their friend. The horsemen bar each well-known passage right and left and set a guard on every outlet. The wood was shagged with thickets and dark ilex boughs; impenetrable briars filled it on every side; through the concealed tracks just gleamed a narrow path.

There, too, Camilla once rode,

leading a column of cavalry and troops resplendent with bronze, a warrior woman; nor had she her woman's hands acquainted with

Minerva's spinning baskets and the distaff—no, not she; but, though a maiden, she was hardened to endure the battle's toil and with swift foot outstrip the winds. She might skim above the highest blades of standing grain untouched and would have left the tender ears uninjured as she ran; or she might hold her way across midsea uplifted by the swelling tide, nor had she moistened in the water her swift feet.

And there occurred also the final scene, when after his last fight Turnus's frame grew chill and motionless at the feet of Æneas, and "his soul, resenting its lot, fled groaningly to the shades."

GREAT MOTHER OF FRUITS, GREAT MOTHER OF MEN

WHEN Virgil wrote the famous lines in praise of Italy,

> Hail, Great Mother of Fruits, Saturnian Land,
> Great Mother of Men,

the Italy of his affection and reverence was already centuries old, and the story of her people traced back into the mists of a prehistoric age. The huge walls of many-sided grey limestone blocks which encompassed then, and today still encompass, the hill towns of the central Apennines to the east of Rome were as little understood by him as they are by us.

Twenty centuries have been added to the story of Italy since the birth of her poet. Two thousand successions of spring, summer, autumn, and winter soon will have rolled over the land since in "many a golden phrase" he sang of her

> wheat and woodland,
> Tilth and vineyard, hive and horse and herd.

The lover of Italy today looks forth upon an Italian land which suffered the long decline and decay of the crumbling Roman Empire, which became the prey of the disorders and dismemberments of the Dark Centuries, which passed through the turbulences of the Renaissance and the stagnation of later days, which endured the depredations and humiliations of foreign domination, which agonized in the nineteenth-century struggle for independence, and which is but recently recovered from the greatest of all wars and the most dangerous of internal dissensions. Yet, despite the ravages of invasion and plague and internal strife with which her history is marked, despite her periods of servitude and inertness, despite the humiliation, neglect, and decay of long centuries, a Virgil of today might address to Italy the same stately apostrophe as his ancient forerunner of Mantua:

Salve magna parens frugum, Saturnia tellus,
Magna parens virum.

The Italian land is still the Great Mother of Fruitage. The same two seas, above and below, wash her extended coast lines and temper the summer's heat and the winter's cold. The same glowing sunshine bathes her fields from May to October in the bright, life-giving light. The same abundant rains of November to April make of valley and plain vast reservoirs of moisture for

Olive, aloe, and maize and vine

through the long summer of uninterrupted sunlit heat, and feed the lakes and streams and springs of a well watered land. The landscape on every hand is the ancient Roman landscape hardly altered; the mountains, the valleys, the plains, the rivers, and the sea, the unchanging country, are eternal. The cities in the plain and on the coast, the towns on hilltop and mountain slope, are nearly all the cities and the towns of Roman times. The sheep and lambs, the long-horned white cattle, the horse, the donkey, the goat, the lizard, the lark, the thrush, the swallow, the owl, the hawk, the eagle, are no more Italian than Roman. The ilex, the pine, the cypress, the ivy, the laurel, the rose, the vine, the olive, the chestnut, the oak, the ash, the fields of golden grain, the trim rows of the orchard and the varied green of gardens, that beautify the landscape of Italy today are the same that gave character to Italy when Virgil praised them in the *Georgics*. "Golden Plenty from a full horn pours forth her fruits upon Italy" as she did in Horace's time. Of no country could it be said more truthfully, in Cicero's phrase, that "the soil never refuses a draft, and always renders back with interest what it has received." But for a few omissions, as of the potato, tobacco, and Indian corn, and but for a few additions, as of larger forests and fuller streams, the landscape and the husbandry of Roman Italy still remain in all the richness and beauty of ancient times.

Perhaps not all the beauty. It may be that with changes in forestation and with alluvial action some hills have lost their denser carpets of leafy green and some streams their one-time volume and speed, and that soft marshes and sluggish rivers and

ORCHARDS AND GRAIN FIELDS NEAR ANCONA

PASTURES AND PINE GROVE NEAR ROME

VINEYARDS AND GARDENS AT AGROPOLI

THE FOREST AT VALLOMBROSA

stagnant lagoons have taken the place of firmer and cleaner shores where the great water systems find their ways to the sea; but the loss of beauty in these respects is more than made up by the charm of hillside and valley and plain long disciplined in form and fruitfulness to meet the needs of modern Italy's millions.

And if the Italian land has continued through the ages to be the Great Mother of Fruits, it is no less true that Italy has never ceased to be the Great Mother of Men. Such has been her yield in humanity since the poet's time that now hardly could even a Virgil fitly sing her praises.

When the poet of the *Georgics* wrote, the pagan era was near its close, but pagan culture was still nearly three centuries and a half from the Constantinian Edict and the final triumph of the new era. The *Æneid* was still to come, the great national poem of Rome and the Roman world. The smiling *Satires* of Horace were already appearing, the exquisite cameos of the *Odes* and the mellow wisdom of the *Epistles* were soon to win their way to permanent fame, along with "Livy's pictured page" and the limpid story-telling of Ovid and the genial contemplations of Tibullus. There were still to come the bitter innuendo of Tacitus, the enlightened pedagogy of Quintilian, the essays and dramas of Seneca, the encyclopædic and ill-digested learning of the Elder Pliny and the suavely artificial *Epistles* of the Younger, the thundering satire of Juvenal, and the witty and kaleidoscopic comment of the world's greatest epigrammatist, Martial. Gossipy and human Suetonius was to preserve the memories of the first emperors, and Ammianus Marcellinus those of the later, Apuleius was to give the world his *Golden Ass,* with the immortal story of Cupid and Psyche, Symmachus was to embody the ideal of the late Roman gentleman, Claudian to reëcho one last time the stately measure of Virgil, Ausonius and Boëthius to mark the fading of paganism into the light of Christianity. The administration of state was to have its Five Good Emperors and the longest known European peace. Many a statesman and many a military genius were to arise, to keep together in order and safety the decaying, disintegrating, and threatened Roman world. The law was to have its Gaius, Papinian, and Ulpian to give literary form to legal theory and practice, and its Justinian to set in order for the benefit of mankind the results of a thousand patient years in the science and art of governing men.

It is true that not all these men were of Roman birth or blood, and that many came from beyond the bounds of Italy. They were hardly less therefore the sons of Italy and Eternal Rome. The language in which they wrote and ruled was the language of Mother Rome, their intellectual, moral, social, and administrative ideals were Roman, they looked to the Rome of the past and the present as the center of their world. Such as were not in flesh the sons of Italy and Rome were their spiritual sons.

But there was the dawning Christianity as well as the setting paganism. The Christian Fathers were to come, and the long line of devotees and martyrs and saints that have made Italy in faith and practice the world's most intensely religious land and its greatest organizer of religious enterprise. There were to come the two hundred and sixty-one heads of the Church, with few exceptions Italian born, to unify her effort and perpetuate her character. There were to come Augustine and Ambrose of Milan, Francis and Clara of Assisi, Filippo Neri and Francesca of Rome. The great monastic establishments were to arise, correctors of abuses, conservers of ideals, protectors and preservers of learning. There were still to come the builders and decorators of wonderful early Christian and mediæval churches. There were the free cities and the guilds and their contribution to individual and collective life. There was to come the Renaissance with its marvelous product of architects and painters and sculptors, and its men of science and letters. There were the musical geniuses, to develop the music of the Church and to accomplish the transition from the sacred to the profane, and to lead the world to opera and symphony. Not least, there were the patriots and martyrs of the Risorgimento to teach the world the value of national liberty and how to suffer for it, and there were its soldiers and statesmen to possess and set in order Italian lands. And today there are the scholars and statesmen, the economists and reformers, the archæologists and educators, the inventors and explorers on land and sea and in the air, who are not without reason in declaring that the Italy they are building is destined soon to become again what she was in the days of the Rebirth of Learning—the teacher of the nations.

Thus the reading of Italy's history since Virgil's time, with its pages made golden by the names of saints and warriors and poets and artists and inventors and patriots and statesmen, leaves men willing still to call her, as Virgil called her, *Magna Parens Virum*.

Yet there is a difference. The Italy of Virgil's praise was the Great Mother of Men sprung only from the Italian land. Since the poet's day the nations of the earth have become the sons of Italy. Some of them are sons by tradition of actual blood in colonization, and more are her sons by tradition of culture. The language of ancient Italy and Rome has become not only that of modern Italy, but of all the great areas to which the Latin races have spread. The architecture, the manners, the laws, the morality, and the religion of these countries, and, in only less measure, of all countries that share our Western civilization, are likewise in the line of descent from Italy and ancient Rome. Whatever our ancestry in race, the tracing of our cultural forerunners leads us back to Italy, and to the City on the Tiber, and to the times of the Latin Classics.

. XXIII .

THE MEANING OF THE ECLOGUES
AND THE GEORGICS

THE first thing to be said in the appraisal of Virgil's meaning is that the meaning of poetry is not constant. It takes two to deliver a message—the speaker and the auditor. The communication of any truth outside the merely tangible or ponderable or measurable will vary with mental habit, with cultural background, with physical and social environment; which is to say, it will vary from person to person, from people to people, from age to age. Virgil to us in the America of the twentieth century is not exactly what Virgil was to Dante or what Virgil was to the Augustan times in which he gave his poems to the world. This itself is a meaning of Virgil's poetry.

Yet physical nature contains much that is constant from age to age and from land to land; and man is composed of much that is unchanging. His physical and mental processes, his senses, and his elemental sensibilities vary little with time. The idle singer of an empty day may utter a substance that will have melted into air before the day is done; but the poet of high emprise will not fail of the universal and the enduring.

Recognizing the fact of the passing and the permanent in the work of the poet, let us consider separately the three works that survive as unmistakably Virgil's own, estimating first the meaning that is not for an age but for all time; second, the meaning that is for our age but not for Virgil's time; and third, the meaning that was for Virgil's age but is not for our own.

Let us look first at the *Eclogues*. The ten short compositions of Virgil's younger manhood days, ranging in length from sixty-three to one hundred and ten hexameters, transport us to the greenery, the fruitfulness, and the freshness and peace of the pastoral regions of Mediterranean lands.

214

Who does not enjoy in imagination the cool grot and the straying green ivy, the mossy spring and the sod softer than sleep, the grass dewy in the dawn, the ash most fair in the forest, the pine in the garden, the poplar by the streamside, the opaque ilex, the somber cypresses, the fir showing black on the high mountains? Who does not delight in thoughts of the lush-leafed vine in the hillside vineyard, the apples and pears of the orchard, the olive slope in grey-green and silver, the flowers and foliage of garden and grove, the fall of refreshing rains upon the parched soil, the coursing of irrigation waters at the roots of languishing plants? Who is not refreshed and recreated as he becomes one with the shepherd and his lambs and the cattle on a thousand hills, reclines with him in the shade of the wide-spreading beech and meditates with him on slender reed the woodland Muse, enjoys with him under the sod-built roof of his cot the mellow fruits, the mealy chestnut, and goodly store of cheese, and feels with him the blessedness of the day's work done as the distant roofs of the farmhouses send up their smoke, and the lengthening shadows descend from the high hills?

> *Et iam summa procul villarum culmina fumant*
> *Maioresque cadunt altis de montibus umbrae.*

And who does not enjoy the dignified and gracious language in which it is all presented?

The *Eclogues* are Virgil's contribution to the poetry of escape. It is to this one charm, the release of the spirit in the peace that flows like a river, that all their single beauties of content and language are minister. This is the meaning of Virgil in the *Eclogues* which is common to our age and his own.

To this universal charm of the *Eclogues,* for our day the passage of time has added the particular charm of literary and natural association. As we read the lovely names of Arethusa and Amaryllis and Galatea, of Corydon and Thyrsis, *Arcades ambo,* of Daphnis and Thestylis and Lycidas, English and American landscape and English and American letters enter the scene as well as Theocritus and Syracuse. We sport with Amaryllis in another shade, and strictly meditate the thankless Muse in new surround-

ings. Arcadia and the Arcadians have travelled far, even to becoming the seventeenth century "plague in every European
capital." We are all Arcadian at times,

Omnes florentes aetatibus, Arcades omnes.

Somewhat, too, has been added to the *Eclogues* in our day by the
breeding of the century and a quarter since Wordsworth's prime
in the sentiment of communion with nature. It is much to be
doubted that we enjoy nature more than Virgil and Horace
enjoyed it; but it is likely that our holding communion with her
various forms is more self-conscious.

Yet there are many respects in which the *Eclogues* meant more
to the ancient. The reader of Virgil's day knew by birthright and
directly the Italy which we must know from fleeting visits or
from description. The beasts, the birds, the plants, the landscape,
and the language, the cicada and the bright-hued lizard, the olive
grove, the vine, the flocks and the piping shepherd, the sacrifice at
the altar, were the tenants of his consciousness from boyhood. The
Roman of Augustan times had the advantage, too, in the personal
phases of the *Eclogues*. The allegory of Daphnis, the prophecy of
the so-called *Messianic Eclogue*, the relations of Gallus and
Lycoris, the elusive identities of Tityrus and Menalcas, the allusions to Virgil's lost farm, were not for him the strange or unex-
plainable matters they soon became and have since remained.
What we call the learning of the poems was less obtrusive. The
mythological and geographical lore was not to him a mere succession of names. The song matches of shepherds were not the
novelty in ancient Italy that they seem to us; the land of *stornelli*
has always known them and still knows them.

Finally, the Roman feeling as to Virgil's imitation of the Greek
pastoral was different from ours today. The *Eclogues* in their first
line and in every poem recall Theocritus; they make use of
Theocritean names and settings, and often phrases, and they are
permeated by Theocritean spirit; yet they are not translations,
they are not adaptations, and they are Italian poems. They were
not written with a Theocritus open before the poet, but, as John
Lowes and E. K. Rand would say, from the deep well of his mind,

which by that time was "filled with the varied splendors of Italy as well as the varied splendors of Theocritus and others who had sung of grottoes and beech trees and shadowy hills." That they recalled the delights of Theocritus was not misunderstood by the Roman, as it is by us, as a fault. The author was bringing to the poetic literature of the Romans, of which we possess now only Catullus and Lucretius and fragments of a cumbersome dramatic and epic-historic product, a new author and a new kind. What to us affords the material for dissertations proving the dependence of the poet was to his fellows an achievement and a benefaction which they admired and for which they were grateful. Who thinks of calling Milton unoriginal because he uses Virgil and the Bible?

If we look next at the *Georgics*, the work of Virgil's middle years, four books of *Points on Farming*, comprising 2,188 hexameters (the *Eclogues* amounted to 831), we find the universals are of a different sort. "What makes the glad harvest, under what stars the earth should be turned and the vine wedded to the elm, what shall be the care of the kine, what nurture in the keeping of the flock, how great the skill of the thrifty bee—these themes now shall employ my song." All ages not savage know of these matters, and to most men in all but the greatest cities the country and its affairs are not unfamiliar.

The *Georgics* treat of permanent factors in the complex of human subsistence. In Book One we have soil-testing, fertilization, plowing, irrigation, the pests of insect, animal, and weed that harass the tiller of the fields, the seasons and their proper tasks, the signs of the skies, lucky and unlucky. In Book Two the themes are the vine, the vintage, the press, the olive and its gathering, the trees, wild and cultivated, the lands of their origin, the soils in which they thrive, the process of grafting, their protection against cropping cattle and nibbling goat, their trimming, the constant working of the dirt about the roots, their uses in fruitage, fodder, timber, shade, and on the winter hearth. Book Three treats of the horse, the ox, the sheep, the goat, the choice of sires, the care of the mother, their feeding and tending, the breeding of the racer, the seasons and times of day for pasturage, the care of wool, the need of salting, the treatment of disease. Book Four astonishes us with the marvels of the bees, their swarming and their battles, their economics and their statesmanship, the opening of their hives, the curing of their ailments, the renewal of the swarm. These main themes, with a thousand homely accompaniments, make up the mass of the world's greatest poem on the country and its life.

But the mere facts of plant and animal husbandry are not all of the *Georgics,* or their claim to greatness would be less than that of the crabbed notes of Cato's *De Agricultura* or the practical chapters of the erudite Varro on the same themes. Virgil is indeed a son of the soil, but not that alone. He knows the country as a child knows its mother. He feels, rather than knows, the oncoming changes of the season, the promise of the skies and air, the wants of plant and animal, the satisfaction of growing things in the rain upon the leaf, the water at the root, the stirring of the soil. And yet the *Georgics* are not a manual of agriculture. They are the poem of one who sees and feels beyond the vine and the tree, the irrigation stream and the rain, the ox and the sheep and the swine, and the toil and trouble of man. The detailing of instructions or description is never long without interruption or transformation. The poem rarely comes to ground, and rarely long remains there. Charged with the ethereal stuff of imaginative sympathy, it overcomes the gravity of its earthy part and mounts to upper air. The waters, the heavens, and the living things of the soil desert their special utilitarian existence and become parts of a spacious whole in whose expression the chief concern of the poem lies. The rain and the stormy wind that bring flood and ruin, and whose coming the prudent farmer for the sake of crop and flock will presage by his accumulated wisdom in the lore of the heavens, in a moment have left the earth and become a titanic affair of sky and sea and mountain, of roaring waves and screaming gulls and rushing streams, and of murmuring forests and crashing thunder in the high hills:

> *Continuo ventis surgentibus aut freta ponti*
> *Incipiunt agitata tumescere et aridus altis*
> *Montibus audiri fragor, aut resonantia longe*
> *Litora misceri et nemorum increbrescere murmur—*

SAINT PETER'S FROM MONTE MARIO

CYPRESSES IN THE VILLA D'ESTE AT TIVOLI

A PASTORAL SCENE BY PINELLI

THE LANDSCAPE AT FERENTINO

Then straight with rising winds the roughened sea
Begins to swell and surge, and on the hills
The crashing of dry timber fills the air,
Or by the shore the loud resounding waves
Are mingled with the roaring of the groves.

What begins as the catalogue of weather signs is transformed
forthwith into a gallery of croaking beasts and birds—the frogs
in the mud with their old complaining song; the reprobate
raven, fit figure for the Japanese brush as with vigorous call de-
manding rain he stalks in solitude and meditation on the dry
sands—

Tum cornix plena pluviam vocat improba voce
Et sola in sicca secum spatiatur harena.

Or the girls of the house are charmingly pictured in the evening
hours at their spinning, and we see them looking up as the oil
sputters and the wick gathers crumbly soot in forecast of the
coming change. The poem rises from the breeding of the mare to
the mad excitements of the glittering chariot race. It rises from
the breeding of the bull to the universal passion that peoples
pasture and fold. It pictures the raging of the jealous beasts as
they charge in the battle that bathes their flanks in black gore
while the woodlands and far Olympus reëcho their bellowings.
The bees are seen at their honey-making, and we marvel to find
them wiser in their ways than men, with occupations and peoples
and clans and high-souled chieftains and battles. The farm-
house and its hard routine are transformed by the poet's love of
the simple, the genuine, the homely, the manners and observances
of olden days, the faith of the "fathers and mothers in Israel," so
to speak, of the eternal and unchanging country.

Even the inevitable toil and drudgery of country life become a
part in the great and unfathomed scheme of "Universal Nature
moved by universal mind." The Father himself it was who willed
that the path of the husbandman should not be easy. It was He
who first with new art turned the fields, sharpening the hearts
of men with cares, and not allowing his realms to decay with
heavy lethargy. Before Jove no tillers of the soil subdued the
acres; it was not right even to mark off the fields or to divide them

with the boundary stone. Men gained their livelihood in common; the earth of its own accord brought forth freely of everything, and none had to demand or seek. The Father it was that added the heavy poison to the dark serpent, bade the wolves to ravage and the sea to roll, struck away the honeys from the foliage, removed fire, and stopped the wine from flowing at its will in streams; decreeing thus in order that use by practice should forge out little by little the various arts, should look to the furrow for the grassy wheat, and strike out the fire hidden away in the veins of the flint.... Toil overcame all things—toil the unwelcome—and heavy need in the midst of hardship.

Such is the appeal of the *Georgics* to the heart of humanity at large. It is not the appeal of the *Eclogues*. This is not the poetry of escape; the Italy of the *Georgics* is not decorative but real. It is the poetry of a deeper emotion—of love for home and reverence for tradition, of love for the beauty as opposed to the prettiness of nature, of love for the justice as well as the joy of life, for the dignity and wholesomeness of work as well as its rewards, for communion with the vast reaches of universal creation. It is no longer the poetry of youth; its author feels all the gravity of life.

There has been no successor of the *Georgics* as there have been successors of the *Eclogues*. The meaning of the *Georgics* has not been so greatly enriched by later association. Unless, as has been suggested by one critic, we are to see in the famous passage on Italy in the Second Book, and in slighter reference elsewhere, the beginnings of scenery in literature, and unless, as was remarked above of the *Eclogues*, we are to think of the modern sensitiveness to nature as superior to that of Virgil's auditors, there seems to be no respect in which we may claim a meaning for the *Georgics* peculiar to our times. On the contrary, the accident of birth two thousand years later and five thousand miles farther west has cost us somewhat.

What did the Augustans see and feel in the *Georgics* that is not audible and sensible to us? Again, as in the *Eclogues*, it may be said that they saw and felt their own land, but in its larger and less local aspects—in its mountains, valleys, and plains, its pastures and its gardens, its flowers and plants and birds and animals, its

rains in winter and its long months of summer sun, its thrice-
ripening fruitage in the year.

Hail, Saturnian land, great mother of fruits!

They saw the operations of farm and pasture, and the mode of
life of shepherd and farmer—the shearing and spinning and
weaving, the bare feet in the vintage, the pressing of the trodden
grape, the white herds in the Clitumnus and the lordly bull at the
altar, the immemorial ways of their sires and grandsires. They
knew and felt their heroic past. Scipio, Marius, the Decii, were
not mere names to them. They thought of their heroes and of
Rome itself as sprung from the soil. Their Italy was mother of
men as she was mother of fruits.

But the Roman reader found in the *Georgics* more than appreciation. He felt in the magnificent lines an exhortation. They
put him in mind of present needs—of the practical need for the
produce of the soil, and of the need, still more, of an Italy one in
sentiment and one in action. It was only fifty years since Italy had
been at war with Rome in rebellion against her unfair treatment
of allies. It was only a few years since Virgil's fellow provincials
received the franchise. The violence and uncertainties of the riots
and civil wars of a hundred years were only now felt to be nearing
their end. The poet who had passed his boyhood on the fertile
acres, who knew Italy from the mountains to the sea and from
Romulus to Julius and Augustus, who had won distinction by
singing of her beauties, who had seen Italy become Rome and
Rome become Italy, who was beginning to see in Rome and
Roman character the hand of destiny—this poet now expressed in
stately verse aglow with feeling the first idealization of Italy's
unity. This was not the least meaning of Virgil in the *Georgics*.

THE MEANING OF THE ÆNEID

AFTER the seven years on the 2,188 hexameters of the *Georgics*, eleven years on the 9,896 of the *Æneid*. If the poet had worked continuously, these figures would mean less than one line a day of the *Georgics*, and a little more than two lines a day of the *Æneid*. We know, or should know, that poets do not always work by schedule; but we should also realize that the Latin tongue, however disciplined and orderly, is not a flexible instrument, and that the hexameter in Latin is not a verse which, in Horace's phrase, one can dash off at two hundred before breakfast or a thousand standing on one foot. Augustan times took expression seriously, whether in verse or prose.

Two commentators tell us of Virgil's "saying that he delivered himself of his verses and licked them into shape" as a bear her cubs. It is not difficult to believe that an average of two a day represents a fairly constant effort of eleven years and the employment, during some periods, of a fairly constant day of many hours. It is not difficult to conceive also that the poem was not given the desirable readjustments and polish, and that the poet on his last bed could not contemplate its release.

The *Æneid* is none the less Virgil's greatest poem, the greatest long poem of his age and people, and one of the world's greatest long poems. It is also the one of his three works to change most—to gain most and to lose most—in the "innumerable series of the years and the flight of time." Let us for the third time attempt the separation of the constant from the accidental.

The Epic of Æneas is a story, a good story, and a story well told. Without its historical trimmings, it might be a children's adventure story. A brave and good prince and his faithful followers have been compelled by a war that destroyed their city, to

AMONG THE RUINS AT OSTIA

A VINEYARD AT TERNI

THE VIRGIL MOSAIC IN TUNIS

THE SOURCES OF THE CLITUMNUS

roam the sea in search of a new home. They have just left Sicily for the Italy which the Fates and the gods through prophecy in vision and oracle told them contains the hidden land of their quest, when a terrifying storm sweeps them in wreck and despair on to the strange coasts of Punic Africa, where a beautiful and unfortunate princess, unjustly driven from her home far away, has recently established her capital. The weary and homeless prince and the lonely and lovely princess meet. At a great feast in her marble palace he tells at her desire the story of the enemy's burning of his city and slaughter of its people, of how he rescued from the flames his princess, his old father, and his little son, of how he lost the princess, of how he wandered for seven years searching in vain for the new home that the gods had promised him, of how his father died in Sicily, and how the storm carried him and the men who were left on and on till they found land. The reader acquainted with Othello and Desdemona knows how it will come out:

> His story being done,
> She gave him for his pains a world of sighs . . .
> She loved him for the dangers he had passed,
> And he loved her that she did pity them.

But this was not the only witchcraft that was used. The fairy protectors of the prince and princess, the loving Venus and the proud and wicked Juno, caused them, or at least the princess, to end with being most hopelessly in love; and then, when she simply could not give him up, the wicked fairy changed her mind and got the King of all the Fairies, Jupiter, to command the prince to sail away and leave the princess. As the prince looked back in the dark he saw a great light in the sky. The princess's heart had broken, and she had stabbed herself with the dagger the prince gave her for a present, and the light was her funeral pyre.

And so on—the Fifth Book and the athletic funeral games; the Sixth and the descent to Avernus; the Seventh, and the treaty with King Latinus in the country at the Tiber mouth, the advent of Turnus, the gathering of the clans, and war; the Eighth, and Æneas' visit to Pallanteum on the site of Rome; the Ninth and its battles, with the episode of Nisus and Euryalus; the Tenth,

Eleventh, and Twelfth with the tumultuous campaign that led to final victory.

Such is the story of the *Æneid*, stripped of its narrative detail and wealth of episode. The *Æneid*, however, is not a mere adventure story. Not even the age that forgot the origins of Rome and in their thought of them confounded the legends of Noah and the Ark and the Tower of Babel with the tales of Saturn and Janus, saw in the *Æneid* so little as that. The *Æneid* is the highly sophisticated story of the antecedents of the founding of Rome. Its actors are the heroic remnant of Troy, a great city tragically cut down; they are acting under divine authority; their chief, Æneas, is Heaven's consecrated instrument; the purpose of it all is the divine will to accomplish the unity of the world under the rule of a righteous power. Every part of the poem is written with Rome and the Roman people and their destiny in mind— *Romanam condere gentem*. Its unity is as nearly perfect as that of most long poems. Its episodes divert and entertain without becoming insubordinate, and are all contributory to the action. If in practice it does somewhat fall apart, it is not so much the poet's fault as our own. We break it apart by reading and teaching the first six books and selections, and by never becoming familiar with the whole.

Further, besides the good story rich in episode and well knit, there has been for the two thousand years of the *Æneid's* readers the appeal of its characters. If Æneas himself is not quite the hero in our eyes, there are many figures who are as admirable and as real as the nature of epic demands or will permit; for it must be remembered that epic is primarily action and not psychology, and that the reality of epic does not aim at the reality of the sociological novel.

There are Virgil's women. There is Dido, a regal figure, living, loving, suffering, and dying in the grand style; perishing not by fate nor in deserved death but pitiably before her day inflamed by sudden madness; Dido, on whom even omnipotent but mischievous Juno had compassion, sending down from Olympus the rainbow goddess, Iris, to free her agonizing soul from the body that enmeshed it, and whom Virgil himself, her creator, could not withstand. There is Camilla, the warrior princess, who might have passed with winged feet over the heads of the unharvested wheat and not harmed the tender stalks in her flight, and whose eternally feminine love for bright array betrayed her to the death. There is the mother of Euryalus, in all the passion and pathos of the war mother's grief.

There is the boy Ascanius in the glare of burning Troy, half trotting, half dragged as he clings to his father's hand, still the reality of boyhood eight years later by the Tiber bank when, as the Trojans in their hunger devour the cakes on which their other viands have rested, he cries out in the delight of discovery, "Look! we are eating our tables"; and continuing in boyish ways when he wounds the favorite stag of Silvia, the royal keeper's daughter, and later sends his first arrow home in the fight. There is Pallas, old Evander's son, the gallant youth who in vain matches himself with Turnus. There is Turnus himself, the ardent, the proud, the headstrong, who in spite of men and gods will fight it out with the Trojan stranger invading his rights. There are Nisus and Euryalus in their moonlight adventure, friends in life and in death—"O fortunate both! If aught my song avail, no day shall ever see you lost from the minds of men." There is Sinon, the wily and plausible Greek.

There are Virgil's lovable and pathetic old men. There is Priam cut down at the altar in the agony of his grief for young Polites as Pyrrhus butchers him before his father's eyes. There is Anchises, borne protesting from Troy on the shoulders of the faithful Æneas. There is the venerable Evander, Arcadian exile reigning in pastoral simplicity on the Palatine Hill, the Rome that is to be, wakened in his humble cottage by the kindly dawn and the matin songs of birds under the eaves, proud father of gallant Pallas going forth to war, and stricken to earth at war's tragic answer to his prayers. There is the reverend king of the Latin folk, Latinus, ruling in long peace his fields and placid towns until rival claimants to his friendship and his daughter perplexed him in the extreme. There is even hateful Mezentius, caring naught for the regard of gods or men, but melted at the sight of dead Lausus, and in his turn standing to the stroke of Æneas with the prayer on his lips, "O protect my body from the bitter hate of my people, and grant me to share the tomb with my son!"—

It is in these old men who lose their all in the death of gallant and loyal sons, and in the young men whom the dark day bears away before their time from the lot of sweet life, that the well known pathos, sadness, gentleness, melancholy, of the poet is especially to be felt. In what other poet is there so deep and so constant and universal sympathy—for the old who feel their hold on this world relaxing, for youth cut off by violence or disease or crossed in hopeless love, for friends or lovers or kinsmen separated, for the wanderer faring on the sea and never coming to the desired haven, for the weary and afflicted everywhere? Who so many times and so deeply sings the boon of rest after toil, of night and sleep descending on weary and care-worn mortals?—

> *Tempus erat quo prima quies mortalibus aegris*
> *Incipit et dono divom gratissima serpit.*

The character of the men and women in the *Æneid* when Virgil is not drawing on Homer for epic effect is the character of our own world and the character of Christian culture. The morality of the *Æneid*, and almost its religion, are our own. Virgil's gods are not the gay and irresponsible and meddlesome beings of the *Iliad*; they partake of the gravity and steadfastness, and even the conscientiousness, of the Roman citizen and soldier, the senator, and the pater- and mater-familias. They, and the Roman religion, and the Roman people, were on the way to the ideas of modern and more gentle days. The sentiment of sacrifice that gives to enduring states and civilizations their permanence is dominant in the *Æneid* as it is in the serious letters and life of Christian times.

If we turn now from the consideration of these constant values of the *Æneid* to those which the passage of time has added for our own enjoyment, we shall find a greater change than in the case of either *Georgics* or *Eclogues*.

In the first place, the great poem which to the poet and his circle had the background of supposedly seven centuries of Roman history, and was in a manner only prophetic of the imperial cen-

ÆNEAS WOUNDED, WITH ASCANIUS, VENUS,
AND THE SURGEON

RAPHAEL'S "PARNASSUS"

turies upon which the State was now entering, has for us the ancient Roman background of the almost thirteen hundred years from the traditional founders' date in 753 B.C. to the year of our Lord 529 when the *Code of Justinian* summed up in restatement the experience of the Roman civilization in the search for justice— the justice which the Roman himself defined in the work of Justinian as "the steadfast and perpetual will to render to every man his right"; adding also, "The precepts of the law are these: to live honorably, to injure no other man, to render to every man his own." To us, the Roman Empire is achievement; to Virgil's time the distinctive term was unknown, and the ship of the Roman State was struggling to gain the harbor—in Horace's verse, its side bare of oarage, its mast splintered and sail-yards creaking, its cables gone, its canvas rent, its navigators in distress.

But the background to our *Æneid* is even more than those thirteen hundred years. The Roman Empire decayed and fell away, but Roman civilization did not die. Roman law, the Latin language, Roman religion and morality, Roman architecture, painting, and sculpture, survived the wreck of the political and military empire of Rome, and became the basis and substance of another Rome. The Rome of the Seven Hills and the Rome of the Mediterranean World became the Greater Rome of Mediæval and Renaissance Europe and the Greater Rome of today. In the language we speak, the buildings we build, the prayers we pray, the sermons we preach, the conduct by which we are inspired and inspire, in the law we obey, we are still citizens of ancient Rome. The *Æneid* may be called the national poem of the Occidental World.

In the second place, the literary associations of the *Æneid* have multiplied. Time has added to the name of Homer many others. Since Virgil's day we have had a Dante, a Tasso, an Ariosto, a Camoëns, a Milton, a Longfellow, a Tennyson. Virgil has attracted to his company the great and the small. *Paradise Lost* has twelve books and its Gathering of the Clans. George Warrington's adventures are told in chapters headed by *"Conticuere Omnes"* and *"Intentique Ora Silebant."* Cassius rescues the tired Cæsar from the troubled Tiber chafing with her shores:

I, as Æneas our great ancestor
Did from the flames of Troy upon his shoulder
The old Anchises bear, so from the waves of Tiber
Did I the tired Cæsar.

Byron has "looked on Ida with a Trojan's eye," and phrases for us "Tully's voice and Virgil's lay and Livy's pictured page." We hear Christopher Morley *Thunder on the Left*, and G.B.S. starts us off well disposed toward an indifferent play by calling it *Arms and the Man*, a title adapted by scores of essayists and story-writers. We find Virgils in fiction and Virgils in life. The high-school graduating class adopts a Virgilian motto. The Archæological Institute of America prints on its device the *Virum Monumenta Priorum* of the Eighth Book. Henry Purcell in the eighteenth century writes the opera *Dido and Æneas*, which was produced once more in 1930. Not least, the "stateliest measure ever moulded by the lips of man" is proven to be exactly that by a long line of versifiers with more enthusiasm than taste who have attempted to employ it in modern tongues.

Again, the *Æneid* has changed with the times because of new styles of thought and sentiment. The advent of chivalry heightened the feeling for Dido, and deepened interest in the first four books. The presence of Christianity and Dante in our thought impregnates the whole Sixth Book with mystic feeling. The nationalism of the past century has done much to make our day understand the poet, so far as purpose is concerned, better than any generation since his time; and the vain attempts at a united or even peaceful Europe serve only to set in relief the achievement of the Empire which for four centuries with an army of 300,000 men and a fleet of rowboats kept together in the Pax Romana the lands today in the process of self-extinction for the sake of self-preservation.

Finally, the *Æneid* has changed with the enlargement of the world through discovery, through the facilitation of travel, and through the growth of knowledge and invention. The *Æneid* published in 17 B.C. was not the *Æneid* known and felt in the summer of 1930 by the member of the American Classical League on the Virgilian Cruise or by the member on the Horatian Cruise in 1935—who was bred in a Christian civilization, who had learned of the limits of the terrestrial sphere and the infinities of the celestial reaches, and who knew the story of the earth from the time when the foundations thereof were laid and the morning stars sang together; who was cultivated in the love of nature, and through literary and real experience had grown sensitive to scene; who was a pilgrim from beyond the Streams of Ocean and from a land with a simple and heroic past and a luxurious and powerful but troubled present which history some day will call the American Republic and the American Empire, a land talking much of destiny but with no poet to detect or create a pattern in a world which longs for union and peace even as the world of Virgil longed for the Pax Romana. The *Æneid* of the Virgil pilgrimage contained many things of heaven and earth not dreamt in the philosophy of the Horatius who was the friend of its author.

Yet not all this widening of horizon and increase of knowledge will serve to compensate the reader of Virgil for his removal from the time and place of the poem. The ancient saw and felt more truly and clearly than any modern reader what the *Æneid* meant in the mind and soul of the poet. What we see through a glass darkly, he saw face to face.

Once more, as in the case of *Eclogues* and *Georgics*, the setting of the poem was the setting of the ancient reader's own life. He knew the Mediterranean better than we; to him it was *Mare Nostrum*—a Roman lake. He knew Italy; it was the land of his birth and nurture and of his fathers unto the twentieth generation. He knew Rome, the Forum, the Palatine, and the Capitol, once old Evander's poor domain and the scene of Æneas's visit. He knew the Tiber winding to the sea, Ostia and the spot of Æneas's landing and camp, the Rutulians, the country of old Latinus, Ardea the capital of Turnus, and Etruria—all the lands and towns of the Gathering of the Clans. He felt something living in the names of Trojan and Latin heroes—Clausus from whom sprang the great Claudian gens; Cloanthus the ancestor of the Cluentii; Sergestus the founder of the Sergians, of whom Lucius Sergius Catiline was the degenerate scion; Mnestheus the original

Memmius. If New England had an *Æneid*, ancestor hunters would wear it to rags. He knew Avernus and the Cumae region. He could not only see the mysterious vapors rise as we can today, but could visit the Sibyl of Cumae and hear the oracular voice at a time when the grot at Cumae was as much a reality in the lives of the faithful as the similar grots of today.

Yet these are externals, though not merely that. The reader of Virgil's times knew Roman character as no one has known it since its disappearance. He knew the old and the young, the urban and the rustic, the youth and the maid, the soldier and the officer, the plebeian and the noble, the shepherd and the artisan, the senator and the rabble, the demagogue and the patriot, all the mingled elements that formed the living background of the poet's creations. He knew how they looked, how they acted, how they felt. He knew as one of them all the details of their dressing, their eating, their thinking, while we know them from lectures on Roman Life. He knew the intricacies of politics as a witness and participant, while we know them from books and courses—perhaps as accurately, perhaps more so, but with far less reality. He knew the sacrifice at the altar, the pouring of libations, the hymn and the prayer, the votive offering or the token of the rescued and the healed, and sometimes the mysteries at whose curtain even the dissertation must halt. The allusions to centuries of history and hundreds of historic places were not always for him mere data or names and spots on the map, or food for the cannonades of heavy annotation. He knew from the times and perhaps from experience what was behind the descriptions of war and why it was *detestatum* by mothers. He knew the ramming and boarding and hand-to-hand of the long triremes; or, on land, the signal for the legionaries to advance, the steady forward march of the lines, the call of the bugles, the double quick to throwing distance, the halt and the hurling of the pilum, the dash with swords into the enemy ranks, the stroke and cut and thrust, the speedy but bloody decision with which came swift death or the joy of victory—in Horace's phrase,

> *Concurritur; horae*
> *Momento cita mors venit aut victoria laeta.*

RAPHAEL'S "POESIA"

AUGUSTUS AS IMPERATOR

Not every reader had participated, as Horace had, but he was near it all. He knew the ardor and the need of loyalty. He knew the weariness and the prayers for peace of a State whose wars for a hundred years had been the horrible encounters of civil conflict.

All these things the Augustan knew with the vividness of the man born in them, reared in their midst, educated into them, forming part of them. We of today have them all to study, to memorize, to attempt to understand. Roman literature as it survives is beyond parallel the literature of a people in action. Its appreciation both requires and confers acquaintance with the public and private affairs of a great and complex civilization.

Not only did the Roman thus born from the same civilization and at the same time as the *Æneid* itself possess the advantage of understanding by nature and with comparatively little effort the thousand details in the national poem that time has since transmuted into leaden archæology, but the poet himself had the advantage of being understood in spirit, in purpose, and in form. The *Æneid* was not for its day a patchwork of plagiarisms. It was the author's glory, not his guilt, that he took the Mæonian as Horace had taken the Æolic measures, and "taught them in Latin numbers for to run," that he made his poem glow with Homeric color by crowding the hexameter with boasting heroes of more than human stature, and by bringing down the gods from high Olympus to mingle in mankind's affairs, that he made it sparkle with Homeric epithet and simile. It was as little his guilt and as much his glory as it was Dante's and Tasso's and Ariosto's and Milton's and Camoëns's to enliven their works with the glow and sparkle of the Virgilian, the Horatian, and the Ovidian line, the Ciceronian or Senecan phrase and paragraph.

Nor was it present to the Roman reader, more than to the English, Italian, or Portuguese, that the poem he read was a foreign poem, or that it was something for which the author and his people should not have credit. The *Æneid* did not consist for him, to use the familiar parrot-phrase, of "the first half imitating the *Odyssey* and the second half the *Iliad*." To him it was a unity, carefully wrought and beautifully adorned, the unhalting story of the Latin Pilgrim Fathers in the long search for freedom and an abode for their household gods that began at Troy and ended with the divine sanction at the Tiber mouth. Its hero was not a colorless prince who weakly and heartlessly abandoned to her tragic lot the beautiful queen, but an exile flying before Fate, much tossed about on sea and land by the might of the gods and sorely tried in war—an *émigré,* a paterfamilias, the high priest of his men-at-arms, a chieftain with divine warrant and under divine command, a man of duty and destiny. The key to Æneas's character is not chivalry, but citizenship. When love conflicts with duty in the founder of the State in which the citizen father as judge or general could condemn to death a son disloyal to the State, love must stand aside. The poet's demonstration of his hero's devotion to duty by the Dido episode does not leave us with admiration for Æneas undiminished, and it may not have been an entire success in his own time, but reason at least should temper our disapproval by the reminder that Virgil was writing a national epic, and that the Dido story *was* an episode.

The *Æneid* is a Roman epic. It is not the natural epic sprung from an early culture, like the Homeric poems, not the doctrinal or theological epic of Dante or Milton, not the purely adventure epic of Moorish legend in Spain of Ariosto, not the historical epic of the Crusades by Tasso, not the allegorical court epic of Spenser, but the epic of a people and a State and a literature in the full tide of life—a conscious epic, a sophisticated epic, a literary epic, an art epic, an epic for the cultivated, a political epic, a partisan and a propaganda and a purpose epic, an Augustan epic, anything but a really Homeric and really Hellenic epic. Behind the Homeric veneer, and furnishing the substance of the poem, is the life and spirit of Italy and Rome. Æneas is no longer a Homeric hero, Latinus is not a Priam, Camilla is no queen of the Amazons; the gods in council are a Roman Senate, the scenes and sentiment belong to the Roman citizen, Roman reality is everywhere, permeating and enveloping even the Homeric adaptations. It is useless and it is unjust to look in Virgil for the brightness and lightness of Homeric speech and action, for the

naïve Iliadic unrestraint of passion and expression, for the airi-
ness and speed of the Homeric hexameter, for the supple and
sensitive language, for the easy invention and swiftly-moving
narrative of the folk-story teller. The *Æneid* is not in that class
of epic, and does not emulate it; but, as an evenly woven tissue
of invention and reality, as a skilful blending of legend, history,
and actual life, as a steadily moving and consistent narrative with
beginning, middle, and end, it has form and unity unequalled in
any natural epic and not surpassed by any epic of its class; as an
example of dignified and sonorous expression it is as supreme in
the style of verse as Cicero is in the style of prose, and has no
rival but Milton; and as a richly furnished record of the greatest
moment in the history of the great governing race who are the
cultural ancestors of Europe and the Western Hemisphere, it is a
human document with no rival at all in the realm of poetry.

Such is the meaning, or such are the meanings, of Virgil—the
poet of the *Eclogues* and relaxation and escape; the poet of the
Georgics and the beauty and blessedness of Italy and the life of
the soil; the poet of the *Æneid* and the divine and human origins
of the Roman State; the revealer of Roman character and the
prophet of Roman destiny; the recorder and preserver of the
Roman ideal.

But this is not all. We were celebrating in the year 1930 something more than the birthday of a famous poet. The meaning of
Virgil is more than the meaning of a single poet or of a single
poem. We were celebrating in 1930, and in this year of 1935,
the year of Horace, we are again celebrating, the power of poetry
and the power of art. Art is an energy and an instrument in
human affairs. Virgil and Horace and Livy and Cicero were not
mere entertainers of the age. They gathered up the serious
thought and the glowing sentiment of the best heads and hearts
of the times regarding the duty of men toward their fellows and
toward the State, and gave it the golden expression without which
it would not have had currency, and without which it would not
have been translated into action. The Emperor and Mæcenas his
counsellor knew what they were about when they gave Horace
the encouragement and the freedom that insured his best effort,

and when they insisted on the publication of the *Æneid*. The poets more than the politicians created the Roman Empire. In the midst of the wreckage to which the passions and perfidies and the disorders and destructions of three generations had reduced the State, they helped men see that there was a pattern and a plan in life. The State and the Emperor existed at their best in the poetry of Horace and Virgil before that best became reality; the poets' ideals were lifted up and drew all men unto them. The poet can bring the future; he can even change the past. By the gifts of vision and expression, he has more than once transformed a Balaclava to victory.

We were and we are celebrating the endurance as well as the power of the poet's art. Imperial Cæsar is long since dead and turned to clay, and the cloud-capped towers and gorgeous palaces of the Empire have left scarce a rack behind. The work of the poet remains. The encyclopædic learning of Varro is all gone but a few pages: the matchless prose of Cicero remains in many volumes.

> All passes. Art alone
>   Enduring stays to us;
> The bust outlives the throne;
>   The coin, Tiberius.
> Even the gods must go;
>   Only the lofty rhyme
> Not countless years o'erthrow,
>   Not long array of time.

We are celebrating the power of poetry as the greatest means of communication and as the greatest bond between men. "Art is the memory of mankind," says Mr. Woodberry. Virgil and Horace and their friends are our memory of a great episode in the history of civilization.

> What should we know,
>   For better or worse,
> Of the long ago,
>   Were it not for verse—
> What ships went down;
>   What walls were razed;
> Who won the crown;
>   What lads were praised?

A fallen stone
  And a waste of sands—
And all is known
  Of the artless lands.
But you need not delve
  By the seaside hills
Where the Muse herself
  All Time fulfills—
Who cuts with his scythe
  All things not hers,
All but the blithe
  Hexameters!

HORACE THE POET OF ITALY

W HAT joy there is in these songs!" writes Andrew Lang of Horace's *Odes*, addressing the poet in *Letters to Dead Authors*. And he continues:

What delight of life, what an exquisite Hellenic grace of art, what a manly nature to endure, what tenderness and constancy of friendship, what a sense of all that is fair in the glittering stream, the music of the waterfall, the hum of bees, the silvery gray of the olive woods on the hillside! How human are all your verses, Horace! What a pleasure is yours in the straining poplars, swaying in the wind! What gladness you gain from the white crest of Soracte, beheld through the fluttering snow-flakes while the logs are being piled higher on the hearth.

To you, the loveliness of your land is a thing to live for. None of the Latin poets your fellows, or none but Virgil, seem to me to have known so well as you, Horace, how happy and fortunate a thing it was to be born in Italy. You do not say so, like your Virgil, in one splendid passage, numbering the glories of the land as a lover might count the perfections of his mistress. But the sentiment is ever in your heart and often on your lips.

It is as true of Horace as it is of Virgil, and as it is true of ancient poetry in general, that his love of nature and of places is incidentally expressed rather than of purpose in descriptive poem or passage. The *Satires* and *Epistles* are concerned with philosophy and criticism of letters and life, and we should hardly expect to find among them whole compositions, or even lengthy passages, celebrating the natural beauties of the land; but the *Odes* themselves, which are lyrics and therefore of a class of poetry much devoted to nature, contain almost no nature poems.

Horace's *Odes* may be divided not very distinctly into seven classes: patriotic or political, invocations or religious, friendship or personal, philosophy of life or *Lebensweisheit*, lighter vein, place, nature. There are about ten which might be classified as

STATUE OF HORACE IN VENOSA

THE BANDUSIAN SPRING

OLIVES IN THE SO-CALLED VILLA OF QUINTILIUS VARUS

MONTE SORACTE

nature poems; yet many of the ten could be placed with equal right under philosophy of life or friendship, and almost no one of them makes of nature an end in itself. Three which might be called spring poems, *Solvitur acris hiems, Diffugere nives,* and *Iam veris comites,* are in reality exhortations to remember the brevity of life and the inevitability of death, and to enjoy what pleasures are possible here and now. One which might be called idyllic, *Velox amoenum,* is the invitation to Tyndaris to come and enjoy Homeric song, cups of innocent Lesbian, and freedom from the passions of jealous lovers in the cool, secluded valley of the poet's Sabine retreat. The exquisite forest scene of the Chloe Ode, *Vitas inuleo,* is a bit of love banter. The prayer to Apollo, *Quid dedicatum,* is an expression of the poet's ideal of the riches of life. The Septimius Ode, *Septimi Gades,* portrays the ideal background of a long and ideal friendship. In only the Bandusian Spring, *O fons Bandusiae,* the Faunus Ode, *Faune nympharum,* and the Second Epode, *Beatus ille,* in spite of its discordant ending—in only these three does nature so predominate that we are willing to call them nature poems; though even these are objective in their treatment, and without the self-consciousness of modern nature poetry.

The translation of the Bandusian Ode by James Beattie, with its freedoms of a hundred and fifty years ago, affords a very pleasant example of the poet claimed entirely by contemplation of natural scene. After praise of the clearness and coldness of the spring and promise of a sacrifice on the morrow, the poem concludes:

> As springs of old renowned, thy name,
> Blest fountain! I devote to fame,
> Thus, while I sing in deathless lays
> The verdant holm, whose waving sprays,
> Thy sweet retirement to defend,
> High o'er the moss-grown rock impend,
> Whence prattling in loquacious play,
> Thy sprightly waters leap away.

With this may be contrasted one of the spring poems, in which the beauties of the landscape, half obscured by mythological intrusions, soon give way to somber thoughts of pallid death:

The Call of Spring

Biting winter's frost is going, and the smiling spring-wind blowing,
    And the sailor rigs his boat along the shore;
Flocks roam now the pasture wide, the plowman leaves the ingleside,
    And the whitened mead with hoarfrost gleams no more.

Now doth Venus tread the tune under overhanging moon,
    Leading Nymphs and comely Graces in the dance,
And the Cyclops' lurid blaze lights up Vulcan with its rays,
    As they ply their ponderous anvils 'neath his glance.

'Tis the fitting season now to adorn the anointed brow
    With the wreath of myrtle green, or firstling flowers;
Meet now, too, to slay a kid, or an ewe, if Faunus bid,
    And to sacrifice to him in woodland bowers.

Pallid Death knocks no more sure at the hovels of the poor
    Than at palaces of kings with turrets high;
Happy though have been thy days, Sestius, life but briefly stays,
    And to build long hopes is vain, with death so nigh.

Even now the night is falling and the fabled Shades are calling,
    And the cheerless home infernal soon will yawn;
Never more will it be thine to be crowned o'er merry wine,
    When to Pluto's distant vale thou once hast gone.

And yet, in spite of the lack of poems devoted to nature, Horace is rich in appreciation of nature's charms. He knows thoroughly and loves the Italian landscape. The feeling for it is indeed ever in his heart and often on his lips. With only the passing word and phrase, he makes us feel all the richness of Italy's charm in tree and plant and flower. From a mind stored with the impressions of a lifetime he throws out to us clear pictures of the ilex opaque in the sun, the white poplar, the huge pine, the rose, the cypress shading the tomb, the oak, the olive groves, the vine wedded to the elm and hanging heavy with purple clusters in colorful autumn, the bachelor plane, the myrtle, the laurel, the parsley, the ivy, the bed of violets, the dark groves on Algidus, the green of meadow and pasture, the gold of ripened grain.

In like manner appear the familiar animals of Italy. Horace has known from childhood the ox keeping holiday with the villagers, the ass with ears dropping as the load becomes too heavy, the kid with his budding horns, the languid flocks and their shepherd seeking the shade by the banks of the stream, the lamb offered up in sacrifice. He gives us glimpses of the horse under the whip of the eager charioteer, the mule jogging along the Appian Way, the greedy little porker, the many-wintered crow, the raven, the little lizard bright in the sun, the timid fawn alone in the forest, the ant accumulating her store, the bees busy about the thyme, the owl, the eagle and the lesser birds, the cock crowing at dawn.

Nor are these concrete objects in nature all. The poet feels also the moods of nature. He knows, and makes his readers know, the dog-days when every breath of wind is stilled, the crashing thunderstorm and its red lightnings, the winds clashing over boiling seas, the morning crisp with hoar-frost or cutting with iciness, the hail-storm deadly to the vines, the snows disappearing under warm west winds, the silences of sunny pastures made still more silent by the fluting of the shepherd, the golden days of plenteous autumn, the cheer of the village holiday, the calm of evenfall in the mountains when the sun lengthens the shadows and relieves the wearied ox of his yoke, bringing on the friendly night. He knows the cheer of the village holiday and feels a kinship with country folk:

The Village Holiday

Faunus, slighted lover of nymphs that yield not,
Passing oft the bounds of my sunny pastures
Gentle be thy step, and may'st ever kindly
    Be to my yeanlings.
Thine a young kid falls when the year's end neareth;
Fails not plenteous wine from the mixbowl streaming,
Venus' chosen mate, and thine ancient altar
    Smokes with much incense.

Sports each flock and herd o'er the grassy pasture
When returns thy Nones of December festal;
Rests the ox from labor, and through the meadows
    Revels the hamlet.
Then 'mong lambs unfrighted the wolf doth wander;
Strews its leaves the forest amain to grace thee;
Smites the hated earth with his foot the delver
    Triple time treading.

Horace is in reality more the poet of Italy than Virgil. The city as well as the country finds expression in him, the life of man as well as the life of nature. If we do not feel in him so pronounced as in Virgil the identification of self with the great sum of things, we do find in him a wider sweep of interest in the ordinary affairs of men on earth. To quote from *Horace and His Influence:*

Where else may be seen so many vivid incidental pictures of men at their daily occupations of work or play? In Satire and Epistle this is to be expected, though there are satirists and writers of letters who never transfer the colors of life to their canvas; but the lyrics, too, are kaleidoscopic with scenes from the round of daily human life. We are given fleeting but vivid glimpses into the career of merchant and sailor. We see the sportsman in chase of the boar, the rustic setting snares for the greedy thrush, the serenader under the casement, the plowman at his ingleside, the anxious mother at the window on the cliff, never taking her eyes from the curved shore, the husbandman passing industrious days on his own hillside, tilling his own acres with his own oxen and training the vine to the unwedded tree, the young men of the hill towns carrying bundles of fagots along rocky slopes, the rural holiday and its festivities, the sun-browned wife making ready the evening meal against the coming of the tired peasant. We are shown all the quaint and quiet life of the countryside. The page is often golden with homely precept or tale of the sort which for all time has been natural to farmer folk. There is the story of the country mouse and the town mouse, the fox and the greedy weasel that ate until he could not pass through the crack by which he came, the rustic who sat and waited for the river to get by, the horse that called man to aid him against the stag, and received the bit forever.

"The mellow charm of Italian landscape and the genial warmth of Italian life" pervade all Horace. His miniatures of men in the city are as vivid as those of the farmer folk. He has looked on at the races in the Circus, at the candidate mingling with the crowds on election day, at the young men at their games and exercises or swimming in the Tiber, at the fortune-teller plying his art, at the young gallant and his lady of the Greek name, at the boisterous drinking party. His memory is filled with pictures of the choir of boys and girls at the temple altar, the suppliant at the shrine, the poet under the vine in his garden, the birthday

THE TORRE DELLE MILIZIE IN ROME

THE TIBER, WITH RARI NANTES SWIMMERS

CASCADES AT TIVOLI, ANCIENT TIBUR

dinner, the meeting of old comrades, the palace with mosaic floors, ceiling of gold and ivory, and columns from Hymettus and Africa, the lovers' quarrel and reconciliation. He has seen the procession with pontifex and Vestal winding up the Capitol, and participated in the celebration of the Sæcular Games. All the motley life of the crowded, busy city has passed before his eyes: the money-lender plying his trade in the Forum, the lawyer started from his sleep by the early client, the shopkeeper, the vendor hawking cheap wares among the people in tunics, the sick man calling in the doctor, the miser gloating over his pieces, the hypocrite courting the rich, the thief, the beggar, the actor, the singer, the dandy posing before the ladies, the poet introduced to his patron, the boy being taken by his father to the schoolmaster, the senator with his train of clients, the vegetable market, the lodger at his bachelor dinner, the funerals of rich and poor, the bore clinging tight to his victim, the crowd gathering at the least excitement, the judge and jury in court, the slave taking liberties with his master on the Saturnalia, the gladiator looking up from the sands for the verdict of the crowd, the philosopher at his meditations, the little boys at their games in the street, the barber and his patrons, the old jurist heavy on his feet and complaining of the distance home. His ears have rung with the noisy din of traffic and voices in the great capital, his eyes have smarted from its dust and smoke, his soul has shrunk from its turmoil.

Thus far we have contemplated Horace as the poet of landscape and life in Italy at large. In the next chapter we shall see him in the definite places of his experience.

. XXVI .

THE HORACE COUNTRY

HORACE not only reflects so well the character of Italian landscape and life in general, but there are so many identifiable scenes both urban and rustic in which as we read his lines we see him present, that familiarity with the Horace country means acquaintance with a great part of Italy.

As might be expected, Horace is the poet, first of all, of the capital. The city of Rome is the almost universal background of his works. Eternal Rome, Rome divinely founded and divinely warranted, the Rome of Destiny, the Rome of Virgil, is indeed also Horace's Rome, though Horace leaves its epic glorification to the fitter hands of the white-souled friend he called the twin of his own spirit.

The Rome of Horace, as contrasted with Virgil's, is the tangible Rome of reality. To be at home with him, we must know the city ancient and modern. We must visit the Palatine and its Temple of Apollo whose dedication the poet attended. We must walk the Sacred Way past the Temple of Vesta and the Basilica Julia, the scene of his perspiring hour with the bore. We must climb the Capitol and see what remains of the Temple of Jupiter Optimus Maximus, where the *Carmen Sæculare* was hymned by the sons and daughters of good old Roman blood, and look upon the stone in the National Museum still showing the record of its authorship, *Carmen composuit Quintus Horatius Flaccus*. We must cross Father Tiber to the Vatican Hill that echoed back the praises of Mæcenas as with Horace he sat in the theater, and visit the immense ruins of the Circus Maximus, where the glowing wheel of the chariot swept the driver on to the victory that made him lord of the earth and equal to the gods. We must walk on the pavements the poet trod in his philosophic rambles among the lowly folk of the city, and frequent the Campus Martius where he had his game of ball until fatigue and the high sun reminded him of the bath, and look down upon the Tiber waters, to be swum three times by those whose itch for writing made them sleepless. We must see the Fabrician Bridge, still bearing today the names of Lollius and Lepidus, in whose consulship Horace completed four times eleven Decembers, and enter the dark vaults of the Mausoleum of Augustus, from 1907 to 1935 Rome's concert auditorium, begun by Augustus in 28 B.C. when Horace was thirty-seven, and five years afterward receiving the ashes of young Marcellus. We must wander on the Esquiline, gloomy with neglected burial grounds until Mæcenas converted it into pleasant gardens near his home—the Esquiline, one day to receive the ashes of Horace himself:

> Horatius Flaccus, B.C. 8,
> There's not a doubt about the date—
> You're dead and buried:
> As you observed, the seasons roll;
> And 'cross the Styx full many a soul
>   Has Charon ferried,
> Since, mourned of men and Muses nine,
> They laid you on the Esquiline.

Horace is the poet also of definite places in Italy outside Rome. The travelling out of no other poet leads to so many charming spots. None other has better claim to be the pocket companion of the classical scholar.

Venusia, the birthplace of Horace, is modern Venosa, a city of eight thousand in the mountains one hundred and fifty miles east of Naples. Near it is the Ofanto, "the far sounding Aufidus at which I was born." Monte Vulture is ancient Voltur, where storied doves covered with fresh leafage of laurel and myrtle the child, perhaps Horace himself, that had fallen asleep tired out with play beyond the bounds of nurse Apulia, his native province. The Acherontia and Bantine headlands and low-lying Forentum of the poet are the Acerenza and Banzi and Forenza of today; and in Venosa itself are a statue to Horace and dubious ancient walls called the house of Horace.

Twenty miles from Venosa toward the east coast is the line of the Appian Way at Canosa. What pleasures have Horatians enjoyed, following the poet from Rome on the Queen of Roads—to Aricia, where he stopped at the modest inn; to Forum Appi, where he took the canal boat for the night, with mosquitoes and frogs to drive sleep away, and boatman and traveller singing of the girls they left behind them; to Anxur, now Terracina, conspicuous with its far-gleaming rocks, and famous for the memories of *Fra Diavolo* the opera and Washington Irving's story *The Inn at Terracina*; to Formia, beautiful on the curving shore at the base of the high hills still famous for the vine; into fruitful Campania, where at Sinuessa the party, already containing Mæcenas, was further enriched by the addition of Plotius and Varius and Virgil; to Capua, in the Vesuvian plain, the city whose comforts reduced the manhood of Hannibal's troopers; through the Caudine Forks, the pass thirty-five miles northeast of Naples where the Roman army passed under the Samnite yoke; to Beneventum, now Benevento, where the busy host almost burned up the place while roasting the thrushes; into the familiar mountains of Apulia; to Canusium, now Canosa, with gritty bread and a scarcity of water that has lasted to our own generation; over wretched roads to Rubi, Ruvo today; to the walls of fishy Barium on the sea, today Bari and still with a plenteous trade in fish; to Brundisium, the end of the journey and the poet's paper, the Brindisi of today, the port of Pompey's flight and Cæsar's pursuit in 49 B.C., the port of Virgil's return and death in 19.

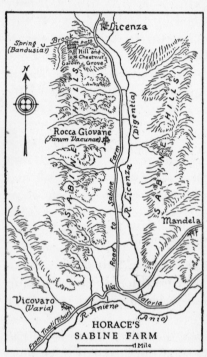

HORACE'S
SABINE FARM
|———————1 Mile

Forty-four miles west from Brindisi is Taranto, the ancient
Tarentum, "where the honey is not second to Hymettus, and the
olive vies with green Venafrum, where Jove makes the springtime long and the winters mild, and where the vale of Aulon,
friendly to the fruitful vine, need feel no envy of the Falernian
grape." This is the little corner of earth that smiled upon the
poet beyond all others. "Happy Horace!" wrote Sainte-Beuve.
"What a fortune has been his! Why, because he once expressed
in a few charming verses his fondness for the life of the country,
and described his favorite corner of earth, the lines composed for
his own pleasure and for the friend to whom he addressed them
have laid hold on the memory of all men and have become so
firmly lodged there that one can conceive no others, and finds
only those when he feels the need of praising his own beloved
retreat!"

Tarentum is only one of the charming spots of the lovely
country Horace knows and loves so well. Its picturesque lane-like
streets, its fragments of ancient temples, its beautiful gulf and
harbor with warships riding at anchor, its inner gulf on whose
banks are heaps of the ancient shell-fish from which the imperial
purple dye was distilled, its leafy surroundings and sunny, orchard-
covered hills, make it a place of great appeal to the Horatian
pilgrim. Green Venafrum, on the Volturnus near Arpinum in
central Italy, is twice linked by Horace with Tarentum; once as
fruitful in the olive, and once in the superb stanzas describing
the departure of Regulus for Carthage after his refusal to be
ransomed: "And yet he knew what the barbarian torturer had
in store for him; but he nevertheless pushed aside the kinsmen
that strove to stay him, and the people urging him not to return,
exactly as if he had finished his cases in court and were leaving
tedious affairs behind, and starting for the fields of Venafrum
or Lacedæmonian Tarentum."

And there is watery Baiae, the charming coast retreat near
Avernus, where Horace's rich man cheats the sea by building
into the water; and the Lucrine Lake, still with its oysters; and
cool Præneste, today Palestrina, and pleasant Antium, Anzio now,
and Pedum with its healthful groves; and Fidenae and Gabii,

ancient towns in the Campagna neglected even in Horace's day, and now marked only by ruin; and the Alban pastures, and Algidus and Soracte mantled in snow, and the fertile fields of fruitful Sardinia, and summery Calabria, and the fields which Liris, taciturn stream, still eats away with its quiet waters. There is Tibur on its slope, founded by the Argive, the Tivoli of today, eighteen miles from Rome, with its vineyards and gardens watered now, as in Horace's time, by the swift-running streamlets, and with its headlong Anio plunging down the cliffs—

> From the green steeps whence Anio leaps
> In clouds of snow-white foam.

Fifteen miles above Tibur, in the Sabine part of the Apennines, a good day's jaunt from Rome, was the poet's Sabine farm, the gift of Mæcenas, adviser to the Emperor and patron of poets, in the year 33 B.C., when Horace was thirty-two years old. This is the most frequent of Horatian excursions. The irregular reaches of the Via Tiburtina, a road of magnificent distances, lead from Rome through the broad rollings of the Campagna to the foot of Tivoli's olive slopes, and at fifteen miles zigzag steeply through the groves to the mountain town on the brow of the Apennines. Past the Anio glen and the Sibyl's temple hanging on its edge, the road becomes on the farther side of the town the Via Valeria, winding through the hills with the Anio below to the right. It passes Vicovaro on the height to its left, and at Mandela turns to the north where the stream Licenza comes down a deep and narrow valley to join the Anio.

Five miles up the Licenza, crowning a steep and detached hill in a little nook at the base of the mountain heights that suddenly end the valley, is the village of Licenza. On the left of the road a half mile before it crosses the stream and enters the village, is a ridge covered by a chestnut grove. Beyond the chestnut ridge, between it and the high opposing slope, about forty rods from the highway and in plain view of Licenza, is a level space containing the floors and foundation walls of an ancient country house. This, with little question, is what is left of the Sabine Villa of Horace. It had numerous rooms, some with tasteful

LICENZA

ROCCA GIOVANE

THE VILLA OF HORACE

THE COUNTRY AROUND THE SABINE FARM

mosaics still preserved, a garden and portico, and a pool supplied by a channel from a precipitous little stream among the vineyards on the mountainside. The site, long claimed as Horace's retreat, was excavated in 1911 and the following years, and the original building found to have been occupied and enlarged in Flavian times a hundred years after Horace. The fragments of wall decoration, pipes, coins, and other movable relics, are to be seen in the little museum in the village of Licenza. Nothing so far dis-

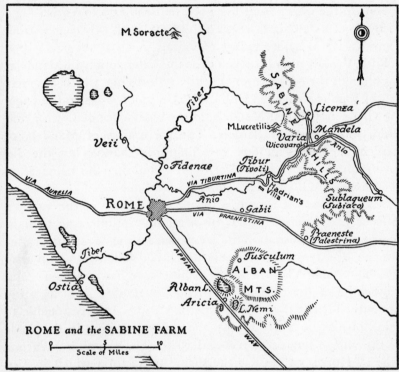

ROME and the SABINE FARM

covered proves absolutely the site as Horace's farm, but few longer doubt its identity, and no one doubts the identity of the neighborhood in general; so perfect is the correspondence of the physical surroundings with Horace's own testimony.

First of all, the estate was in the Sabines. Horace declares himself "rich enough with just his Sabine place," and mentions riding "into the steep Sabines."

Second, it was in the Tivoli neighborhood. The poet mentions

Tibur and the Anio so much indeed that it is suspected he had a retreat at Tibur as well as farther in the mountains. The venerable George H. Hallam firmly believed that his villa on the outskirts was once the property of Horace.

Third, it was in the valley of a cold stream that needed attention to keep it from flooding the fields, and was called Digentia. The modern Licenza is an easy change from the word Digentia, and the stream in times of rain or thaw soon overflows.

Fourth, the estate "sent five good householders to Varia." The Vicovaro of today, six or seven miles away, is an easy change from Vicus Variae, meaning village of Varia.

Fifth, the Digentia is spoken of as the water supply of Mandela: "as often as the cool stream Digentia restores me, which Mandela drinks, hamlet shrivelled with cold." Up to a few generations ago, the village now called Mandela, at the confluence of Licenza and Anio, was known as Bardela. The corruption of Mandela to Bardela represents another easy linguistic change; but the discovery on the spot of an inscription containing the name Mandela makes the linguistic argument superfluous.

Sixth, at Rocca Giovane, a town on the brow of the valley a mile or two from the villa ruins, an inscription came to light recording the restoration in Vespasian's time, a century after Horace, of a temple to Victoria which had fallen into ruin with age. The name Victoria in the Sabine speech was Vacuna, and Horace in an Epistle tells his friend Fuscus that he is dictating the letter behind the rotting fane of Vacuna. It is reasonable to think of him on a stroll down the valley, stopping in the shade of the village temple to rest and write. The crumbling Vacuna fane of Horace's time was the shrine to Victoria which in Vespasian's time had collapsed.

Finally, both the position of the valley as described by Horace, and its general character, accord with the physical facts.

So that you need not ask me, dearest Quintius [he writes] whether my farm supports its owner with land under plow, or makes him rich with the fruit of the olive, whether with apples, or meadows, or the elm draped with vines, the form and position of my acres shall be herein described at length. The hills are uninterrupted except that a shady valley separates them, and in such a way that the sun at his coming looks upon its right side, and at his departure with retreating chariot veils its left in mist. You would praise the climate. What, if I should tell you that the benevolent thickets supply ruddy cherries and plums? That the oak and the ilex delight my herds with much food, their master with much shade? You would say that Tarentum with all its greenery had been transported hither. There is a spring, too, big enough to give its name to the stream; the Hebrus winding through Thrace is not colder or purer. Its water is good for an ailing head or an ailing stomach. This beloved retreat—and charming, too, if you will believe it—keeps your friend in health through the September hours.

The Licenza valley does in reality run north and south. It has the variety of lands and products mentioned by the poet. The waters of spring and stream are icy cold; and the chemists have declared that they also have curative properties.

Here, then, we may imagine Horace coming "to his citadel in the hills," "when the first fig and the heat call out the funeral director and his train of dark-clad lictors, when every father and fond mother are pale with anxiety for their children, and the petty obligations of the Forum and the halls of the great bring on the fever and unseal wills." Perhaps it was here that, as he wandered in the Sabine forest singing of Lalage, the dreadful wolf met him and left him unharmed. Here, perhaps, was the falling tree that narrowly missed its master. Perhaps the water splashing over the rock and down the hill above the ruins today is the spring made so famous by Horace:

> O crystal-bright Bandusian Spring,
>   Worthy thou of the mellow wine
> And flowers I bring to thy pure depths:
>   A kid the morrow shall be thine.
>
> The day of lustful strife draws on,
>   The starting horns begin to gleam;
> In vain! his red blood soon shall tinge
>   The waters of thy clear, cold stream.
>
> The dog-star's fiercely blazing hour
>   Ne'er with its heat doth change thy pool;
> To wandering flock and ploughworn steer
>   Thou givest waters fresh and cool.

Thee, too, 'mong storied founts I'll place,
Singing the oak that slants the steep
Above the hollowed home of rock
From which thy prattling streamlets leap.

Here Faunus roamed, frightening the nymphs; here the ancient altar smoked with much incense, and the flock and the herd kept holiday with the villagers themselves, and the delver rejoiced to beat in triple time the hated earth. Here the vale resounded with the melodious pipe of Tyndaris, and plenty, rich in the honors of the country, poured forth to the full her fruits from kindly horn. Here were the trackless hills in whose woodlands the timid fawn quaked at the sound of bright little lizards rustling the dry leaves:

Chloe, thou fliest me like a fawn
That on some lonely upland lawn,
Seeking its dam, in winds and trees
Imaginary dangers sees.
Does Spring's fresh breeze the foliage shake,
Or lizard rustle in the brake?
At once it quakes in heart and limb.
Yet I, sweet girl, no tiger grim,
No fierce Gætulian lion am.
Then, no more, fawn-like, seek thy dam,
But bury all thy fond alarms—
'Tis time thou should'st—in true love's arms.

And here, standing in the morning sunshine at the door of his beloved retreat, Horace surveyed his lands and his lot in life, and found them good. "What I prayed for was this: a measure of land not so large, where I could have a garden, a flow of never-failing water near the house, and a little woodland besides. The gods have been more kindly and generous than I asked."

This was the place he longed for as he endured the heat and dust and trivialities of the capital. "O country, when shall I ever look upon thee? When can I quaff sweet forgetfulness of life's anxieties, now from the books of the men of olden time, now from sleep and hours of idleness?"

This was the scene of neighbor Cervius's old-wives' tales told to the point. "For if anyone in his ignorance praises the lot of rich but anxious Arellius, he begins in this fashion: 'Once upon a time a country mouse, they say, welcomed a town mouse to his hole—old friends they were, the host unpolished and close, but still not incapable of loosening up his soul to entertain a friend.' "

The country mouse, we need not doubt, is the philosophic Horace, happy in his modest possessions and in the knowledge that "much is wanting to him who desires much; well is it with him to whom with sparing hand God hath given just enough." At the end of the story the country mouse is Horace still, when "in terror they scurry across the floor, in still wilder fright as the high chamber resounds with the barking of Molossian dogs," and the country mouse declares, "Not this the life for me, and so fare you well; my scant living, and my hole in the ground in the woods to keep me safe from dangers, will be good enough for me."

He is the same Horace who elsewhere addresses his friend Fuscus:

You keep to the city; I am for the streamlets of the charming country, its moss-covered rocks, and its groves. *Que voulez-vous?* I live and am a king as soon as I have left behind the things you noisily praise to the skies. . . . Do you know any place better than the blessed country? Is there a place where the winter is milder, where the breeze more pleasantly softens the rage of the dog-star and the attacks of the Lion when in his fury he has welcomed the blazing sun? Is there a place where envious care breaks in less upon one's sleep? Are the scent and color of the sod inferior to Libyan mosaic? Is the water that tries the lead in the city purer than that which murmurs in the streamlet bustling down the slope? . . . This I am writing you behind the rotting fane of Vacuna, happy in everything but this, that you are not here with me.

In no better place or mood could we say good-bye, with Andrew Lang, to the poet of nature and men in Italy. "Farewell, dear Horace; farewell, thou wise and kindly heathen; of mortals the most human, the friend of my friends and of so many generations of men."

. XXVII .

THE SEASONS

THERE is in Roman literature so much of the calm and contemplative, and there is so much beauty in Italian landscape and climate, that one is surprised not to find in the Latin authors the abundant reference to the seasons that characterizes English and American literature.

The fact is due to several causes. In the first place, the contrast between the seasons of heat and cold in Mediterranean countries is less pronounced than in England, not to say in New England, and therefore the stimulations of delight and dislike are less. The Italian winter is short and mild; the lingering roses of autumn have scarcely disappeared when the flowers of spring begin to blow. The whole round of the year is rich in beauty and in yield.

In the second place, the ancient Roman looked upon a disciplined and limited landscape. Vineyard, olive orchard, garden, grain field, and pasture, with the pine, the cypress, the ilex, and the poplar to decorate them, were constantly before him, and the mountains or the sea were the definite and not distant bounds of his vision. The mountains concealed no mysteries, for they were filled with charming valleys, and on their cliffs and headlands and slopes were the little hamlets, like so many posts of occupation held by the soldiers of the soil. Even the sea was a well managed Roman lake. There were no horizons disappearing into the infinities of sea and plain, no dark and endless, unexplored forest recesses, as there were in the Northern lands, to encourage the romantic sentiments of wonder and mystery. Ausonius, of Bordeaux, writing the *Mosella* while professor at Trèves four centuries after Virgil's death, is called the first of the modern poets of Europe because, in Mackail's phrase, he "unites Virgilian rhythm and diction with the new romantic sense of the beauties of nature." It is not so much the passage of four hundred years and the development of feeling for landscape that make the *Mosella* modern as it is the Northern scene in which the poem is written. The romantic movement of the nineteenth century and the humanization of nature were due less to reaction from the pseudo-classic than to the fact that the discovery of the out-of-doors and the migration of poetry from the study to the fields took place in the North.

Let it not be thought that the ancients are silent on the seasons. It is only that they are more objective in their thought and expression, and therefore treat the seasons less at length.

Winter

Winter in the Latin authors is the season of inaction. "The inert winter returns," says Horace—*bruma recurrit iners*. "When Aquarius saddens the inverted year," the hard-working little ant no longer comes forth. When winter spreads its snow on the Alban Hills, Horace will go down to the sea and huddle up and read. In severer climes there is the *glacies iners*, the deadening ice. In Virgil, winter is the season of inaction and unproductiveness for the farmer, the season of storm and lying in the harbor for ships.

The poets of the world have never loved winter as they have loved other seasons. If their thoughts of winter touch beauty at all, it is the beauty of placid moments when all the earth is folded in white, as on one rare morning Horace saw Mount Soracte:

> You see how, deep with gleaming snow,
> Soracte stands, and, bending low,
>   Yon branches droop beneath their burden,
> And streams o'erfrozen have ceased their flow.

If the poets conceive of happiness in winter, it is not the happiness of external nature, but the good cheer of men and women enjoying shelter and fire, or the delight of boys and girls at play in the keen air, or the exhilaration of sportsmen defying the rigors of the season, or the resignation of the husbandman as he turns his hand to this and that while waiting for life to reawaken, or the contentment of beasts in fold or steading. It is the negative happiness of making necessity a virtue. When Virgil praises the winter of his Italy, it is as the season of enforced rest, and yet the season of pressing tasks:

> When the yield is past the farmers oft enjoy the season of cold, and pleasantly meet each other around the board. Festal winter beckons to them and releases them from cares, as when the laden ships have at last reached harbor and the glad sailors hang wreaths of flowers upon them. But still, then is the time to strip the oaks of acorns and to gather laurel berries and the olive and the blood-red myrtle. Then is the time to set snares for the crane and nets for the deer, and to hunt the long-eared hare. Then is the time to hurl the stone from the hempen Balearic sling and strike down the doe—when the snow lies deep and the streams push forward the ice.

Horace's winter is much the same: "But when the wintry season of thundering Jove brings on the rains and snows, with many a hound the rustic either drives from this side and that the boar into the opposing nets, or with smooth rod spreads the delicate net to betray the greedy thrush, and with the snare takes the timid rabbit and the migrant crane as joyful prizes."

Yet happiness of nature there is none. Winter is the cruel season, the season without pity. When at its oncoming "the vineyard drops to the ground its last leafage, and chill Aquilo strikes from the groves their honor, even then the alert husbandman looks anxiously forward to the needs of the coming year." If in Virgil's Italy it is thus unwelcome, in the colder North it is the season of driving snow and pitiless cold, of ugly inertness and death. Spenser sees it with a familiarity and a vividness hardly possible to poets of the Italian land.

> Lastly, came Winter clothèd all in frieze,
>   Chattering his teeth for cold that did him chill;
> Whilst on his hoary beard his breath did freeze,
>   And the dull drops, that from his purpled bill
>   As from a limbec did adown distill:
> In his right hand a tippèd staff he held,
>   With which his feeble steps he stayèd still;
> For he was faint with cold, and weak with eld;
> That scarce his loosèd limbs he able was to weld.

A RARE DAY IN ROME

A SPRING LANDSCAPE

SUMMER IN THE VILLA BORGHESE

A WHEAT HARVEST SCENE

Winter is the tragic season, and December is the tragic month. In Austin Dobson's fresco of *A Masque of the Months,*

> Last of all the shrunk December,
>   Cowled for age, in ashes gray;
> Fading like a fading ember,—
> Last of all the shrunk December.
> Him regarding, men remember
> Life and joy must pass away.

No, the winter is an unlovely season. If we praise it, it is only when happy escape from its cruelties is uppermost in fancy; or when thoughts of the joy of defiance and the exaltation of victory set imagination aglow.

> Then let the icy North wind blow
>   The trumpets of the coming storm,
> To arrowy sleet and blinding snow
>   Yon slanting lines of rain transform.
> Young hearts shall hail the drifted cold
>   As gaily as I did of old;
> And I, who watch them through the frosty pane,
> Unenvious, live in them my boyhood o'er again.

SPRING

Biting winter in Horace "is dispelled by the pleasing change of spring and Favonius"; "the cold grows mild under the Zephyrs." Favonius is the West wind, the "favoring" wind, and Zephyrus, son of Astræus the Titan wind-father and Aurora the Dawn, is also the West wind. The breezes are the "companions of spring." They melt the frosts and swell the streams, they bring forth the flowers and start the bees to work. In Cowper's England,

> Spring hangs her infant blossoms on the trees,
> Rocked in the cradle of the western breeze.

In Chaucer,

> The season pricketh every gentle herte,
> And maketh him out of his sleep to sterte.

The fulness of the spring is in May. May in Italy sees the end of the rains and the coming of the season of unbroken sunshine.

May in England is the month of May Day and May poles and May
dances, the merry month. It could not be without its place in the
Masque of the Months:

> May the jocund cometh after,
>   Month of all the Loves (and mine);
> Month of mock and cuckoo laughter,—
> May the jocund cometh after.
> Beaks are gay on roof and rafter;
> Luckless lovers peak and pine.

At mention of spring the mind is filled straightway with imag-
inings of sunshine and flowers, of plantings and sowings, of rising
sap and swelling seed and bud and opening blossom, of love and
mating, of the joyous upward thrust of life. Sweet lovers love the
spring.

> For love is crowned with the prime
> In the spring time, the only pretty ring time.

Spring is the season of Venus, the one deity Lucretius cannot keep
out of this world's affairs.

> Mother of Rome, delight of Gods and men,
> Dear Venus that beneath the gliding stars
> Makest to teem the many-voyagèd main
> And fruitful lands—for all of living things
> Through thee alone are evermore conceived,
> Through thee are risen to visit the great sun—
> Before thee, Goddess, and thy coming on,
> Flee stormy wind and massy cloud away,
> For thee the dædal Earth bears scented flowers,
> For thee the waters of the unvexèd deep
> Smile, and the hollows of the sérene sky
> Glow with diffusèd radiance for thee!
> For soon as comes the springtime face of day,
> And procreant gales blow from the West unbarred,
> First fowls of air, smit to the heart by thee,
> Foretoken thy approach, O thou Divine,
> And leap the wild herds round the happy fields,
> Or swim the bounding torrents. Thus amain,
> Seized with the spell, all creatures follow thee,
> Whithersoever thou walkest forth to lead.

And thence through seas and mountains and swift streams,
Through leafy homes of birds and greening plains,
Kindling the lure of love in every breast,
Thou bringest the eternal generations forth,
Kind after kind. And since 't is thou alone
Guidest the Cosmos, and without thee naught
Is risen to reach the shining shores of light,
Nor aught of joyful or of lovely born. . . .

In the more practical and more serenely poetic Virgil of the
Georgics,

Spring is useful to the leafage of the grove, and useful to the forest.
In the spring the soil swells and demands the begetting seed. Then the
Omnipotent Father Ether descends in fecund rains into the bosom of
his happy bride, and mightily mingling with her mighty body fosters
growth in every kind. Then do the pathless thickets resound with
tuneful birds, and the herds when their time is come seek out their
mates. The nurturing field brings forth, and the plowed fields open
their bosoms to the warming breezes of the West wind; in all of them
abounds the tender moisture. Now do the new-springing seeds dare
safely to trust themselves to new suns; the vine leaf fears not the rising
South wind nor the rain driven from the sky by the blasts of the North
wind, but pushes forth its buds and unfolds all its leafage. One could
believe that at the first beginnings of the growing world the days that
shone were not different nor had other character. It was the spring
then, it was the spring that the mighty earth was living in, and the
East winds spared their wintry blasts when the first flocks were drinking in the light and the iron race of man was rearing its head from
the hard fields, and the beasts were let into the forest and the stars
into the sky. Nor could tender creatures endure the hardship of this
world were not so great a calm to go between the cold and the heat
and did not the mercy of the skies attend upon the earth.

Higher praise of the spring could hardly be uttered; nor could
higher praise be given the climate of Italy than Virgil's: "Here
spring is long lasting, and summer lingers in months not her own."

Yet spring, like autumn, is a season not exempt from storm.
In Shakespearean phrase,

Unruly blasts wait on the tender spring.

Spring is not entirely an amiable season, unless indeed to those
themselves in the spring of life. Spring is not reposeful. It is above

all the season of restlessness and movement. The incomparable invocation of the spring spirit by Lucretius is almost a tribute to violence. Spring is the masculine season, the young Hercules of the seasons, crude, rough, violent—

> When proud-pied April, dressed in all his trim,
> Hath put a spirit of youth in everything.

It is the youth of the year, and it has the faults of youth:

> Oh, how this spring of love resembleth
> The uncertain glory of an April day,
> Which now shows all the beauty of the sun,
> And by and by a cloud takes all away.

Spring is impatient, heedless, boisterous, importunate, presumptuous, eager, arrogant, violent. It bursts the seed and cleaves the soil and crumbles the wall and fires the blood. It is fickle. It laughs and weeps, it frolics and sulks, it smiles and rages, in the same day, in the same hour. It is like youth, and we love it and forgive it as we love and forgive youth, because of its beauty and its promises, because of its increasing calm. "At the very last of the winter, when the spring is now calm," says Virgil, "then are the lands fat, then is the wine at its mellowest, then is the season of sweet slumberings and deep shadows in the mountains."

Virgil has a genuine feeling for spring. His mentions of it in the *Georgics,* supposedly meant to be practical, go beyond the prosaic and end in the realm of poetry. In Horace, we have a difference. In the three nature poems already mentioned, spring appears not for its own sake but as a background. The seventh ode of Book IV may be taken as an example.

The Lesson of Spring

> The quickening year dissolves the snow,
> And grasses spring, and blossoms blow;
> Through greener plains the stream once more
> Glides lessening by the silent shore;
> Again th' awakening forests wear
> Their pendent wealth of wreathed hair;
> While nymphs and graces, disarrayed,
> Dance fearless in the mottled shade.

The circling year, the fleeting day,
Are types of nature's law, and say
That to frail earth the fates deny
The gift of immortality.
All, all is change. 'Neath Spring's warm sighs
Hoar-headed Winter wakes, and dies;
Summer succeeds to vernal showers;
Autumn comes next with fruits and flowers.
The Winter lays his icy hand
Once more upon the sleeping land.
Through heaven's blue depths swift-sailing moons
Repair the loss of vanished suns:
But when we reach the fated shore
Which kings and heroes trod before,
What are we? Clay to dust returned,
A shade, forgotten and unmourned.
We live today; tomorrow's light
May not be ours: then live aright;
With generous heart thy riches share,
And disappoint the grasping heir.
When Minos, throned in Stygian gloom,
Relentless judge, shall speak thy doom,
Torquatus, thee nor proud descent,
Nor wit, nor wisdom eloquent,
Nor piety itself, shall save
From the dark silence of the grave.
In vain the huntress queen implored
Hades' inexorable lord
To free her chaste Hippolytus:
The might of Theseus strove in vain
To sunder the Lethean chain
Which bound his loved Pirithous.

Here it is to be noted that all four seasons are mentioned, and that each is briefly characterized. It is to be noted also that spring is the one to receive most attention, and that spring itself and the whole cycle as a unit are the background for Horace's moral of the brevity of life.

This poem, in method and purpose, and in substance somewhat, is a repetition of *Solvitur acris,* already quoted. There also spring is characterized at length. In the third of Horace's nature poems the depiction of the season is more extended.

Now blows the gentle Thracian breeze,
Herald of spring, to calm the seas
    And fill the flowing sails;
The fields are stiff with frost no more,
Nor do the snow-fed torrents roar
    Impetuous down the vales.

The swallow builds her nest of clay,
And seems to mourn with plaintive lay
    Young Itys' cruel fate—
Of Cecrops' house the curse and bane,
For that too savage vengeance ta'en
    On royal lust and hate.

The guardians of the woolly sheep
Stretched on the grass sweet concert keep
    Of flutes with varied trills,
And charm the god who haunts the groves,
The god who tends the flocks, and loves
    Arcadia's purpled hills.

This charming description of the spring already advanced to
summer heat and suggesting thirst is the prelude to a friendly
invitation to dinner graced with choice wine and perfume. Its
conclusion, however, after three genial stanzas, is a recurrence to
the familiar theme:

Come, quit those covetous thoughts, those knitted
        brows;
    Think on the last black embers, while you may,
And be for once unwise. When time allows
    'T is sweet the fool to play.

But spring is overtaken and displaced by summer. "And summer tramples upon spring," sings Horace.

June the next, with roses scented,
    Languid from a slumber-spell;
June in shade of leafage tented;
June the next, with roses scented.
Now her Itys, still lamented,
    Sings the mournful Philomel.

SUMMER ✓

The name of summer is enveloped in flowers and heat. It recalls the scent of rose and clover blossom, the aroma of drying hay, the wholesome perfume of rain-soaked earth and growing plants. It fills the imagination with color and richness; with glistening verdure waxing luxuriant under a golden sun, with flowers in field and hedge, with berries flaming in the foliage of bush and vine, with mown acres and skimming swallows and drowsy bees, with waves of heat rising at noonday over fields of yellowing grain, with patient cattle standing in shady pools. It revives to the ear the cricket and locust etching the deep, hot silences of late July.

In summer did lonely and hopeless Corydon lament to hills and groves:

Ah, cruel Alexis, care you nothing for my songs? Have you no pity for me? You will some day bring on my death. Now even the flocks are courting the shady places and coolness, now the green lizards the thorny thickets hide close, and Thestylis is bruising the garlic and wild thyme and savory herbs for the reapers wearied by the consuming sun; yet here am I following your footsteps, with the cicadas in the trees under the blazing sun singing back their songs to me.

The summer of the Latin poets is not so well defined as spring or winter. The rustic festival of Tibullus is so enveloped in summer atmosphere that one must remind himself that the indeterminate season here represented is usually thought to be spring, and sometimes even winter. Autumn bears fruits, and so does summer. The heat of late summer and the heat of early autumn are much the same. The *Eclogues* of Virgil, with their universal out-of-door character, might be expected to name or define the season; yet in only one, the second, is summer clearly the season, because there are cicadae and harvesters; in one, the first, the tender chestnuts and mellow apples, and the roofs of the farmhouses sending up smoke at sunset, bespeak the early autumn; in two of them, the sixth and the eighth, no season is distinguishable; and in the remaining six we are sure only that the season is not winter, but some time in late spring, mid summer, or early autumn. The *formosissimus annus* of the third, "the year at its greatest beauty," may describe either spring or summer. The whole seven are best described as summery, and even the two whose settings indicate no season are suggestive of the warmth and foliage of summer. In the *Georgics* also, summer is undefined. We have seen Virgil's beautiful lines on the perfect days of spring. The spring is a time of active beginnings, the autumn a time of realization. When Virgil in the second book of the *Georgics* describes the round of the year, the summer receives no such eloquent passage as that on spring two hundred lines preceding. It is there only by implication.

The husbandman cleaves the earth with curved share: hence the yield of his labor, hence his support of his native land and his little household gods, hence his herds of cattle and his deserving oxen. There is no interval; the year is rich with apples or the young of the flocks or the sheaves of grain, and loads the furrows with increase and overflows the granary. Winter approaches: the Sicyonian olive is crushed in the oil mill, the swine come home glad with acorns, the woodlands yield the arbute; autumn drops her varied fruits, and the vintage seasons itself on the sunny rocks.

It is like Horace, who uses the spring as the background for exhortation to seize upon life, to use summer in the same manner. "Now doth the father of Andromeda bring forth clearly his hidden fires; now doth Procyon rage, and the star of the furious Lion, as the sun brings once more the days of drought; now doth the shepherd with languid flock wearily seek out the shade and the stream and the thickets of shaggy Silvanus; now is the silent bank abandoned by the straying breeze—and you are taking anxious thought of the State." Horace's summer is not the friendly season of Virgil that envelops the fields in heat that transforms itself into ripened grain and mellow fruitage. It is the atrocious season of the blazing Dog-star, the season "when the first fig and the heat decorate the funeral manager with gloomy lictors, and every father and fond mother grow pale with concern for their children, and close application to duty and the petty tasks of the forum bring on fevers and unseal wills."

But Horace was living the life of the city man when he wrote these words, and was forgetful of the secluded valley to which he invited Tyndaris, far from the heat of the Dog-star, and "rich to overflowing with the kindly abundance of the honors of the country."

Summer is the constant season. It is no longer the season of beginnings and promise; it is already the season of first fruits. It is the ardent season, the season of the love that no longer deceives. Spring is masculine, and youthful; summer is feminine, a ripened woman. If any days are perfect, the days of summer are perfect days:

> Then Heaven tries earth if it be in tune,
> And over it softly her warm ear lays.

AUTUMN

But behold autumn, most blessed of the seasons, "the Sabbath of the year." The days of promise fulfilled are at hand. Under skies turbulent no more with the impetuous moods of spring, nor glowing with the heat of summer, nor as yet darkened by the rains of winter, the "apple-bearing autumn" of Horace "lifts from the fields her head beautiful with mellow fruits," or "with golden plenty pours from full horn into the lap of Italy." Horace may fear "the South wind injuring health in the autumn" and the "leaden South wind and heavy autumn," or the season dangerous to rustic Phidyle's sweet yeanlings in the apple-bearing time of the year; but the sirocco blowing up from the Sahara is only an incident. The poet who coins Horace's beautiful phrases about autumn and the mellow fruits and golden plenty, and the livid-green clusters growing into purple ripeness among the leaves, was sensitive to the loveliness of the season. Autumn is the season of the Faunus Ode. It is probably the season when Horace sat drinking under the thick-shading arbor and bade Davus not to search where the late roses lingered. Autumn in Virgil is the season of the olive and the dropping of the fruits and the foliage. The souls waiting to cross the Styx are "as many as the leaves that fall in the forest when loosened by the first cold of autumn." At the persuasion of autumn the grape that has ripened on the terraced rocks pours forth its liquor. Autumn brings the vintage.

> Laden deep with fruity cluster,
>   Then September, ripe and hale;
> Bees about his basket fluster,
> Laden deep with fruity cluster.
>   Skies have now a softer lustre;
>   Barns resound to flap of flail.

With the vintage and such light labor come gladness and merriment. The joy of autumn, however, is not the intoxication of mirth. It is the deeper satisfaction of peace and plenty. Granary and bin are filled. Basket and crate are warm with the color and rich with the perfume of ripened fruits. We never tire of autumn's praises:

> Season of mists and mellow fruitfulness,
>   Close bosom-friend of the maturing sun;
> Conspiring with him how to load and bless
>   With fruit the vines that round the thatch-
>   eaves run;
> To bend with apples the mossed cottage-trees,
>   And fill all fruit with ripeness to the core.

Like summer, autumn is feminine. She is the summer grown to full perfection. She is not a lover; she is a friend, a benefactress, a mother, a deity. Her embrace is infinitely calm and pure. She is of all the seasons the one most at peace with herself:

> There is a harmony
> In autumn, and a lustre in its sky
> Which through the summer is not heard nor
>   seen,
> As if it could not be, as if it had not been.

Poet and sculptor of the ancient day when nature appeared to man in human form delighted to give autumn the ample lines and benevolent mien of a nobly beautiful woman. She was a matron glorified, a mother goddess, a Roman Ceres, a Greek Demeter; such as Theocritus saw her at the harvest-feast in Cos, when "once upon a time went Eucritus and he, and for a third Amyntas, from the town to the Haleis," the day he met with Lycidas:

> All of rich summer smacked, of autumn all:
> Pears at our feet, and apples at our side
> Rolled in luxuriance; branches on the ground
> Sprawled, overweighed with damsons; while
>   we brushed
> From the cask's head the crust of four long
>   years . . .
> All by Demeter's shrine at harvest-home.
> Beside whose cornstacks may I oft again
> Plant my broad van: while she stands by and
>   smiles,
> Poppies and cornsheaves on each laden arm.

For autumn to take on divine form, and to be adored, was in the way of nature. Our Pilgrim ancestors, setting in autumn the Festival of Thanks for the increase of their little fields, were moved by the same impulse that reared the altar to Demeter and Ceres. Yet somehow they seem to be on less intimate terms with nature; to think of the blessings of the autumn season as bestowed by the providence of the One God the Father may be more in accord with reason or theological fashion, but it is hardly as beautiful as to feel their source in the loving-kindness of a divine woman.

But autumn has another aspect. The garnered stores, the bare fields, the leafless trees that soon follow the close of summer, all declare the season of decay, to be followed by the season of death. Autumn in our zone is unique among the seasons. It is a dual season, and yet a unity. It is at once the happiest and the saddest time of the year—the "season of mists and mellow fruitfulness," and the season of "the melancholy days."

Above all in the later days, when suns are low and the light more sombre, when the first frost has dropped the leaves to earth and "the chill year drives the birds beyond the sea to sunny lands," when skies are thick and gray and the cold rains begin, when

> Gone hath the Spring, with all its flowers,
>   And gone the Summer's pomp and show,
> And Autumn, in his leafless bowers,
>   Is waiting for the Winter's snow,

then is autumn indeed the saddest of the seasons. Its image lives
in the mind as that of no other season:

> The melancholy days are come, the saddest of the year,
> Of wailing winds, and naked woods, and meadows brown
> and sere.
> Heaped in the hollows of the grove, the autumn leaves
> lie dead;
> They rustle to the eddying gust, and to the rabbit's
> tread;
> The robin and the wren are flown, and from the shrubs
> the jay,
> And from the wood-top calls the crow through all the
> gloomy day.

Yet autumn is not of two separate and diverse characters. It is
a unity.

The suggestion of melancholy is indeed always at hand in
autumn. When the fruits are still mellowing on the trees, when
the tents of corn are still pitched in the fields, before the russet-
yellows and scarlets and red-browns have spread their carpet in
the wood, before "November chill blaws loud wi' angry sugh,"
autumn is already the season of sadness and solemnity. From the
first linkèd-long-drawn-out chant of the locust in the soft nights
of summer, melancholy enters upon her reign. She waxes as the
weeks go by. In the midst of the year's abundance, in the midst
of calm and repose in field and forest, there is felt on every hand
the presence of the Great Enemy—or the Great Friend. Fulfilment
is always solemn; fruition is less joyous than promise. The journey's end finds the pilgrim more sober than its progress. The
ending of growth is the beginning of decay. Our ancestors-in-the-
spirit about the Mediterranean were in keeping with nature when
long ago they placed in autumn the Day of the Dead their northern children know as All Souls'. The ways of autumn suggest
death, as those of spring suggest life. Autumn is melancholy.

But autumn is none the less the happiest season, the season of
melancholy indeed, but of divinest melancholy.

> Hail, thou goddess, sage and holy,
> Hail, divinest Melancholy!

The essence of the matter is that autumn is a harmony, a blending in perfection of happiness and sadness. Her gayety is tempered to soberness by the solemn witness everywhere of work completed and death at hand. Her sadness is tempered to acquiescence by the suggestion on every hand of fulfilment accomplished and repose assured. At no other time is nature's invitation to rest so gentle and so consoling. Autumn is the season neither of joy nor of sadness: she is the season of blessedness.

All the seasons are rich. Autumn only, so deeply of the spirit is her harmony, is most golden. The temperate year is a rich diversity of rich seasons. Fortunate, more than fortunate, did they know their own blessings, they who receive year after year the rich gift of God!—

> Rich gift of God! A year of time!
>   What pomp of rise and shut of day,
> What hues wherewith our northern clime
>   Makes autumn's dropping woodlands gay,
> What airs outblown from ferny cells,
> And clover-bloom and sweet-brier smells,
> What songs of brooks and birds, what fruits and
>   flowers,
> Green woods and moonlit snows, have in its round
>   been ours!

HORACE AND LIBERTY

AT about the age of twenty-six Horace was introduced to Mæcenas, the intimate adviser of Augustus who is sometimes called his prime minister. About six years afterward, the poet received from Mæcenas the Sabine Farm, thus coming into possession of the much beloved retreat thirty miles from Rome which he thought of as his "citadel in the mountains." Mæcenas continued throughout life to be his patron and friend. His dying request of the Emperor, in 8 B.C. a few months before the death of his poet friend, was to "keep Horatius Flaccus in mind as you would me myself."

Horace had from the first been in the good graces of Augustus also. His biographer tells us that the Emperor, after reading several of the *Satires* and finding no mention of himself, complained because Horace did not choose to address him—"or are you afraid you will lose your reputation with posterity because you seem to have been my friend?" As a result, the poet began his second book of *Epistles* with four lines addressed to Augustus. The first book had been dedicated to Mæcenas, as had been the first three books of *Odes* and the first book of *Satires*.

"While you are engaged single-handed in so many great undertakings," Horace writes to the Emperor in this introduction, "while you are safeguarding the fortunes of Italy with arms, adorning her with morals, improving her with laws, I should be sinning against the general good were I to consume your time in a long address, O Cæsar."

Ten years after the publication of *Odes* I-III, in 13 B.C. at the bidding of Augustus the poet published a fourth book of *Odes* containing poems in honor of the Emperor and his stepsons Tiberius and Drusus. Horace was thus at the age of fifty-two the court poet or laureate.

The patronage of Mæcenas and the friendly interest of Augustus made Horace financially independent and gave him social currency for the last thirty of his fifty-eight years. This did not, however, take from him his freedom of action and opinion, or make him servile. In one of the *Epistles*, he declares his readiness to surrender all that Mæcenas has given him if he is not to be allowed his liberty. The favors of the minister have been bestowed not as a charity but as the reward for genuine worth. The manner of Horace's assertion of independence is such as to make Mæcenas stand well with the reader, but it is also not the sort of declaration a dependent would make.

Horace, writing to his patron, used one of his many simple country stories to point his moral:

A little fox had crept through a narrow opening into a bin of grain, and after feasting was trying in vain with his full body to get out again. To him a weasel looking on: "If you want to get safely out of there," said she, "you must come back to the narrow hole thin just as you went into it thin." If this figures my obligation in this case, I make over to you again everything. I am not the one to praise the sleep of the poor while I am surfeited with dainty living, and I will not exchange my perfect freedom for the riches of the Arabians. You have often praised me as a modest man, and you have heard yourself called by me patron and father to your face, and I have called you so as freely in other company. Try me, and see whether I cannot give you back your gifts, and gladly.

Nor with the Emperor was the poet less independent. Not only did he not until urged by Augustus include him among the many prominent men addressed in his writings, but he declined the Emperor's appointment of him as private secretary. Nor can it be said that his praises of the Emperor and others of the imperial family were insincere. His long maturing conviction that Roman fortunes were in good hands was manifest years before he was invited to celebrate the achievements of the new régime.

To assume that Horace's relations with the Emperor and his minister and court carried with them no constraint whatever, would be to credit him with a degree of detachment rarely attained in the sorry history of human behavior. We need not hesitate, however, to believe that his esteem for them as persons, his approval of their purposes, and the consciousness of the sincerity and value of his coöperation, left him with the feeling of independence and dignity.

But being independent morally was not Horace's whole conception of liberty. He was a poet, and wanted the command of his time for the courting of inspiration and the application of the file. He wanted no prescribed duties to keep him from the Muse, and to leave him fatigued and unfit at the end of their discharge. It may be mentioned, too, that he was a man of indolent tastes who did not marry, who liked to do as he pleased in the matter of rising and retiring, who liked contemplation whether by himself in his chamber or as he went on leisurely rambles and observed the human scene, and whose mind worked best when left to work at its own bidding.

Then I go to my night's rest, not worried because I must rise early next morning and go to face Marsyas and business. Up to the fourth hour I lie abed. After that I take a stroll, or read or write by myself to suit my mood, and then take an olive-oil rub. But when I am tired by exercise and the mounting sun admonishes me to go and bathe, I desert the field and the three-cornered ball game. After a sparing lunch, only enough to keep me from going through the day with an empty stomach, I take my leisure by myself. This is the life of those free from the burdens and miseries of ambition.

Nor was freedom from imperial constraint and from the restrictions of settled occupation all that entered into Horace's ideal of the poet's liberty. More important than either were the freedom and repose of the contented mind: freedom from ambition for a place in the government employ or for the prestige of the socially ostentatious; freedom from the desire to increase his wealth beyond what reasonably satisfied the need of an unpretentious poet and philosopher. There are open to liberty-loving men two roads to freedom, as to ambitious men there are open two roads to wealth. "I shall better increase my scant revenues by contracting my desires," says Horace, "than if I were lord of Phrygia and added thereto the realms of Crœsus: to those who desire much, much also is wanting"; meaning what Carlyle meant when he said that the fraction of life increased in value not so much by increasing the numerator as by lessening the denomina-

GARDEN OF ALBERGO DEL SOLE AT POMPEII

VENAFRO AND ITS OLIVE GROVES

A POSSIBLE BUST OF HORACE

"NEQUE ME SUB ARTA VITE BIBENTEM"

tor. In like manner, the freedom of men may be made more ample by the contracting of desire. The constraints of poverty are less to those who fix their desires less upon the riches of this world.

We are always charmed by Horace's gospel of contentment with little—"to those who demand many things, many things are lacking: well is it for him to whom God with sparing hand hath given enough." His prayer before Apollo on the dedication day of the temple on the Palatine, October 9, 28 B.C., near the close of his thirty-seventh year, is one of the world's wisest and most human prayers:

> Health to enjoy the blessings sent
> From heaven; a mind unclouded, strong;
> A cheerful heart; a wise content;
> An honored age; and song.

Horace's ideal of liberty went further still. It included freedom from the domination of the more elemental passions—the passion of anger, the passion of cruelty, the passion of miserly greed, the passion of fear, the passion of the drunkard, the passion of the lover. Here again, he would have us lessen the denominator. The fear of ingloriousness will not enslave the man who dominates the desire for glory. The constraint of physical fear will not lie upon the man not bound by the desire to live at any cost.

Spurn from thee the pleasures of sense; pleasure purchased with pain is harm. The avaricious man is always in want; set definite ends to thy desires. The envious man grows thin as he views the riches of another; the tyrants of Sicily invented no torture greater than envy. Anger is brief madness; rule thy spirit. . . . To look upon nothing with covetous eye is the only thing that can make and keep one happy.

If we are to ask how strictly Horace conformed to his ideal of freedom from the passions, we must first remember that a total abstinence from them—from wine, from love, from ambition, from gain, even from anger—was not his purpose. Not renunciation, but control, was his platform. When appetite began to demand satisfaction rather than to accept, it was already on the way to demand the mastery. The passion that did not minister but was ministered unto was a destroyer of happiness. It was not a question of the all or nothing of Ibsen's Brand, but of the how much or how little.

We must not look to Horace for asceticism or for sympathy with it. If we could recall him from the Elysian Fields to which we trust the kindly Fates allowed him entrance, and if we could discourse with him of liberty as it affects the ordinary relations of living, Horace would be in agreement with us. If we were to push on to the purchase of liberty through the austerities of self-denial and self-sacrifice, he would probably call us extreme, and even fantastic. With what might be termed the ecstasy of self-domination he would have little patience. Life and its gifts, for Horace, were to be used, and were to be used in this life. They were to be used because they gave pleasure here and now, not renounced in order that through renunciation they might be the means of demonstrating the stern virtue of self-control. He would have been quite sure to remind us of the Golden Mean.

We can easily imagine the poet indulging in a good-natured little homily, to this effect:

I am in accord with you as regards the virtues. Be faithful to family, friends, religion, and State, and let not inordinate desire for any of the goods of this life take from you your independence; but, on the other hand, do not go so far in the quest of liberty as to defeat your own ends and miss the very purpose of liberty. Go slowly, use your reason, and don't be overanxious to penetrate the secret of existence. You will never know the All, and it was never meant that you should, but you do know what is about you.

> Seek not to pierce the morrow's haze,
> But for the moment render praise.

If there really is a purpose in the Universe, be sure it will be fulfilled without your taking too much thought. You talk about the other world and the gods—or God, as you please. Why not leave something to them?

> All else entrust the gods to keep.
> Whose nod can lull the winds to sleep,
> Vexing the ash and cypress agèd,
> Or battling over the boiling deep.

But let us not inquire further as to Horace's consistency. Above all, let us not make the mistake of those who match the philosophy of life of his more mature years with the gross conduct implied (and only implied) in his youthful works. Whether or not Horace indulged in wine or women to the hurt of his happiness is not so important as the fact that his ideas on liberty are always stimulating, and have inspired many men to profounder thought and happier living. A pagan and unaware of the Christian philosophy of life soon to add so much to his own, he starts us nevertheless into paths of pleasant thinking. To adopt his own figure from *De Arte Poetica,* he functions "in the manner of the whetstone, able to give a keen edge, though itself not cutting."

. XXIX .

THE EMPEROR AT HOME

AUGUSTUS has been called the Architect of the Roman Empire. He took the material assembled by Julius Cæsar, shaped it, and erected it into a solid and enduring edifice. This is perhaps not giving enough credit to the Dictator. Julius Cæsar had not only assembled what he found and what he created, but had begun its erection. Both in the city of Rome and in Roman territory at large, Augustus found a basement and framework whose need was not so much amplification as it was solidifying, partitioning, finishing, and providing with the means of operation. He began the task, a boy of eighteen and a half, when in early April, 44 B.C., he left school at Apollonia in Epirus for Brundisium and Rome to claim his inheritance. On January 1, 27, when he entered the Senate to announce the restoration of constitutional authority, it could be assumed that the task was finished.

By far the largest portion of Augustus's lifetime was spent inside the city of Rome, as by far the largest part of Julius Cæsar's was passed abroad. The Dictator's work was done in person and on the spot and with his own hands. Augustus wrought with the hands of others. From the hour he set foot on Italian soil, a youth with no official standing and no troops, "he acted with the circumspection, the caution, the astuteness, and the adroitness of an experienced politician." He somehow kept a cool head and perhaps a clear one in the uncertain times before Philippi destroyed the hopes of the old régime and made him part master of a disordered world. At Philippi he profited by Antony's military genius, and later by the soldierly capacities of Agrippa, Messalla, and Tiberius. In only two of his foreign wars, the Cantabrian and the Illyrican, did he participate in person. For advice in the statesmanship of reconstruction he drew on Agrippa and

Mæcenas, on the ablest of the old governing class, and on friendly talent wherever found. The governors of the provinces were his personal choice, and personally responsible.

Not least of all did the Emperor use the literary talent of the day. Once he had brought to its end a century of violence and the world had seen in the fact his divine warrant, Virgil and Horace by expressing the admirations and hopes of the times not only crystallized the ideal of Emperor and Empire in the minds of men, but set the standards by which thenceforth they must measure themselves.

Augustus was born in Rome on the 23rd of September, 63 B.C. He first left the city and Italy at little more than sixteen, when he pleased his granduncle Julius by making his way to join him unexpectedly in Spain in the campaign ending with the defeat of the Pompeians at Munda in March, 45 B.C. Soon after the return, he was sent to Apollonia, across the Adriatic, where he was still in school when the news of Cæsar's assassination came. The campaign at Philippi took him away from Italy in 42 B.C.; the protracted troubles on the sea with Sextus Pompeius called him to Sicilian waters in 36 B.C.; from 35 to 33 B.C. he was engaged much of the time in the subjugation of Illyricum; the latter part of 31 B.C., all of 30 B.C., and the first half of 29 B.C. were occupied by the campaign at Actium and the expedition to Egypt and the East against Antony and Cleopatra; from 27 to 24 B.C. he was in Spain, compelling to obedience a country which had been rebellious for two centuries; and in 16 to 13 B.C. he was three years in Gaul, laying the permanent foundations for its government. After his fiftieth year, he seems not to have gone outside the borders of Italy, and he was probably not long away from Rome. His total absence from Italy was about twelve years of the seventy-seven of his life.

Nor was Augustus's life away from Italy the dashing and adventurous sort so fascinating in the story of Julius Cæsar. It is not likely that even a commentary by his own hand would shed upon the safe and sane campaigns of the Emperor the glamour of Cæsar's great adventure in Gaul. It is to the life of Augustus in the city and in his home that the reader will turn for greater interest. The pages of Suetonius transform the calculating auto-crat, the unfeeling man of blood and iron whose image is carried in the minds of most of us, into a human being for whom it is possible to feel a sympathy, or even compassion.

Augustus was born just before sunrise on the ninth day before the Calends of October in the consulship of Marcus Tullius Cicero and Gaius Antonius, at the Ox-Heads in the Palatine quarter....

At the age of four he lost his father. In his twelfth year he delivered a funeral oration to the assembled people in honor of his grandmother Julia. Four years later, after assuming the gown of manhood, he received military prizes at Cæsar's African triumph, though he had taken no part in the war on account of his youth....

He lived at first near the Forum Romanum, above the Stairs of the Ringmakers, in a house which had belonged to the orator Calvus; afterwards, on the Palatine, but in the no less modest dwelling of Hortensius, which was remarkable neither for size nor elegance, having but a short colonnade with columns of Alban stone, and rooms without any marble decorations or handsome pavements. For more than forty years too he used the same bedroom in winter and summer; although he found the city unfavorable to his health in the winter, yet continued to winter there. If ever he planned to do anything in private or without interruption, he had a retired place at the top of the house, which he called "Syracuse" and "technyphion." In this he used to take refuge, or else in the villa of one of his freedmen in the suburbs; but whenever he was not well, he slept at Mæcenas's house.

For retirement he went most frequently to places by the sea and the islands of Campania, or to the towns near Rome, such as Lanuvium, Praeneste, or Tibur, where he very often held court in the colonnades of the Temple of Hercules. He disliked large and sumptuous country palaces, actually razing to the ground one which his granddaughter Julia built on a lavish scale. His own villas, which were modest enough, he decorated not so much with handsome statues and pictures as with terraces, groves, and objects noteworthy for their antiquity and rarity; for example, at Capreae the monstrous bones of huge sea monsters and wild beasts, called the "bones of the giants" and the "weapons of the heroes."

The simplicity of his furniture and household goods may be seen from couches and tables still in existence, many of which are scarcely fine enough for a private citizen. They say that he always slept on a low and plainly furnished bed. Except on special occasions he wore common clothes for the house, made by his sister, wife, daughter or granddaughters; his togas were neither close nor full, his purple stripe neither narrow nor broad, and his shoes somewhat high-soled, to make him look taller than he really was. But he always kept shoes and clothing to wear in public ready in his room for sudden and unexpected occasions. . . .

To enable more men to take part in the administration of the State, he devised new offices: the charge of public buildings, of the roads, of the aqueducts, of the channel of the Tiber, of the distribution of grain to the people, as well as the prefecture of the city. . . . He desired also to revive the ancient fashion of dress. . . . To show that he was a prince who desired the public welfare rather than popularity, when the people complained of the scarcity and high price of wine, he sharply rebuked them by saying: "My son-in-law Agrippa has taken good care, by building several aqueducts, that men shall not go thirsty." . . .

He exchanged social calls with many, and did not cease to attend all their anniversaries, until he was well on in years and was once incommoded by the crowd on the day of a betrothal. When Gallus Cerinius, a senator with whom he was not at all intimate, had become blind and had therefore resolved to end his life by starvation, Augustus called on him and by his consoling words induced him to live. . . .

No one suffered for his freedom of speech or insolence. He did not even dread the lampoons against him which were scattered in the senate house, but took great pains to refute them; and without trying to discover the authors, he merely proposed that hereafter such as published notes or verses defamatory of anyone under a false name should be called to account. . . .

Since the city was not adorned as the dignity of the Empire demanded, and was exposed to flood and fire, he so beautified it that he could justly boast that he had found it built of brick and left it in marble. He made it safe too for the future, so far as human foresight could provide for this.

He built many public works, in particular the following: his forum with the Temple of Mars the Avenger, the Temple of Apollo on the Palatine, and the fane of Jupiter the Thunderer on the Capitol. His reason for building the forum was the increase in the number of the people and of cases at law, which seemed to call for a third forum, since two were no longer adequate. Therefore it was opened to the public with some haste, before the Temple of Mars was finished, and it was provided that the public prosecutions be held there apart from the rest, as well as the selection of jurors by lot. He had made a vow to build the Temple of Mars in the war of Philippi, which he undertook to avenge his father; accordingly he decreed that in it the Senate should consider wars and claims for triumphs, from it those who were on their way to the provinces with military commands should be escorted, and to it victors on their return should bear the tokens of their triumphs. He reared the Temple of Apollo in that part of his house on the Palatine for which the soothsayers declared that the god had shown his desire by striking it with lightning. He joined to it colonnades with Latin and Greek libraries, and when he was getting to be an old man he often held meetings of the Senate there as well, and revised the lists of jurors. He dedicated the shrine to Jupiter the Thunderer because of a narrow escape; for on his Cantabrian expedition during a march by night, a flash of lightning grazed his litter and struck the slave dead who was carrying a torch before him. He constructed some works too in the name of others, his grandsons to wit, his wife and his sister, such as the Colonnade and Basilica of Gaius and Lucius; also the colonnades of Livia and Octavia, and the Theater of Marcellus. More than that, he often urged other prominent men to adorn the city with new monuments or to restore and embellish old ones, each according to his means. And many such works were built at that time by many men; for example, the Temple of Hercules of the Muses by Marcius Philippus, the Temple of Diana by Lucius Cornificius, the Hall of Liberty by Asinius Pollio, the Temple of Saturn by Munatius Plancus, a theater by Cornelius Balbus, an amphitheater by Statilius Taurus, and by Marcus Agrippa in particular many magnificent structures.

He divided the area of the city into regions and wards, arranging that the former should be under the charge of magistrates selected each year by lot, and the latter under "masters" elected by the inhabitants of the respective neighborhoods. To guard against fires he devised a system of stations of night watchmen, and to control the floods he widened and cleared out the channel of the Tiber, which had for some time been filled with rubbish and narrowed by jutting buildings. Further, to make the approach to the city easier from every direction, he personally undertook to rebuild the Flaminian Road all the way to Ariminum, and assigned the rest of the highways to others who had been honored with triumphs, asking them to use their prize money in paving them.

The recognizable Augustan monuments in Rome today are the remnants of the Rostra, removed from the Comitium and enlarged in 42 B.C. or soon after; the great floor of the Basilica Julia, a building begun by Cæsar, finished after his death by Augustus, burned, and rededicated in 12 B.C.; the foundations of the Temple of Julius Cæsar, dedicated 29 B.C.; the shell of the Mausoleum, 28 B.C.; the foundations of the Arch in the Forum, 19 B.C.; the shell of the Theater of Marcellus, 13 B.C.; the towering walls of the Forum

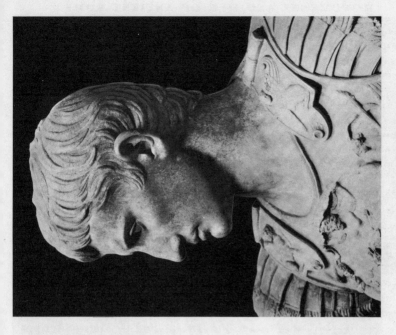

AUGUSTUS AS IMPERATOR

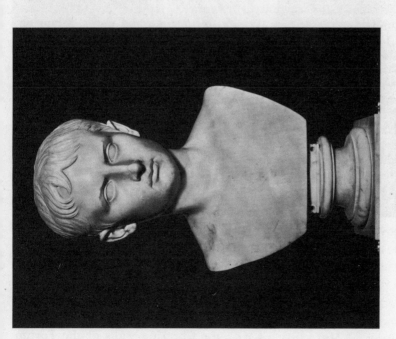

THE YOUNG AUGUSTUS

AUGUSTUS AS PRIEST

of Augustus, with its Temple of Mars, 2 B.C. The house of the
Emperor, perhaps the one called now the House of Livia, perhaps the ruins under the Flavian Palace floor, was built from the
public funds, and finished in 27 B.C. The Temple of Apollo on
the Palatine, whose dedication on October 9, 28 B.C., was wit-
nessed by Horace and Propertius, is seen by some scholars in the
great foundations to the east of the House of Livia.

He surpassed all his predecessors in the frequency, variety, and mag-
nificence of his public shows. He says that he gave games four times
in his own name and twenty-three times for other magistrates, who
were either away from Rome or lacked means. He gave them sometimes in all the wards and on many stages with actors in all languages,
and combats of gladiators not only in the Forum or the amphitheater,
but in the Circus and in the Sæpta; sometimes, however, he gave
nothing except a fight with wild beasts. He gave athletic contests too
in the Campus Martius, erecting wooden seats; also a sea-fight, con-
structing an artificial lake near the Tiber, where the grove of the
Cæsars now stands. On such occasions he stationed guards in various
parts of the city, to prevent it from falling a prey to brigands because
of the few people who remained at home. . . .
But at the height of his happiness and his confidence in his family
and its training, Fortune proved fickle. He found the two Julias, his
daughter and granddaughter, guilty of every form of vice, and ban-
ished them. He lost Gaius and Lucius within the span of eighteen
months, for the former died in Lycia and the latter at Massilia. He
then publicly adopted his third grandson Agrippa and at the same
time his stepson Tiberius by a bill passed in the assembly of the
curiae; but he soon disowned Agrippa because of his low tastes and
violent temper, and sent him off to Surrentum.
He bore the death of his kin with far more resignation than their
misconduct. For he was not greatly broken by the fate of Gaius and
Lucius, but he informed the Senate of his daughter's fall through a
letter read in his absence by a quæstor, and for very shame would
meet no one for a long time, and even thought of putting her to
death. At all events, when one of her confidantes, a freedwoman
called Phœbe, hanged herself at about that same time, he said: "I
would rather have been Phœbe's father." . . .
On the last day of his life he asked every now and then whether
there was any disturbance without on his account; then calling for a
mirror, he had his hair combed and his falling jaws set straight. . . .
While he was asking some newcomers from the city about the daughter of Drusus, who was ill, he suddenly passed away as he was kissing

Livia, uttering these last words: "Live mindful of our wedlock, Livia, and farewell," thus blessed with an easy death and such a one as he had always longed for. . . .

His body was carried by the senators of the municipalities and colonies from Nola all the way to Bovillae, in the night time because of the season of the year, being placed by day in the basilica of the town at which they arrived or in its principal temple. At Bovillae the members of the equestrian order met it and bore it to the city, where they placed it in the vestibule of his house. . . .

His eulogy was twice delivered: before the Temple of the Deified Julius by Tiberius, and from the old Rostra by Drusus, son of Tiberius; and he was carried on the shoulders of senators to the Campus Martius and there cremated. There was even an ex-prætor who took oath that he had seen the form of the Emperor, after he had been reduced to ashes, on its way to heaven. His remains were gathered up by the leading men of the equestrian order, bare-footed and in ungirt tunics, and placed in the Mausoleum. This structure he had built in his sixth consulship between the Via Flaminia and the bank of the Tiber, and at the same time opened to the public the groves and walks by which it was surrounded.

THE EMPEROR'S LAST RESTING PLACE

B ESIDES the foundations of the arch erected in 19 B.C.
to commemorate the return of the standards lost in the
battle of Carrhae in 53 B.C., the substructures of the
Temple of Julius Cæsar, dedicated in 29 B.C., the foundations of
the Basilica Julia, rebuilt by Augustus and dedicated by him in
12 B.C., various beautiful fragments of the Altar of Peace, and the
Theater of Marcellus, recently disengaged from mediæval and
modern buildings and made a national monument, there are two
grand monuments remaining from Augustan times. One is the
Forum of Augustus, excavated and disengaged within the past
few years, and now to be seen with its mighty enclosure walls and
temple remains in all their immensity. The other is the
Mausoleum, the tomb in the grand style in which the Emperor's
ashes were laid to rest.

The Mausoleum is the most personal and the most moving of
all the Augustan monuments. Let us look for a moment upon the
eventful fortunes of the famous pile.

Rising between the Tiber and the northward road from Rome
in 28 B.C., forty-two years after the birth of Virgil and thirty-five
after that of the Emperor, when he was "in the middle of the
course of our life"—

Nel mezzo del cammin di nostra vita—

the Mausoleum was used for the first time in 23 B.C., in his fortieth
year, when the groanings of the brave were wafted from Mars's
broad field to Mars's mighty town as Father Tiber, flowing past
that new-built sepulchre, beheld Marcellus, the hope of the
Emperor and the hope of Rome, dead at twenty, carried into its
solemn portals. It continued for a hundred and twenty-one years
more as the burial place of the Julio-Claudians and some of their

successors, though denied the ashes of the two Julias and of Nero, until with Trajan the imperial dead were laid elsewhere, and it settled into stately and venerable dignity as a historic monument. For the four hundred and thirty-eight years that passed from its erection to Alaric's time, it remained a mighty witness of its founder's greatness.

In the days succeeding the night of August 24, 410 A.D., when Alaric entered the gates of the aging and helpless city, the Mausoleum probably first felt the hand of violence. This made easy the descent to abandonment and desolation. Despoiled, crumbling, neglected, in the centuries leading into the darkness it towered a lonely ruin above the general ruin of the sinking city. In the twelfth century it was a fortress of the Colonna. On May 30, 1167, in their hatred of the Colonna prince, the Romans destroyed the fortress. In 1225 it was again in Colonna hands, in 1241 once more it was stormed. On October 11, 1354, in a place called Campo dell' Austa, the body of unhappy Cola di Rienzo was burned.

The Orsini succeeded the Colonna. Decay was reinforced by destruction. The precious marble and firm travertine were stripped from the great pile or pried from its interiors, broken into convenient sizes, and burned into lime or worked into the makeshift walls of a mediæval town. The upper interior crumbled and collapsed, and left the great tomb roofless. The ages of dismantling and decay left behind so little of travertine and marble that none but the expert would think of the ancient building as other than the vast bulk of brick and concrete still standing solidly but imbedded in modern building and all but invisible.

In the early 1500's, the church and hospital of San Rocco were built at the south entrance of the Mausoleum, where part of one of the two obelisks flanking the portal still survived. Peruzzi's sketches in the Uffizi are proof that the marble revetment of the great drum was at least in part still there. Then came the Soderini, converting the whole into an Italian garden, trim with landscape architecture and decoration of antique statuary; and then the Fioravanti; and then the rich Portuguese, the Marquis Benedetto Correa de Sylva, who in 1780 rented it to Bernardo Matas, a

Spaniard, who conducted an inn lodged in its ruins and transformed the garden interior into a Plaza de Toros or arena for
bullfighting—the *toros,* however, being the familiar Italian buffalo. The enterprise not succeeding, after three years Bernardo
Matas surrendered his holding to the Marquis Vincenzo Correa,
who added to the buffalo tournaments "singing daily and nightly,
the chase of the wild boar, the bucket-game, the sack race, fireworks on festa evenings, and the aerostatic globe." Such was his
success that the Corea, as it was called, became the vogue—"the
favorite resort of beauty and elegant youth." A permanent amphitheater was begun in 1796. In 1810 a stage was erected, and there
were late afternoon performances, which were suspended at Ave
Maria while the bells of San Rocco rang.

This dramatic period, the most brilliant in the history of the
ruin, came to an end in 1829 with the prohibition of the jousts
and fireworks because of damp and the fear of malaria, an equestrian circus after a time taking the place of the old performance.
Nor did the glass roof of Count Telfener halt the declining fortunes of the place. The Roman audiences, hitherto attracted by the
privilege of enjoying the open air, fell away, and the Public Safety
ultimately ordered a closing because of insufficient exit facilities.

For many years the Mausoleum stood closed and empty. It was
proposed to make it a museum for sculptural casts, and it did
finally come into use for a time as the atelier for the equestrian
statue of Victor Emmanuel II which now adorns the Monument
on Piazza Venezia.

Then came the twentieth century and a new era. In 1907, the
city of Rome obtained the unhappy monument from the State,
refitted it, and made it the concert theater of Rome, the Augusteo.
In its 3,600 seats, usually priced from 25 cents to $1.50, for over
twenty-five years the thousands of Rome's music lovers, with thousands of the music lovers among the world's lovers of Rome, had
the supreme delight of the world's masterpieces performed by
Roman orchestras in one of the world's most comfortable, most
novel, and most inspiring concert halls.

Many who have attended concerts in this great musical studio
of Rome have seen, on their passing in and out, certain gigantic

walls of concrete and facings of reticulate masonry, with many blocks of travertine, suggesting the presence, below the modern floor of the hall and the corridors leading to it, of the massive lower parts of the structure, which were covered by the falling in of the roof and upper members and have remained untouched since the Soderini gardens were planned. In the summer of 1926, and again in the autumn of 1927, the exploration of these parts was undertaken.

The proposed undertaking had to be carried out by means of shafts and galleries; the Augusteo continued throughout as the usual auditorium. To enter these passages was like traversing the tunnels of an ordinary mine. They have made possible for the first time in modern centuries, not only the penetration of the inner chambers of the tomb, but the accurate understanding of its ground plan.

The Mausoleum of Augustus was 90 metres, or 290 feet, in diameter. The modern street level and the main floor of the Augusteo are some twenty-one feet above the floor of the ancient tomb. The gigantic shell, once heavily veneered with marble, and up to 1935 visible only in the court which is entered from Via Ripetta, is bordered within at the base by twelve empty chambers crossed by spurs of masonry—the whole for no purpose other than to form a support for the great mass above them. These twelve are paralleled within by other twelve which have the same function. Inside these two concentric rings of twelve structural voids is a third concentric ring, this time of uninterrupted void, forming a corridor from which two doorways lead into a fourth ring or corridor like the third, whose inner wall enclosed the actual crypt. Here, around what was either a central pillar of stone or masonry which rose through the entire massive building to its summit to form a support for the statue which was at its apex, or, less likely, a shaft serving the same purpose but also containing a stairway mounting to the upper air, is a final corridor, this time with niches.

In this innermost corridor about the central shaft or pillar, and perhaps in the second corridor surrounding it, in the niches and on the floor against the walls, were placed the urns that en-

CANINA'S IDEA OF THE MAUSOLEUM OF AUGUSTUS

PLAN OF THE MAUSOLEUM OF AUGUSTUS

THE TIBER AND THE ROOF OF THE AUGUSTEO

THE MARCELLUS INSCRIPTION

veloped the ashes of the imperial dead from Marcellus in 23 B.C.
to Nerva in 98 of the Christian era. In these precincts, which had
lain in cold obstruction and darkness for the many hundreds of
years since last the spoiler had mined them for their marbles and
travertine, were found, in 1926, a base with a dedication to the
Emperor Nerva; and, in 1927, besides a statue fragment and the
mutilated blocks of marble in whose upper parts were the cavities
into which had been placed the urns containing the ashes of the
Augustan dead, another giant block of marble, inscribed in the
grand style, already reduced by the cutting away of upper and
lower parts, and half prepared for a further division into two by
a chisel which had been driven along the course of a line of the
most magnificent capitals in history. The letters cancelled and the
letters preserved are not the epitaph of Augustus, but the names
of his sister and his sister's son.

MARCELLUS G F	OCTAVIA
GENER	SOROR
AUGUSTI CAESARIS	AUGUSTI CAESARIS

"Marcellus the son of Gaius, son-in-law of Augustus Cæsar;
Octavia, sister of Augustus Cæsar." Hither, in the year 11 of the
old era, twelve years after Marcellus had been left in the dark
profundity of the tomb strewn with full hands of lilies and bright-
hued flowers, came the mother to join the son—the son whose
name in Virgil's verse as he read before her she could not hear
without a piercing of the heart; to be followed, after five and
twenty years of care and disillusionment and loneliness, by the
aged and weary but unbroken Emperor who in the last hour
called in his friends and asked them whether he seemed to them
to have acted well the comedy of life, and then added:

> Since well I've played my part, all clap your hands,
> And from the stage dismiss me with applause.

. XXXI .

A CENTURY OF EMPERORS

THE city which Augustus found brick and left marble, and the State which he found in chaos and left a well-ordered and established Empire, did not cease in their development when the Emperor made his exit from the stage on which he had played his part. The play was not yet played out; there were other actors to come.

Tiberius, son of Livia and stepson of Augustus, succeeded A.D. 14 at the age of fifty-six to the place from the hope of which early death had removed, first, Marcellus, son of Octavia, the Emperor's sister, and, next, Gaius and Lucius, sons of Julia, his daughter. Accomplished campaigner, able administrator, and of sterling character, thrust by force of circumstance quite as much as by the intrigues of Livia into a position for whose diplomacies and finesse the soldier's active directness and honesty were not sufficient qualifications, the twenty-three years of his reign so tried and warped the nature of Tiberius that during his later years he removed himself both from the sight and from the sympathies of men. The villa on the heights of Capri saw more of him than the imperial residence on the Palatine Hill which, with a memorial arch and the rebuilding of the Temple of Castor and Pollux in the Forum, was his contribution to the building growth of Rome.

The Palace of Tiberius, on the brow of the Palatine facing the Temple of Jupiter Optimus Maximus across the deep Vela-brum on the Capitoline Hill, was enlarged and in part replaced by the Palace of Caligula, his successor, twenty-five-year-old son of Germanicus, who was grandson of Empress Livia, and Agrippina, daughter of Agrippa and Julia the daughter of Augustus. Its huge foundations, utilized and covered by later builders, may be seen here and there in the great masses of brick

CALIGULA

TIBERIUS

THE CLAUDIAN AQUEDUCT

and concrete ruin overhanging the Temple of Castor and Pollux in the southeast corner of the Forum. It was in this temple that the crack-brained young Emperor "Little Boots," so nicknamed by the soldiers in camp with whom his father and mother were popular, inserted himself between the twin gods Castor and Pollux in order to share with them the adoration of worshippers; and it was probably over its roof and that of the neighboring Basilica Julia that the notorious "bridge" ran by which Caligula crossed from the palace to his communions with Jupiter Best and Greatest in the temple on the Capitoline. The great circus of Caligula, into whose ruins Constantine built the original Church of Saint Peter's, succeeded in the sixteenth century by the present Saint Peter's, was the place in which the Christians of Nero's time, charged with being incendiaries and with hatred of the human kind, "were made to afford sport for the people by being covered with the skins of wild beasts and torn in pieces by dogs, or by being affixed to crosses to be set on fire, so that when the daylight had failed they might furnish light for the night as they were consumed."

Caligula, murdered by his own men in the underground gallery of his own palace, was succeeded by Claudius, his uncle, fifty-one years old, grandson of Livia, a compound of weak-mindedness, overeducation, and virtue reminding us of the sovereign sixteen hundred years later described as "the wisest fool in Christendom." Builder of a great temple on the Cælian opposite the Palatine called the Claudianum, some of whose fragments are still visible, creator of the great aqueduct whose ruins in the Campagna near the city are among the wonders of the Roman world, improver of the harbor at Ostia, organizer of the expedition to Britain A.D. 43 which completed the work of Julius Cæsar by effecting a permanent occupation, author of learned treatises on philology, and dupe of Messallina and the court, Claudius died A.D. 54 by Agrippina's poisoned mushrooms.

Nero, for whose sake not only Claudius but his son Britannicus had had to die, and for whom later Octavia his daughter, last of the line, was to die, reigned from A.D. 54 to 68. He was great-great-grandson of Augustus and great-grandson of Mark Antony, and came to the throne at seventeen. Less mad and longer in power than Caligula, youthful, impulsive, and attractive, not without gifts and generous traits, Nero was an example of character not unduly bad by nature made irresponsible by the possession of power. What his Government accomplished, as well as the extent of his goodness and badness, are still not quite definitely appraised. Estimates of his character and achievement, like his character itself, are likely to be out of balance. What he is chiefly remembered for by the average reader is his association with the martyrdom of Christians, his presumed sanction of the greatest of all Rome's fires in July, A.D. 64, which raged for nine days and nights and left the city all but annihilated, his building of the Golden House in part of the ruined area, a great assemblage of pleasure grounds and palaces a mile in extent which he described as "at last a home fit for a man," his pretentious appearances as poet and singer, and his terrible last night of wandering flight across the city and out by the Via Salaria to a shameful death. What the visitor to Rome sees to remind him of the Emperor is part of an aqueduct near the Lateran, certain chambers of the Golden House on the Esquiline above the Colosseum, and foundations beneath the Flavian Palace on the Palatine.

The year of Nero's death saw three emperors succeeding to the throne only to meet one after another with violent death. Galba made way for Otho, Otho made way for Vitellius, and Vitellius made way for the Flavian line in Vespasian and his sons Titus and Domitian. Vespasian, mountaineer, sixty years old, veteran soldier, rugged, economical, conscientious, not without humor, wrecker of Nero's Golden House, on part of whose area, restored to public use, he erected the Colosseum, builder of the Forum and Temple of Peace, and Titus, forty, conqueror of Jerusalem, who succeeded him A.D. 79 after ten years, stocky and strong like his father, "counting the day lost on which he had done no man a kindness," called "the delight of his times," commemorated in the Arch of Titus, seemed almost to demonstrate that human character after all could stand under the strain of autocratic power, and that the Augustan example of concentrated authority was not a mistake; but the younger brother Domitian, succeeding to power

NERO

CLAUDIUS

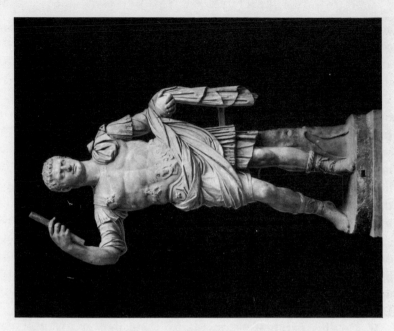

DOMITIAN

VESPASIAN

at thirty, "tall of stature, with a modest expression and a high color," "handsome and graceful," soon proved a manner of Nero, and in the fifteenth year of his reign fell victim to the violence that had removed Caligula, Claudius, Nero, Galba, Otho, and Vitellius. Besides the Colosseum, most wonderful of the world's monuments to the glorification and the commercialization of sport, and the best known of triumphal arches, preserving in sculptural relief the famous Golden Candlestick, the Flavian monuments still visible include the Temple of Vespasian at the head of the Forum, a part of the pavement of the Forum of Peace, the foundation and in part the walls of the immense and luxurious Palace on the Palatine, and remnants of the Baths of Titus.

With the Senate's election of Nerva, wise and just, considerate of the people, corrector of the wrongs of Domitian, began the happier period of the Five Good Emperors, four of whom were adoptive successors to the purple. The disappointing career of Domitian had been a manner of darkness before dawn.

It was this darkness before dawn, these days of tyranny and treachery, of irresponsible extravagance, empty-headed ostentation, and unbridled immorality, that were responsible for the rise of the greatest satirist of ancient times.

XXXII

ROME AND THE SATIRISTS

WRITTEN or literary satire in Rome began with Ennius about the end of the third century before Christ, but was hardly then the biting product usually meant by the term satire. A satire, *satura*, of Ennius was a miscellany of prose and verse which might be called a literary entertainment. Real satire began about a half century later with Lucilius, a champion of the Scipios who with vigor and directness assailed the enemies of his patrons and the enemies of virtue in general, not hesitating to use names. Not all the work of Lucilius was personal satire. The thirteen hundred and more lines of fragments preserved from his thirty books by dry-as-dust Nonius Marcellus of the fourth Christian century show that he wrote also, and perhaps principally, in the manner of Ennius.

Horace, who honored Lucilius by imitation and by willing confession of his debt, so increased the proportion of biting criticism in his satires, which he called *Sermones*, a title best translated as *Talks* or *Causeries*, that the character of satire from that time forth was established; though he describes his method as "telling the truth with a smiling face." In Persius, the young follower of Horace, A.D. 34-62, there is much less breadth of outlook, and the tone of satire is sharper.

The *Satyricon* of Petronius Arbiter, belonging to Nero's time, is still of the *mélange* type, containing both prose and verse, but is to be classed as satire in the ordinary sense as well. In Juvenal, satire becomes bitter even to violence, and there is not only no longer the pleasant miscellany of Ennius, but even the good-natured raillery of Horace has disappeared. Satire has reached its full stature.

Satire is the witty exposure of vice or folly. The epigrammatist of the W. S. Gilbert memorial on the Thames Embankment unconsciously gave it an expressive definition:

> His foe was folly
> And his weapon wit.

Satire is not mere scolding, though both have their origins in displeasure. Scolding is an angry dealing with facts or opinions which concerns two parties only, the scolder and the scolded; it is realistic and literal and direct. To be satirical, scolding or censure must concern three parties: the censor, the censured, and the disinterested or ideal audience. To concern the audience, it must be witty in content and artistic in form. If it does not amuse, if it does not stir to disapproval, if it in no wise arouses interest and liberates æsthetic emotion, it remains a matter of two parties and remains only scolding. If it does amuse or emotionally interest, it is satire, and, if recorded, becomes literary satire. If no third party is present, but scolder or scolded, or both, become conscious of witty and artistic effect, the fact of their consciousness makes them spectators, and the third party is thus supplied as the ideal audience.

The necessity of emotional interest explains why literary satire is usually in verse. There have been many satirical prose writers, but few in whom satire so predominated as to make them satirists. Thackeray, and Dickens less so, are satirical novelists, but remain novelists and not satirists. Aristophanes is a satiric writer of comedy.

The springs of satire are in the moral convictions. The bitter satirist is consumed with moral indignation; he disapproves with his whole nature. He sees wrong exaggerated, multiplied, and threatening the ruin of individual character and society. The milder type of satirist looks on, reflects, philosophically accepts the fact, and even allows it to amuse him. He is not, however, indifferent. He disapproves, but his disapproval is tempered by philosophy. Those who disapprove of nothing will never make satirists. Those who disapprove of everything are common scolds.

It is thus clear that temperament enters into satire. It is the product of feeling as well as thinking. "Life is a comedy to those who think, a tragedy to those who feel." One who is all feeling will make as poor a satirist as one who is all thinking. The disapproval caused by spite results in slander rather than satire. Disordered health and egotism are the enemies of successful satire. Excess of feeling is prejudicial, but there is the danger also of false and unwarranted feeling. A proper definition of the satiric cast of character might be, moral indignation tempered by philosophy, and a proper definition of satire, the witty and literary expression of moral indignation tempered by philosophy. It hardly need be said that wit includes humor but it is by no means always identical with it.

It should be remarked further that satire is a sophisticated kind in literature, and belongs to advanced experience in society. Satire springs from observation and reflection, and reflection presumes experience, comparison, and appraisal. It was no accident that satire came to full stature in the Roman State, in Rome the capital, and in Rome under the Empire.

The Greek State never reached the firmly embracing, well knit, and well centered character of the Roman Empire. The Athenian Empire was an easily dissolved confederation, the Athenian City State a miniature world in which literary satire was an incident of comedy; the Hellenistic State of Alexander the Great had no great capital center, but many centers which were widely separated and practically independent one of another. The virtues and the vices and follies were there, and the satiric faculty as well, but whether from the oversophistication of age and decadence which had resulted in skepticism and lack of moral indignation, or from the lack of cosmopolitan feeling regarding right and wrong, or from the actual decay of character attributed to them by the Romans, the Greeks did not leave behind them literary satire as a kind.

Satire needed the Roman State, an organism in which the virtues were all-important and in which the vices and follies of the citizen were of concern to a society quickly conscious of danger to the general good. It needed a great, cosmopolitan, capital city where the vices and follies were visible in the grand style. It needed a time when the menace of evil character and evil conduct was so great as to be imminent and startling. The Rome of Juvenal, imperial, cosmopolitan, reckless, was ripe for the satirist.

The Rome of Ennius had been a rambling, ill built, unhygienic city of several hundred thousand inhabitants. Its manhood not only belonged to an expanding State but were participators in it— as legislators, as soldiers, as administrators, as voters. The attention of the citizen during Ennius' prime was drawn to matters of moment at home and to great ventures abroad. Growth, action, and a future full of promise do not promote the satiric spirit. The pessimism, discouragement, and alarm of the moralist which underlies satiric indignation were not invited forth, and would have made but a weak bid for popularity.

The Rome of Lucilius' prime was the Rome of the final conquest of Carthage and Greece and the destruction of the cities of Carthage and Corinth. The Scipios who were the poet's patrons, and who with their followers of the Scipionic Circle were still the best expression of the Roman State, had begun to feel the enmity of radical circles, and by the time of Scipio the Younger's death in 129 B.C. the upward thrust of the popular party under the leadership of the Gracchi was far advanced.

In Horace's young manhood a century's political and personal quarrels came to a head in the decade of struggle between Cæsar the radical and Pompey the conservative, and came to an end at Actium with the ultimate removal of the enemies of Augustus from the scene. The *Sermones* of Horace, including *Epistles* as well as *Satires*, began before Actium and continued to about 13 B.C. when the poet was fifty-two and Augustus fifty, when the Roman Empire had become stable and well knit, and when the capital was growing fast into the city of marble. Horace is already thirty when the first of the *Satires* appear, and when the Second Book is published the last threat against the Augustan State has disappeared. Horace is a genial man disposed to charity, the times have brought peace, and the future under the new régime holds out bright promise. On the whole, it is folly rather than vice at which Horace directs his arrows—at men's wrong ideas of life's values, at their inconsistencies and bad taste, at their discontentment, at their silly ambitions. These foibles are not causes for alarm; rather, they are amusing to look upon. They work no great injury to the State as a whole, and, in Horace's tolerant mind at least, are not fatal to the single citizen.

But by Juvenal's time the passage of a hundred years had disabused men's minds of the expectation of a Messianic future. The marble Rome of Augustus, like the Augustan idea of "the great round of the ages beginning again," had lost much of its brilliance and all its novelty. The inrush of foreigners and the rise of the newly freed and the newly rich and the newly noble had filled the capital with a new race. The very success of the Empire had bred an irresponsible citizenry, and into the void of civic default created by paternalism, easy wealth, and idleness flowed the vices of the world. The ordinary honest citizen found his quarters endangered by falling buildings, the streets unsafe with gangsters and rich bullies, his living uncertain because of lying Greek and Oriental competitors. The new woman—the unendurable wealthy woman, the over-educated woman, the cruel woman, the adulterous woman, the woman fanatical over fortune-telling, religion, beautification, or mannishness—filled the streets of the capital. And at the other end of the scale from the unprincipled and insolent rich were the multitude of the poor and idle on the dole from rich man or State, who had learned to expect and demand as a right the favors they received, and who were as unprincipled and insolent as the wealthy patrons they flattered and insulted. The descendants of the old-time Romans had forgotten the honesty, the austerity, the pride, the loyalty and constancy, the *gravitas*, of their sires. The new Romans and their sons had never known those virtues.

Satire is exaggeration. All truth is relative, and the emphasis of any truth is in some measure a distortion of the truth as a whole. Juvenal distorts the truth as to ancient Roman society.

The readers of Juvenal in Roman times, living as they did in the presence of the total truth, were able to make allowances as they read. The reader of today, remote from the scene and bred to another environment, if he is not to be carried away by the thundering condemnations of the satirist and to be possessed by an idea of the Romans of the first century as a people hopelessly lost in morality and behavior, is in need of a corrective. He may

find it in a more generous and observant reading of Roman literature, in the letters of Pliny, for example, written in Juvenal's own
generation; he may find it in the study of the material remains of
the Empire in museums and in their proper sites; or he may find
it, as we have been finding it, in the contemplation of Romans
whose personalities, like the monuments in the grand style, have
nobly survived the assaults and obscurations of time.

In our search for the realities of Roman character in high
places, let us not be content with the story of the emperors of the
first hundred years, even though that story includes an Augustus
made human by age and experience, a Vespasian unspoiled by
power and riches, and a Titus more than worthy of his father.
Let us see what the second hundred years brought forth in imperial character.

XXXIII

THE EMPEROR ABROAD

JULIUS CÆSAR in the conquest of the Empire, and Augustus in its organization, knew at first hand the greater part of the Mediterranean world. Augustus was by far the more constant resident in Rome; yet Suetonius says of him, "I believe there is no province, excepting only Africa and Sardinia, which he did not visit; and he was planning to cross to these from Sicily after his defeat of Sextus Pompeius, but was prevented by a series of violent storms, and later had neither opportunity nor occasion to make the voyage."

The journeyings of the first two Cæsars, however, were largely compelled by necessity of arms. It is not until Hadrian that we have the Roman Empire's greatest example of personal supervision and personal interest. It is worth while to contemplate Hadrian's life as a third illustration of the imperial character.

Hadrian was born on January 24, 76 A.D., in Italica, the Roman town in Spain afterward eclipsed by the city of Seville six miles away. Italica had been founded about 205 B.C. as a veterans' colony, and the original Hadrian in Spain, whose descendants may have married into Spanish families, had migrated thither from Hadria, an Italian city on the Adriatic. The future Emperor was cousin to Trajan, twenty-two years his senior, also a native of Italica, who became his guardian on the death of Hadrian's father in A.D. 85.

Taken to Rome soon after this to be educated, he was so eager in his studies of Greek letters and Greek subjects that his schoolmates called him "the little Greek." In his fifteenth year he returned to Spain to be taught the military art, at the same time enjoying himself as a vigorous huntsman. In the year 93, at the age of seventeen, he was invited to Rome by Trajan, who was

THE EMPRESS SABINA

THE EMPEROR HADRIAN

THE COLUMN AND FORUM OF TRAJAN

PORTICO IN HADRIAN'S VILLA

already an experienced and trusted soldier, and became his protégé. The following year, at eighteen, he held certain minor civil offices in Rome, and at nineteen joined the Second Legion as tribune at what is now Budapest and was then Aquincum. At twenty he was in Mœsia, at twenty-one on the Rhine, and thus became acquainted with the Empire's entire northern boundary in Europe.

In A.D. 98, at the end of Hadrian's twenty-second year, his cousin Trajan became emperor. Spending the winter finishing his under-takings on the Rhine, Trajan in 99 took Hadrian with him to Rome, where in the following year the young man of twenty-three was married to Vibia Sabina, the Emperor's grandniece. In 101, at the age of twenty-five, Hadrian was quæstor on the Danube in Trajan's operations against the Dacians in the Rou-manian country. The years 103 to 105 he passed in Rome, returning in 105 to Dacia in the second expedition as commander of a legion for the first time. In 106, at thirty, he was prætor in Rome, and at the end of the year returned to Pannonia. In 108 he was consul, thus completing the regular round of offices.

Now came six years of comparative quiet. The statement that in 112 the Athenians made him archon may mean that in that year he visited Athens. He was with Trajan on the successful expedition against the Parthians in 113, and was said not to be enthusiastic for the Emperor's policy of thus pushing farther into the East. In 117 he was appointed governor of Syria and went to Antioch. In August of the same year, on the death of Trajan by paralysis in his sixty-fourth year at Selinus, two hundred and fifty miles from Antioch on the way toward Rome by the Cilician coast road, he became emperor, assuming authority in Antioch on the eleventh of the month, three days after the death of his predecessor. To the buildings of the magnificent Forum of Trajan, which already included the Ulpian Basilica and the famous Col-umn, the new Emperor added the Temple of Trajan and Plotina.

It was not until 118 that Hadrian arrived in Rome. After an impressive funeral celebration, including a triumph of the dead Emperor, who appeared in effigy riding in his chariot, the new Emperor departed for the Danube frontier to quiet certain rebellious tribes. This accomplished, in 121 he began the travels which occupied him almost continuously the remaining seventeen years of his life and made him one of the most remarkable of all the imperial line. Their bare enumeration is a description of his character as ruler and man.

The travels begun in 121 kept Hadrian away from Rome until 126. He went through Italy into Gaul, and thence to the upper Rhine and along its course to the sea. He crossed to Britain, and is thought to have built the famous wall, nearly eighty miles long, whose remains from Solway to Tyne are so impressive today. He returned by way of Gaul to the Mediterranean, visiting the cities of Provence now called Avignon and Nîmes, and the neighborhood. Thence he passed to Spain, visiting especially Tarraco, now Tarragona, and made an expedition into Mauretania and what is now Algeria.

These travels in the West, which included all manner of administrative and military activities, occupied two years. In 123, the Emperor left Spain for Ephesus, and began an extensive inspection of the East which lasted three years. This took him in 124 to the western coast of the province of Asia, including visits to Troy and the Hellespont, and perhaps the founding of Hadrianopolis; back to Ephesus for the winter; in 125 to Phrygia, Rhodes, and Athens, where he passed the winter; and in the spring of 126 to many cities of Greece. Returning to Rome by way of Sicily, he climbed Mount Ætna.

The Emperor arrived in Rome toward the end of 126, and remained in his capital about a year. In 128, he set out once more, this time beginning with Africa, where we learn of him at Carthage, Theveste, Timgad, and Lambæsis, all important posts of occupation and represented by many ruins today. He continued in Greece, visiting Athens, Sparta, Arcadia, Mycenae, Argos, Corinth, Megara, Thespiae, Delphi, and Eleusis, where he was initiated into the Mysteries, and returning again to Athens. It was probably on this last visit that he finished and dedicated the gigantic Temple of Olympian Zeus, 676 by 424 feet, begun three centuries before, of which fifteen colossal columns still stand— "the only temple on earth of a magnitude worthy the greatness of the god," Livy says of it. The famous Arch of Hadrian also survives, inscribed on one side, "This is the City of Theseus," and on the other, "This is the City of Hadrian."

The Emperor went on. He visited Ephesus, went up the Mæander to Laodicea, crossed the mountains to Tarsus in Cilicia, called at Samosata, the town of Lucian the satirist, returned once more to Antioch, where he climbed Mount Casius, and continued to Palmyra, Damascus, Judæa, and Egypt. At Pelusium in the Delta, he honored the neglected tomb of Pompey. In Alexandria, he enjoyed the Library and the city's men of learning. He went up the Nile to Thebes, and on November 21, 130, waited for the Memnon to utter the mystic sound of sunrise. He was probably in Rome again in 131, and left it only for the expedition to quell an uprising in Jerusalem.

It must not be thought that in these journeyings on sea and land the Emperor was merely taking his pleasure, though there is no doubt he had from travel all the intellectual and physical delight of the robust cultivated man. A walk or a march of twenty miles, bareheaded in the sun, was only pleasure to him; and his knowledge made every ancient town and monument a joy. He did not flit from place to place, and he was not idle during sojourns in them. His path was marked by new bridges, roads repaired, the erection and restoration of statues, temples, baths, and porticoes, the inauguration of aqueducts, the repair of monuments and buildings. "He built something in almost every city."

Nor were beautification and utility the Emperor's final purpose. In his busy moving from city to city and province to province he was governing the Empire. A thoroughly practised soldier, in every garrison town he reviewed the army. He studied the workings of the courts and the law in both their local and imperial effects; it was in his reign that Salvius Julianus codified the prætors' edicts, one of the Empire's greatest services to ancient and modern times. He studied administration, local and universal; he was one of the Empire's greatest organizers. His passion for system and efficiency is even charged with increasing the bureaucratic burden which was one of the causes of the Empire's ultimate decay.

It was probably after the return from his travels about 131, at the age of fifty-five, that the magnificent villa bearing his name was completed. Fifteen miles from Rome, on a rise of ground between two little streams at the base of the Sabine Hills at Tibur, the Villa of Hadrian was a wonderful combination of art and nature. More than four miles in circumference, its gushing waters, its groves, gardens, promenades, and palaces were mingled in charming disarray to delight the veteran traveller of many lands who had built, laid out, and named the villa's parts to remind him of pleasures in distant climes. There were the Greek Theater, the Stoa Poikile, and the Academy, from Athens, the Canopus from Alexandria, the Vale of Tempe, the Libraries, and even the Inferno. There were baths, and chambers for guests, and quarters for attendants innumerable. Their ruins in the season of the spring violets are among the wonders of the Italian land, as they were in the time of Pius the Second, Æneas Sylvius Piccolomini, the humanist Pope, five centuries ago: "Time has disfigured everything. Ivy now covers the walls in place of paintings and gold-embroidered tapestries. In the seats where of old sat senators clad in togas of purple grow thorns and brambles, and serpents make their lair in the bed-chamber of the Empress. So perishes all earthly, swept away by the stream of years." The notes of Pius contain many like examples of eloquence.

But death with impartial tread came to the master of the princely towers of Hadrian's villa, as it had come to the master of the lowly villa of Horace in the hills not many miles away. On January 24, 138, as he entered his sixty-third year, the Emperor appointed before the Senate as his successor Titus Aurelius Antoninus Pius, fifty-one years old, sometime governor of Asia and now one of the four circuit prætors of Hadrian's reform for Italy. Antoninus Pius was respected and honored, and good to look upon; in Gibbon's phrase, "a senator blameless in all the offices of life"; the one of the Five Good Emperors who best deserves the title.

The Emperor was ill, and the end approaching. On July 10, 138, at lovely Baiae on the Bay of Naples, where he had spent the months in helpless and intense suffering, he parted at last from the "little soul" that so pleasantly had kept him company in the long and varied journeys of his life; the little soul so plaintively addressed by him in his only surviving verse:

Animula vagula blandula,
Hospes comesque corporis,
Quae nunc abibis in loca,
Pallidula, rigida, nudula,
Nec ut soles dabis iocos?

Soul of mine, pretty one, flitting one,
Guest and partner of my clay,
Whither wilt thou hie away,
Pallid one, rigid one, naked one,
Never to play again, never to play!

The Emperor's ashes rested first in the villa of Cicero at Puteoli near by, and after its completion in the following year were laid away in the Mausoleum which today still stands by the Tiber. The mighty platform of the Temple to Venus and Rome, near the Colosseum, with the Pantheon of Agrippa, reërected by him, are the greatest of Hadrian's other monuments in Rome.

THE PHILOSOPHER ON THE THRONE

AMONG the best known monuments of ancient Rome in the Rome of today are the equestrian statue of Marcus Aurelius and the Triumphal Column, one hundred feet high, that bears his name.

The statue has not always been in its present place in the Piazza del Campidoglio, where its benign presence fills the quiet square looked upon by three of Italy's historic palace façades. From its erection until its transfer in 1538 it stood in the Lateran Square, not far from where the imperial rider was born.

The great Column of Marcus Aurelius, decorated, like the similar Column of Trajan, with the sculptured story of the imperial campaigns, and containing a spiral stairway by which ancient visitors to Rome ascended to its summit, today gives its name to Piazza Colonna, as from early mediæval times it gave the name Colonna to the third of the city's thirteen *rioni* or wards. In Roman times, the Column stood by the Via Flaminia, the Broad Way of the capital, in the spacious ninth *regio* which comprised the Campus Martius and was known, from its greatest building, as Circus Flaminius. The statues of Marcus Aurelius and Empress Faustina which once from its top looked forth upon the city had long since disappeared when Sixtus V, 1585-90, erected in their place the figure of the Apostle Paul. The great interpreter and example of Stoicism gave way to the great interpreter and example of Christianity.

Besides these two great monuments, there are also in Rome, in the Palazzo dei Conservatori, three great sculptured reliefs from a triumphal arch, showing the Emperor on horseback receiving in submission the conquered barbarians, and again driving in triumph to sacrifice in the Temple of Jupiter on the Capitoline, and again with veiled head in the act of the sacrifice. Portrait busts

ANTONINUS PIUS

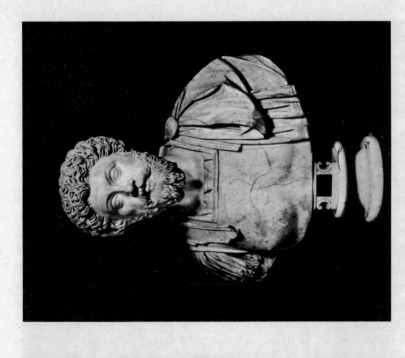

THE EMPEROR MARCUS AURELIUS

THE YOUNG MARCUS AURELIUS

of the Emperor are numerous, two of the best being the Vatican example found in Hadrian's Villa, and the engaging youthful head in the Capitoline Museum representing him at about seventeen.

When Marcus Aurelius Antoninus, last of the Five Good Emperors, was born, on April 26, 121, Hadrian, the third in that line, was in his forty-sixth year and in the fourth year of his reign, and Antoninus Pius, in his thirty-fifth year and as yet unconscious that he was to be Hadrian's successor, had finished his consulship, thus completing the *cursus honorum*, or round of offices, and had retired to his country estate at Lorium on the Aurelian Way twelve miles west of Rome. When Hadrian was about sixty and Marcus Aurelius fifteen, the Emperor adopted as son and successor his friend and favorite, Lucius Verus, who had a son also named Lucius Verus. The elder Lucius dying the first day of the year 138 and his son being only seven, the Emperor during the month following adopted in his place Antoninus Pius, who had soon been recalled from his country retreat to the public service, and for the past sixteen years as district governor in Central Italy, proconsul in Asia, and member of Hadrian's council of advisers, had abundantly demonstrated a dignified and stable character. When at Baiae on July 10, 138, after long illness whose pain had driven him all but mad, the Emperor's "little soul, guest and partner of his clay," took its mournful flight, Antoninus had in reality already been emperor the four and a half months since his adoption.

By the terms of the adoption, Antoninus himself in turn adopted his nephew, Marcus Aurelius, together with Lucius Verus, son of the Verus deceased six months before Hadrian's death. The father of Marcus had died soon after his son's birth. The father's sister, Faustina, was the wife of Antoninus Pius. Marcus's mother, Domitia Lucilla, was a woman of cultivation, and with him after his adoption left their home near the present Lateran Church to live on the Palatine where the imperial residences, an interconnected mass of buildings consisting of the Palace of the Flavians and the much altered palaces of their Julio-Claudian predecessors, now covered a great part of the Hill.

Marcus Aurelius, now called also Antoninus because of his adoption, was thus at the same time nephew and adoptive son of Antoninus Pius, and adoptive grandson of Hadrian. At about the age of twenty-four, probably in 145, he was married to Faustina, his cousin, daughter of Antoninus Pius and Faustina. His education, at the hands of private teachers, had culminated in the retention of one of them, the famous Fronto, a native of Cirta in Africa, as an intimate friend and literary adviser and correspondent until Fronto's death, perhaps in the year of the great plague of A.D. 166, brought to Italy by the soldiers returning from the Parthian campaign.

The peaceful reign of Antoninus Pius lasted from A.D. 138 to 161. He died at the age of seventy-four in his home at Lorium, leaving the State to Marcus Aurelius, now forty years of age. When Hadrian on adopting Antoninus had presented him to the Senate, he said: "I have found you an emperor, noble, mild, obedient, sensible, neither headstrong and rash through youth nor careless through old age." His conduct of the State and of himself during the twenty-two years of his reign was only the continuation of a career which, public and private, was grounded in wisdom, justice, and temperance. The Senate on his accession to power made manifest their recognition of his qualities by conferring upon him the hitherto unused title of Pius, and no man since his death has raised a voice in question of his meriting the title as much after its bestowal as before. A biographer of a century and a half later expresses the universal opinion when he sums up: "He was a man distinguished by good looks, noted for his character, clement, noble, of reposeful countenance, remarkable talent, polished speech, and excellent handwriting, well-poised, a devoted cultivator of the soil, gentle, generous, considerate of others' rights, and all these things with measure and without ostentation; in a word, praiseworthy in everything, and deserving of the verdict of good men when they compare him with Numa Pompilius."

Marcus Aurelius himself wrote in later years of Antoninus:

In my father I observed mildness of temper, and unchangeable resolution in the things which he had determined after due deliberation;

and no vainglory in those things which men call honors; and a love of labor and perseverance; and a readiness to listen to those who had anything to propose for the common weal; and undeviating firmness in giving to every man according to his deserts. . . . And the things which conduce in any way to the commodity of life, and of which fortune gives an abundant supply, he used without arrogance and without excusing himself; so that when he had them, he enjoyed them without affectation, and when he had them not, he did not want them. . . . He took a reasonable care of his body's health, not as one who was greatly attached to life, nor out of regard for personal appearance, nor yet in a careless way, but so that, through his own attention, he very seldom stood in need of the physician's art or of medicine or external applications. . . . He always acted conformably to the institutions of his country, without showing any affectation of doing so. Further, he was not fond of change nor unsteady, but he loved to stay in the same places, and to employ himself about the same things; and after his paroxysms of headache he came immediately fresh and vigorous to his usual occupations. His secrets were not many, but very few and very rare, and these only about public matters; and he showed prudence and economy in the exhibition of the public spectacles and the construction of public buildings, his donations to the people, and in such things, for he was a man who looked to what ought to be done, not to the reputation which is got by a man's acts.

Such was the emperor, uncle, and adoptive father with whom Marcus Aurelius was on terms of confidence, intimacy, and affection from his entrance into the imperial household on February 25, 138, at the age of seventeen, to the death of Antoninus on the probable date of March 7, 161. We have already referred to Domitia Lucilla, the mother of Marcus, and to Fronto, his teacher. Antoninus was not only his father by adoption, but filled the place of the real father whom the young Marcus had probably never known. Being of a most earnest and most impressionable nature, and being so fathered, so mothered, and so tutored, it is not to be wondered at that the last of the Five Good Emperors came to the throne at forty a most serious, dignified, devoted, generous, and intellectual character, and a capable ruler.

Loyal to his adoptive grandfather Hadrian, though under no legal obligation and but little encouraged by the example of his imperial father, who reigned alone, Marcus Aurelius made Lucius Verus, ten years his junior, associate on the throne. The striking

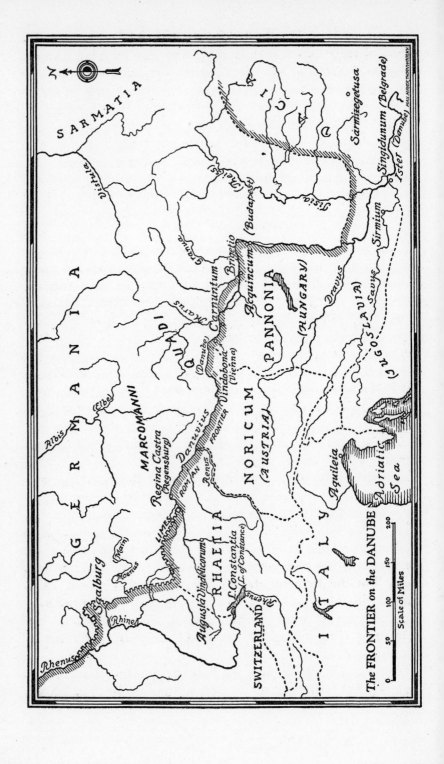

The FRONTIER on the DANUBE

Scale of Miles

0   50   100   150   200

events of their lives and their reign were the Parthian invasion of Syria in A.D. 163, and the despatch of Lucius Verus to take command in the East, where he placed the Syrian army in charge of the experienced soldier Avidius Cassius; the marriage of Lucius Verus to the Emperor's daughter Lucilla in 164, perhaps at Ephesus; the successful conclusion of the two years' Parthian campaign in 165; the great and universal pestilence following the return of the army in 166 to their far separated homes in Italy and elsewhere in Europe, a plague which depleted terribly the manhood of the Empire and impelled it toward decline; the incursions of the Northerner, soon after the plague, into the provinces of Pannonia and Noricum south of the Danube and the successful campaign of the two Emperors against them, during which Lucius Verus was taken ill and died; and a second outbreak of the plague, a second barbarian attack, and the return of Marcus Aurelius to the front in 169, there to spend the most of the not many years of life that remained to him.

The Marcomanni and the Quadi, in the unsubdued country beyond the Danube today occupied by Bohemia and Moravia in Czechoslovakia, continued their hostilities. In A.D. 174 there took place the famous battle in which the miraculous rain and lightning storm turned the tide of victory in favor of the all but vanquished Roman army, as pictured in the sculpture of the Column at Rome.

The next year, while the Emperor was contemplating a campaign to end these border troubles by annexing the territory to the north of the river, the rebellion of Avidius Cassius, who had been left in command in the East eight years previously, after the Parthian War, interrupted his course. Avidius Cassius was murdered by his own officers three months after his rebellion began, but the Emperor, taking Faustina and their son Commodus with him, continued the journey East he had entered upon with the purpose of meeting Cassius, visited Alexandria and Antioch, and, after certain diplomatic meetings with foreign leaders, faced about for the return.

On the road, still in Asia, the Empress Faustina grew ill and died. She had been married to Marcus Aurelius thirty years, and had borne him thirteen children, of whom eight died before his death; and the plain historical facts regarding their life together must surely outweigh the later charge of unfaithfulness on her part. After his return with Commodus by way of Smyrna and Athens to Rome, and after his honoring of the dead Empress at home in every possible way, in deference to the wish of the Senate he gave to Commodus the title Augustus, providing thus in what seemed at the time a wise manner for the orderly succession to the throne, and returned with him to the Danube frontier.

The enemies to be held in check there were a constant threat to the two well-ordered provinces of Noricum and Pannonia, the former represented now by Austria, and the latter by the western part of Hungary. Four city-camps of the Romans lay along the south side of the Danube the one hundred and seventy-five miles of its course from Vienna to Budapest. The westernmost city-camp was Vindobona. It lay within the limits of the Vienna of today, and centered about the Hoher Markt. The next was twenty-eight miles east, and lay along the bluffs of the river between modern Petronell and Deutsch-Altenburg. This was Carnuntum. The third was Brigetio, seventy miles farther on, where today is Szöny, near Komarom, and the fourth was Aquincum, four miles north of modern Budapest.

Of these four military stations, that of Aquincum faces due east across the Danube, which fifteen miles to the north has suddenly turned from its eastward course and started on the southward flow which leads in about two hundred miles to Singidunum, modern Belgrade, where it is joined by the Save, whose valley, beginning near Trieste, formed the grand route from Italy to Dacia. Sirmium, on the Save, fifty miles west of Singidunum, today Mitrovitz, was one of the chief strongholds on this route.

About half way between Aquincum and Brigetio and on the northern side of the Danube, the river Granua came flowing from the Carpathians through the country of the Quadi and poured its waters into the great river. Opposite the camp-city of Carnuntum, the Marus or March came down, also through the lands of the Quadi. Where it joined the Danube, lies the classic battlefield of the Marchfeld. Here in 1809 Napoleon fought and de-

THE COLUMN OF MARCUS AURELIUS

MARCUS AURELIUS IN TRIUMPHAL PROCESSION

feated the Archduke Karl in the battle of Wagram, after his own defeat near-by two months earlier. Here in the thirteenth century fought Bohemians and Hungarians and Austrians. Here, too, was the scene of battles between the Romans from Vindobona and Carnuntum and the Marcomanni and Quadi from the Bohemian forests; and here were spent the last active days of the Emperor philosopher.

· XXXV ·

THE EMPEROR ON THE FRONTIER

NOTHING in Rome—not the great Column, not the great statue on the Capitoline, not the almost living portraits in the museums—so brings us into communion with the spirit of the philosopher Emperor as a visit to the Vindobona and Carnuntum country. Across the face of the clock in the Hoher Markt in Vienna whose hours are marked by the passing of historical figures, among them Maria Theresa and Master Joseph Haydn, at midday sedately moves the figure of Marcus Aurelius, whose prætorium, the headquarters of the army, was perhaps beneath our feet. Here, perhaps, is the scene of his death on March 17, 180. "I bid you farewell," he said to his friends, "and I go on before you"; and to an officer, "Go to the rising sun, for I sink to my setting."

The Roman Museum, in the Rainergasse, is eloquent with the rough relics of the Roman occupation come to light in the Hoher Markt neighborhood and in the surrounding country. In it are to be seen coins, armor, artillery, stone cannon-balls, a pottery oven, a well enclosure, wall and aqueduct remnants, graves, tombstones, skeletons, and milestones, one of them inscribed *M.P. IIII a Vindobona,* "four miles from Vindobona." The great Art History Museum with its abundance of Roman specimens is voiceless and cold as compared with this rugged and familiar collection in its unpretentious home.

But more eloquent of the Emperor's presence are the wide fields, the long road, the ruins, the far vistas, of the camp-city Carnuntum. Petronell, twenty-seven miles east of Vienna, is the modern Carnuntum. In the fields near-by are the ruins of the Heidentor, the Heathen Gate, perhaps a tomb, and the recently excavated amphitheater, nearly four hundred feet in diameter.

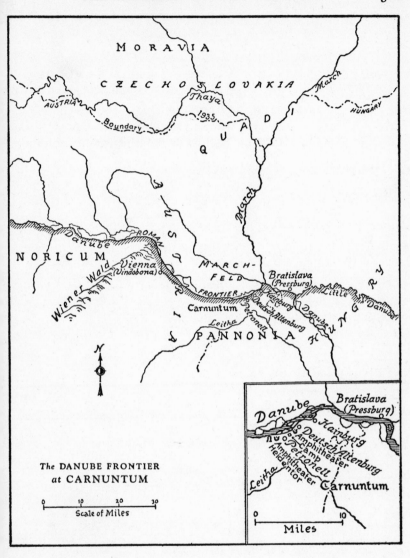

The DANUBE FRONTIER
at CARNUNTUM

Farther east on the highway, a road leads to the estate of Graf
Traun, in whose château is a small but attractive museum of
three rooms containing relics from excavations made on the estate
and afterwards filled in. There are also tombs and other monuments of soldiers of the Fifteenth Legion called Apollinaris; a
relief of the Mithraic sacrifice such as is found in almost every

camp, for Mithras was the soldier's god; monuments to Jupiter and Diana; mosaics indicating the presence of wealth and good homes; and the usual fibulae and other minute domestic objects. On one of the tombstones, not that of a soldier but a civilian, it is recorded that "Gaius Arruntius Lentulus, son of Gaius, at the age of five, Gaius Arruntius Ligus, son of Gaius, at the age of three, are buried here, and Varena Candida, at the age of thirty-five. Gaius Arruntius, free born, erected this to his sons and wife."

The amphitheater and the Heidentor, the museum, and the excavations on the park-like estate of Graf Traun represent the civilian part of the camp-city of Carnuntum. The military establishment of which it was a suburb adjoined it along the great highway running northeast on the brow of the Danube to where the valley narrowed at Hainburg and formed a river gateway to Pannonia, today Hungary. Civil and military portions thus formed a settlement three miles long. The camp itself lies on both sides of the present highway, which was the Via Principalis or main street of the camp. Its excavated portion lies to the left or northwest of the highway, and shows the complicated lines of the various buildings usual in the camp-city. We must imagine them representing the prætorium, the officers' quarters, the barracks of the cohorts, the stables of the cavalry, the quæstor's office and the stores, the hospital, baths, and smithies. Around the camp ran the vallum and the ditch, enclosing an area about one third by one quarter of a mile. Still farther along the high road is the soldiers' amphitheater, somewhat smaller than the presumably civilian example already seen farther west. An altar to Juno Nemesis still stands, there was a box or loggia on the north side, and the main lines of the structure are well preserved. There seems to be a space for cages. The wild animals used in exhibitions were sometimes provided by the legion itself. A centurion in an inscription at Cologne thanks Diana, the huntress deity, for fifty bears captured in six months.

When the uncertainties incident to the murder of Commodus in 192 and Pertinax the following year came to an end in the accession of Septimius Severus, it was in Carnuntum that the

election took place, on April 13, 193. Henceforth known as
Colonia Septimia Carnuntum, in 308, after more than a century
during which little is heard of it, it is the scene of a conference
between Emperor Diocletian and his partner in administration,
Galerius. In 375 it is once more important in the Empire's affairs. The rough peoples beyond the Danube are again troublesome, and Emperor Valentinian spends three summer months in
a punitive campaign against them, with headquarters in the old
camp-city, now called by Ammianus Marcellinus, the historian of
the times, "a town which today is deserted and squalid." It could
not have been long afterward that Carnuntum came to a violent
end. In the cannon-balls and various weapons that lay scattered
about the camp interior as if thrown down and abandoned, and in
the loaves of bread, ready for the oven but unbaked, the story
seems plainly told. There came a time when the Northerners
crossed the great river and were not driven back.

The long reaches of the highway continue another mile to
Deutsch-Altenburg, in which the beautiful Museum Carnuntinum houses a fine collection of monuments from the camp-city
and its neighborhood. Excavation of Carnuntum on a small scale
was begun in 1875. In 1885 an antiquarian society was formed,
in 1904 the Museum was opened, and in 1910 there was published
a study of the exploration and excavation of Carnuntum and
vicinity. By 1925 only one fifth of the extensive and fruitful site
had been excavated.

Nothing survived of either military or civil Carnuntum except
what was covered or protected by accident. Petronell at the one
extremity, and Deutsch-Altenburg a mile beyond the other, rising
in the tenth or eleventh century, no doubt took their levies of
what could easily be moved, as perhaps did Hainburg, farther
away, built about 1050. The farmers who tilled and pastured
the fields for generations have cleared away the remnants ob-
structing their crops and cattle raising. The Heidentor looks as if
the missing half had been either torn down or destroyed by ex-
plosives.

It is along this road, in the sheltered seating of the amphitheaters or among the foundation stones of the camp, or on the high,

grassy bank at the roadside above the broad and mournful Danube flats, with the great river shining out here and there from among the trees and thickets until it leads the vision to the Marchfeld and distant blue mountains at Hainburg, that the *Meditations* of the Emperor philosopher are best read and mused on. The twelve books of *Marcus Aurelius Antoninus the Emperor to Himself*, as the manuscript title reads, begin with what may be called a preface occupying one book, seemingly the one to have been written last, in which the imperial author looks back upon his nearly sixty years of life and his nearly twenty years as ruler of the far-flung Empire, and makes acknowledgment to those whose counsels and character have entered into and formed his manhood and who are the real authors of whatever worth he possesses. No more human and moving document has come to us from ancient times than this humble confession of debt.

The Emperor begins:

From my grandfather I learned good morals and the government of my temper.

From the reputation and remembrance of my father, modesty and a manly character.

From my mother, piety and beneficence, and abstinence, not only from evil deeds, but even from evil thoughts; and further, simplicity in my way of living.

From my brother, to love my kin, and to love truth, and to love justice.

From my tutor, I learned endurance of labor, and to want little, and to work with my hands, and not to meddle with other people's affairs, and not to be ready to listen to slander.

From Maximus, my teacher of philosophy, not to be led aside by anything; and cheerfulness in all circumstances as well as in illness; and to do what was set before me without complaining.

In my father—

But we have already seen the moving tribute paid the character of Antoninus Pius.

This Book was written "among the Quadi at the Granua."

The Second Book concludes, "This in Carnuntum." With it begin the thoughts of the Emperor to himself, the meditations of the Roman Stoic mind on the frailty and the brevity of life, the

THE SOLDIERS' AMPHITHEATER AT CARNUNTUM

THE CAMP SITE AND DANUBE AT CARNUNTUM

THE EMPEROR MARCUS AURELIUS

fleeting nature of the goods we most prize, the orderliness and inevitability of the world of which we are a part, the necessity of our conforming to its laws if we are to live rightly and happily.

Every moment think steadily as a Roman and a man to do what thou hast in hand with perfect and simple dignity, and feeling of affection, and freedom, and justice; and to give thyself relief from all other thoughts. And thou wilt give thyself relief, if thou doest every act of thy life as if it were the last, laying aside all carelessness and passionate aversion from the commands of reason, and all hypocrisy, and self-love, and discontent with the portion which has been given to thee. Thou seest how few the things are, the which if a man lays hold of, he is able to live a life which flows in quiet, and is like the existence of the gods; for the gods on their part will require nothing more from him who observes these things....

Since it is possible that thou mayest depart from life this very moment, regulate every act and thought accordingly. But to go away from among men, if there are gods, is not a thing to be afraid of, for the gods will not involve thee in evil; but if indeed they do not exist, or if they have no concern about human affairs, what is it to me to live in a universe devoid of gods or devoid of providence? But in truth they do exist, and they do care for human things, and they have put all the means in man's power to enable him not to fall into real evils.

How quickly all things disappear, in the universe the bodies themselves, but in time the remembrance of them; what is the nature of all sensible things, and particularly those which attract with the bait of pleasure or terrify by pain, or are noised abroad by vapory fame; how worthless, and contemptible, and sordid, and perishable, and dead they are—all this it is the part of the intellectual faculty to observe. To observe too who there are whose opinions and voices give reputation; what death is, and the fact that, if a man looks at it in itself, and by the abstractive power of reflection resolves into their parts all the things which present themselves to the imagination in it, he will then consider it to be nothing else than an operation of nature; and if anyone is afraid of an operation of nature, he is a child. This, however, is not only an operation of nature, but it is also a thing which conduces to the purposes of nature....

Of human life the time is a point, and the substance is in a flux, and the perception dull, and the composition of the whole body subject to putrefaction, and the soul a whirl, and fortune hard to divine, and fame a thing devoid of judgment. And, to say all in a word, everything which belongs to the body is a stream, and what belongs to the soul is a dream and vapor, and life is a stranger's sojourn, and after-fame is oblivion. What then is that which is able to conduct a man? One thing and only one, philosophy. But this consists in keeping the dæmon within a man free from violence and unharmed, superior to pains and pleasures, doing nothing without a purpose, nor yet falsely and with hypocrisy, not feeling the need of another man's doing or not doing anything; and besides, accepting all that happens, and all that is allotted, as coming from thence, wherever it is, from whence he himself came; and, finally, waiting for death with a cheerful mind, as being nothing else than a dissolution of the elements of which every living being is compounded. But if there is no harm to the elements themselves in each continually changing into another, why should a man have any apprehension about the change and dissolution of all the elements? For it is according to nature, and nothing is evil which is according to nature.

This in Carnuntum.

The Emperor concludes in the Twelfth Book:

Consider nothing to be great except to act as thy nature leads thee, and to endure that which the common nature brings.

How does the ruling faculty make use of itself? for all lies in this. But everything else, whether it is in the power of thy will or not, is only lifeless ashes and smoke.

This reflection is most adapted to move us to contempt of death, that even those who think pleasure to be a good and pain an evil still have despised it.

The man to whom that only is good which comes in due season, and to whom it is the same thing whether he has done more or fewer acts conformable to right reason, and to whom it makes no difference whether he contemplates the world for a longer or a shorter time—for this man neither is death a terrible thing.

Man, thou hast been a citizen in this great state [the world]: what difference does it make to thee whether for five years [or three]? For that which is conformable to the laws is just for all. Where is the hardship then, if no tyrant nor yet an unjust judge sends thee away from the state, but nature who brought thee into it? the same as if a prætor who has employed an actor dismisses him from the stage.— "But I have not finished the five acts, but only three of them." Thou sayest well, but in life the three acts are the whole drama; for what shall be a complete drama is determined by him who was once the cause of its composition, and now of its dissolution; but thou art the cause of neither. Depart then satisfied, for he also who releases thee is satisfied.

"Private devotional memoranda," the *Meditations* are called by C. R. Haines, their translator in the Loeb Classical Library Series. "He is not trying to teach anyone. He is reasoning with his own soul and championing its cause against the persuasions and impulses of the flesh." "Never were words written more transparently single-hearted and sincere. They were not merely written, they were lived."

"By nature a good man," says Dio Cassius, writing not long after the Emperor's death, "his education and the moral training he imposed upon himself made him a far better one."

"As was natural to one who had beautified his soul with every virtuous quality," writes Aristides, a teacher of the time, "he was innocent of all wrong-doing."

An epigrammatist of the *Greek Anthology* reflects even more clearly the esteem in which the *Meditations* were held:

On the Book of Marcus

If thou would'st master care and pain,
Unfold this book and read and read again
Its blessed leaves, whereby thou soon shalt see
The past, the present, and the days to be
With opened eyes; and all delight, all grief,
Shall be like smoke, as empty and as brief.

"We carry in our hearts mourning for Marcus Aurelius," says Renan, "as if he had died yesterday."

Much more might be said, both of the Emperor and of his fellow-searchers after the secrets of life and death and human conduct; but our purpose is already accomplished. In the character and action of Antoninus Pius and Marcus Aurelius we have seen the heights to which it was possible for Romans in the seat of power to rise. In Marcus Aurelius, the philosophy of the Stoics reaches its culmination both in theory and in practice. All that morality is capable of without religion, appears in him. To reach greater heights, humanity had first to have that sense of companionship with and help from a Power not only Infinite but also Personal which was the inspiration of a new religion.

But our concern has been with the pagan era.

ANNOTATIONS

THE following notes are compiled for the convenience of those who desire either to read in amplification of what is contained in the text or to "control" the author's evidence. For the sake of those who prefer to read without being interrupted by learned and not always necessary remarks, and who enjoy a clean page, the usual reference numerals are not obtruded in the text; those who desire notes will easily find and connect them with the appropriate passages. Translations not specifically credited to others are by the author.

CHAPTER I

T. E. Peet, *The Stone and Bronze Ages in Italy and Sicily* (Oxford, 1909).

David Randall-MacIver, *The Etruscans* (Oxford, 1927); *Italy before the Romans* (Oxford, 1928); *The Iron Age in Italy* (Oxford, 1927).

Giuseppe Sergi, *The Mediterranean Race,* English edition (London, 1901).

For Roman remains in Italy, the most convenient means of acquaintance is Baedeker, *Italy from the Alps to the Sea,* or any other reputable guide; for the remains of Rome, S. B. Platner, *Topography and Monuments of Ancient Rome,* second edition (Allyn and Bacon, 1911), and S. B. Platner and Thomas Ashby, *A Topographical Dictionary of Ancient Rome* (Oxford, 1929).

CHAPTER II

For the chief Roman monuments in England, Belgium and Holland, the Rhine, Germany, Austria, Czechoslovakia, Hungary, Palestine and Syria, Greece, Dalmatia, western Jugoslavia, Albania, Egypt, Spain and Portugal, and France, see the Baedeker *Guides* for these areas.

For those of northern Africa, Baedeker's *Mediterranean;* Byron Khun de Prorok, *Digging for Lost African Gods* (Putnam, 1926); and Guido Calza in *Art and Archæology,* October, 1925.

For Turkey and other remote Mediterranean sites, Meyer's *Mittelmeer.*

For England, F. J. Haverfield, *The Roman Occupation of Britain* (Oxford, 1924); Katharine Allen, "Some Glimpses of Roman Britain," *Classical Journal,* XXIV (1929), 254, and "The Roman Wall in England," *ibid.,* VIII, 2.

For the *Limes,* Katharine Allen, "Some Glimpses of the Rætian Limes," (*Classical Journal,* XI, 1915), 95.

For Carnuntum, W. Kubitschek, *Führer durch Carnuntum* (Wien, 1923).

CHAPTER III

R. V. D. Magoffin and Emily C. Davis, *Magic Spades* (Holt, 1929).

August Mau, *Pompeii, Its Life and Art,* translated by F. W. Kelsey (Macmillan, 1899).

Wilhelm Engelmann, *New Guide to Pompeii* (Wilhelm Engelmann, 1929).

Matteo della Corte, *Pompeii, The New Excavations.*

Page 26, line 18. Esther Boise Van Deman, *The Building of the Roman Aqueducts* (Carnegie Institution of Washington, 1934).

Page 26, line 20. Marion E. Blake, *The Pavements of the Roman Buildings of the Republic and Early Empire,* Memoirs of the American Academy in Rome, VIII, 1930.

Page 26, line 31. M. I. Rostovtzeff, "Das Mithræum von Doura," *Mitteilungen des Deutschen Archäologischen Instituts,* Römische, Abteilung 49, 1934.

Page 27, line 2. M. I. Rostovtzeff, *Caravan Cities,* translated by D. and T. Talbot Rice (Oxford, 1932).

Page 27, line 6. A. Poidebard, *La Trace de Rome dans le Désert de Syrie, Introduction de Franz Cumont* (Paris, 1934).

Page 28. For Charles Eliot Norton and the Schools, see Grant Showerman, "America in Ancient Rome," *Art and Archæology,* February, 1925.

CHAPTER IV

Grant Showerman, *Eternal Rome,* Chapter IX, 2.

Rodolfo Lanciani, *The Destruction of Rome* (New York, 1899).

Page 37, lines 13 *ff.* Quoted from Grant Showerman, *Eternal Rome,* p. 371, with permission of Yale University Press.

CHAPTER V

Christian Huelsen, *The Roman Forum,* translated by Jesse Benedict Carter (New York, 1909), pp. 1-57. Also *The Forum and the Palatine,* translated by Helen Tanzer (Bruderhausen, 1928).

CHAPTER VI

Page 47. Guido Calza in *Art and Archæology,* October, 1925.
Page 48. Tenney Frank, "The People of Ostia," *Classical Journal,* April, 1934.
Wilhelm Engelmann, *New Guide to Pompeii.*
Page 51. Amedeo Maiuri in *Art and Archæology,* November, 1931.

CHAPTER VII

Corrado Ricci, Antonio M. Colini, and Valerio Mariani, *Via dell' Impero* (Rome, 1933).

CHAPTER VIII

S. B. Platner, *Topography and Monuments of Ancient Rome,* Chapter I.
Pages 68, 69. Ulrichs, *Codex Urbis Romae Topographicus* (Würzburg, 1871), assembles the chief ancient and medieval Latin evidence on the monuments.
Pages 69, 70. Francis M. Nichols, *The Marvels of Rome* (London, 1889).
Page 72. Thomas Ashby, *The Roman Campagna in Classical Times* (New York, 1927).
Page 73. M. I. Rostovtzeff, *A History of the Ancient World,* Vol. II, *Rome* (Oxford, 1927); *The Social and Economic History of the Roman Empire* (Oxford, 1926).

CHAPTER IX

Page 75. Sallust, *Catilina,* 61.
Pages 75-78. *In Catilinam,* I, 1; II, 4; III, 2; IV and V.
Page 78. *Catilina,* 55, translated by Watson.
Page 79. Christian Huelsen, *The Forum and the Palatine,* trans-

lated by Helen Tanzer, 5-8; Ruth Witherstine, "Where the Romans Lived in the First Century B.C.," *Classical Journal*, XXI, 8; W. B. MacDaniel II, "Cicero and His House on the Palatine," *Classical Journal*, XXIII, 9.

Page 80, line 14. *Ad Atticum*, I, 9.

Page 80, line 17. *Ibid.*, II, 6.

Page 80, line 22. *Ibid.*, II, 11.

Page 80, line 25. *Ibid.*, IV, 10.

Page 80, line 29. *Ad Familiares*, VII, 1.

Page 80, line 32. *Ad Atticum*, XII, 15.

Page 80, line 35. *Ibid.*, XIII, 52.

Pages 83-85. *De Legibus*, I, 5, 15; II, 1-3; II, 3, 6.

Page 85. Macrobius, *Saturnalia*, VI, 4, ¶ 8.

O. E. Schmidt, *Ciceros Villen.*

G. A. Harrer, "A Trip to Cicero's Home," *Classical Journal*, XIX, 2.

H. J. Leon, "Cicero's Birthplace," *Classical Journal*, XIX, 5. The phrase, "it straightway plunges into the Liris," *praecipitat,* is not absolute proof that Carnello is not meant as the island.

CHAPTER X

J. L. Strachan-Davidson, *Cicero* (Putnam, 1903).

W. W. Fowler, *Julius Cæsar* (Putnam, 1907).

T. R. Holmes, *Cæsar's Conquest of Gaul* (London, 1903).

Page 90. *De Bello Gallico*, I, 38.

CHAPTER XI

Page 95. *Ad Familiares*, VIII, 14, 4; XVI, 12, 2.

Page 96. *Ad Atticum*, VII, 22, 1; VIII, 13; translated by Winstedt, Loeb Classical Library.

Pages 98-100. *Ibid.*, IX, 6a, 11a; IX, 16; IX, 18; X, 3a; X, 8b.

Page 101. *Ibid.*, X, 3a, X, 8b.

Page 102. Plutarch, *Cicero*, 39. *Ad Atticum*, XIII, 52.

CHAPTER XII

Page 104. Suetonius, *Cæsar*, XLVI, translated by Rolfe, Loeb Classical Library.

Page 105, line 16. *Ibid.*, X.

Page 105, line 24. *Ibid.*, XX.

Page 106, line 3. *Ibid.,* LXXIV.
Page 106, line 18. *Ibid.,* XX.
Page 107. *Ibid.,* XXXVII.

CHAPTER XIII

Page 111. Suetonius, *Cæsar,* LXXXVII, translated by Rolfe.
Page 115. *Ibid.,* LXXXII.
Page 118. *Ibid.,* LXXXIV and LXXXV.
Page 120. *Ibid.,* LXXXVIII, LXXXIX.

CHAPTER XIV

Page 121. *Philippics,* II, 118, 119, translated by R. S. Conway.
Page 122. Translated by Horace White in appendix to Book IV of Appian, *Civil Wars,* Bohn Library.
Page 124. Appian, *Civil Wars,* Book IV, Ch. IV, 12 and 13, 20. Plutarch, *Cicero,* 49.
Page 125. Pliny, *Natural History,* VII, xxx, 117.
Page 126. *Ad Familiares,* IV, 5, 4. *Childe Harold,* IV, 44 and 45.

CHAPTER XV

Much of the substance of this chapter appeared in my essay entitled "Cicero the Stylist: An Appreciation," in *Classical Journal,* VIII, February, 1913. Consult also John C. Rolfe, *Cicero and His Influence,* in Our Debt to Greece and Rome Series.

CHAPTER XVI

Francis Galton, *Hereditary Genius* (Appleton, 1891), 340 *ff.*

CHAPTER XVII

Page 151. *Academics,* I, 3.
Page 151, line 29. See introduction to *De Finibus,* Loeb Classical Library.
Page 155, paragraph 2. *De Officiis,* I, 2, translated by Walter Miller, Loeb Classical Library; *ibid.,* I, 5.

Page 155, paragraph 3. *Ibid.*, I, 43; I, 6; I, 7.

Page 156, line 8. Columbia University, 1925.

Page 156, line 16. *De Finibus*, V, 23, translated by Rackham.

Page 156, paragraph 3. *Ibid.*, III, 9, 31.

Page 157, paragraph 1. *Somnium Scipionis, De Republica,* VI, 13 and 14.

Page 157, paragraph 5. *De Officiis*, I, 9.

Page 157, paragraph 6. *Ibid.*, I, 15.

Page 157, paragraph 7. *Ibid.*, I, 11.

Page 158, paragraph 2. *Ibid.*, I, 20.

Page 158, paragraph 3. *Ibid.*, I, 25; I, 14.

Page 158, paragraph 4. *De Republica*, I, 47; I, 49; I, 53; I, 68.

For Cicero and democracy, see Margaret Henry, *Dogmatism and Scepticism in Cicero's Philosophy,* p. 110.

Page 159. *De Republica*, I, 65-67, translated by Keyes, Loeb Classical Library.

Page 159, paragraph 4. *De Officiis*, I, 26.

Page 160, paragraph 2. *Ibid.*, I, 28.

Page 160, paragraph 4. *Ibid.*, I, 35.

Page 160, paragraph 6. *Ibid.*, I, 35.

Page 161, paragraph 2. *Ibid.*, I, 29.

Page 161, paragraph 4. *Ibid.*, I, 37.

Page 161, paragraph 6. *Ibid.*, II, 15.

Page 161, paragraph 8. *Ibid.*, III, 10.

Page 161, paragraph 10. *Ibid.*, II, 14.

Page 161, paragraph 12. *De Senectute,* 35, 36.

Page 162. Goethe's *Faust,* Part I, 682, 683.

CHAPTER XVIII

Page 168, line 2. *Tusculan Disputations,* I, 74, translated by J. E. King, Loeb Classical Library.

Page 168, line 9. *On Divination,* II, 148.

Page 168, line 19. Quotation by Miller, introduction to *De Officiis,* p. xii.

Page 168, paragraph 5. *De Senectute,* 84.

Page 169, paragraph 3. Rolfe, p. 168.

CHAPTER XIX

The substance of this chapter appeared in my essay, "On Living in Harmony with Nature," *University of Wisconsin Studies in Language and Literature,* No. 15.

Page 172, paragraph 5. *De Senectute,* 5, 70, 71.

Page 174. *The Thoughts of Marcus Aurelius Antoninus,* translated by Long, VII, 55; II, 1; V, 16; IV, 4; VIII, 54.

Page 175. *Ibid.,* IV, 48; II, 17.

Page 179. Thomas Gray, "The Progress of Poesy."

Page 180, paragraph 2. The Thoughts of Marcus Aurelius Antoninus, III, 4.

CHAPTER XX

Page 183, paragraph 2. Milton, *Lycidas; Georgics,* III, 14, 15.

Page 185. *Satires,* I, 5.

Page 187. Donatus, *Vita.*

Page 188. Jerome, *Epistles,* CXXVII, 12.

Page 189. Augustine, *Confessions,* I, 21.

Page 190, line 9. *Inferno,* I, 85.

Page 190, line 16. *Maphæus Vegius and His Thirteenth Book of the Æneid,* edited by Anna Cox Brinton (Stanford University Press, 1930).

Page 192. *Inferno,* IV, 80.

CHAPTER XXI

Page 193. *De Senectute,* 51.

Page 197. R. S. Conway, *The Vergilian Age* (Harvard University Press, 1928).

Page 198. E. K. Rand, *In Quest of Virgil's Birthplace* (Harvard University Press, 1930).

Page 199. *Georgics,* II, 146-148; 159, 160.

Page 200, line 7. Günther, *Pausilypon,* 201.

Page 200, paragraph 3. F. S. Dunn, "Vergil's Vanishing Tomb," *Art and Archæology,* January, 1930.

Page 202, paragraph 2. *Æneid,* VI, 81, 82; 98-100, translated by Conington. All Virgil translations in this chapter are from Conington.

Page 203, paragraph 2. *Ibid.,* VI, 201-204.

Page 203, paragraph 3. *Ibid.,* VI, 232-235; 236-242.

Page 204, line 15. *Ibid.,* VI, 893-901.

Page 204, line 19. *Ibid.,* VII, 1; 8, 9; 24, 25.

Page 205. *Ibid.,* VII, 25-36; 41-45.

Page 205, line 32. *Ibid.,* VIII, 94-96.

Page 206. *Ibid.,* VIII, 97-110.

Page 206, paragraph 3. *Ibid.,* VIII, 314-317; 366-369.

Page 207, paragraph 1. *Ibid.,* VIII, 455-463.

Page 207, paragraph 3. *Ibid.*, XII, 134-137.
Page 207, paragraph 5. *Ibid.*, IX, 375-383.
Page 207, paragraph 6. *Ibid.*, VII, 803-811.
Page 208, line 9. *Ibid.*, XII, 950-953.

CHAPTER XXII

Grant Showerman, *Eternal Rome,* Chapter XIII.
Page 210. *Georgics*, II, 173, 174.

CHAPTER XXIII

Page 215. *Eclogues*, I, 80-84.
Page 216. *Eclogues*, VII, 4.
Page 217. *Georgics*, I, 1-15.
Page 218. *Georgics*, I, 356-359.
Page 219. *Georgics*, I, 386-392.
Page 219, paragraph 2. *Georgics,* I, 121-146.

CHAPTER XXIV

Page 226, line 15. *Æneid,* II, 268, 269.
Page 228, line 12. *Æneid,* VIII, 312.
Page 230. *Satires,* I, 1, 7, 8.
Page 234, paragraph 1. See R. S. Conway, "Horace," in *The Great Writers of Rome* (London, 1930).
Page 234, paragraph 2. From Austin Dobson's adaptation of Théophile Gautier.
Page 234, bottom. This exquisite little poem, entitled *Verse,* appeared a number of years ago in *The Irish Statesman,* over the signature O. G.

CHAPTER XXV

Page 240. Quoted from Grant Showerman, *Horace and His Influence,* with the permission of Longmans, Green and Company.

CHAPTER XXVI

Page 243. From Austin Dobson, *Ad Q. H. F.*
Page 243, paragraph 4. *Odes,* III, 4.

Page 244. *Satires*, I, 5.

Page 245, paragraph 1. *Odes*, II, 6.

Page 245, paragraph 2. *Odes*, III, 5, 49-56.

Page 246. *Macaulay's Lays of Ancient Rome.*
See also Katharine Allen, "From Rome to Formia," *Art and Archæology*, VI, 4.

Page 247. Giuseppe Lugli, *La Villa d'Orazio* (Rome, 1930).
W. Sellin, *Das Sabinische Landgut des Horaz* (Schwerin i. M., 1896).

Page 248. George H. Hallam, *At Tibur and the Sabine Farm* (Harrow School Bookshop, 1927).

Page 248, bottom. *Epistles*, I, 1-16.

Page 249. *Epistles*, I, 7.

Page 250. *Odes*, I, 23, translated by Goldwin Smith. *Satires*, II, 6.

Page 251. *Epistles*, I, 10.

CHAPTER XXVII

The nucleus of this chapter appeared in my essay entitled "Of Autumn," *Sewanee Review*, October, 1921.

Page 254. *Georgics*, I, 300-310. Horace, *Epodes*, II, 29-36. *Georgics*, II, 404-406. Spenser, *Faerie Queene*, VII, 31.

Page 255. Whittier, "The Last Walk in Autumn," XXV.

Page 256. *De Rerum Natura*, I, 1-23, translated by William Ellery Leonard.

Page 257. *Georgics*, II, 323-345.

Page 258. *Georgics*, I, 340-342.

Page 260. *Odes*, IV, 12.

Page 261. *Eclogues*, II, 6-18.

Page 262. *Georgics*, II, 513-522. Horace, *Odes*, III, 29, 17-26; *Epistles*, I, 7, 5-9.

Page 263, line 1. *Odes*, I, 17, 14-18.

Page 263, line 16 ff. *Odes*, IV, 7, 11. *Epodes*, II, 17, 18; *Epistles*, I, 12, 28; *Odes*, II, 14, 15; *Satires*, II, 6, 18; *Odes*, III, 23, 5-9; *Odes*, III, 18; *Odes*, I, 38; *Æneid*, VI, 309.

Page 264, bottom. *Idylls*, VII.

Page 267. Whittier, "The Last Walk in Autumn," VI.

CHAPTER XXVIII

Page 269. *Epistles*, I, 7, 29-39.

Page 270. *Satires*, I, 6, conclusion; *Odes*, III, 16, 39-43.

Page 271. *Odes*, III, 16, 33-35; *Odes*, I, 31; *Epistles*, I, 2, 55-59, and I, 6, 1 and 2.

Page 272. *Odes*, I, 9.

Page 273. *De Arte Poetica*, 304, 305.

CHAPTER XXIX

J. B. Firth, *Augustus* (New York, 1903).

Page 276, paragraph 2. Suetonius, *Augustus*, V.

Page 276, paragraph 3. *Ibid.*, VIII.

Page 276, paragraphs 4 and 5. *Ibid.*, LXXII.

Page 276, paragraph 6. *Ibid.*, LXXIII.

Page 277, paragraph 2. *Ibid.*, XXXVII, XL, XLII.

Page 277, paragraph 3. *Ibid.*, LIII.

Page 277, paragraph 4. *Ibid.*, LIV and LV.

Page 277, paragraph 5. *Ibid.*, XXVIII.

Page 277, paragraph 6. *Ibid.*, XXIX.

Page 278, paragraph 2. *Ibid.*, XXX.

Page 279, paragraph 2. *Ibid.*, XLIII.

Page 279, paragraphs 3 and 4. *Ibid.*, LXV.

Page 279, paragraphs 5 and following. *Ibid.*, XCIX and C.

CHAPTER XXX

S. B. Platner, *Topography and Monuments of Ancient Rome*, for the ancient structures.

Page 280, paragraph 3. *Æneid*, VI, 872-874.

Page 285, bottom. *Ibid.*, 883; Suetonius, *Augustus*, XCIX.

CHAPTER XXXI

For monuments, see S. B. Platner, *Topography and Monuments of Ancient Rome*, index; for the emperors, Suetonius, *Lives*, translated by Rolfe, Loeb Classical Library.

Page 287, line 14. Tacitus, *Annals*, XV, 44.

CHAPTER XXXII

Grant Showerman, *Rome and the Romans*, Chapters XXXIII, "Satire and Its Targets," XXXIV, "A Dinner with the Newly Rich."

CHAPTER XXXIII

Page 296, paragraph 1. Suetonius, *Augustus*, XLVII.
Page 298, line 37. Livy, XLI, 20, 8.
Spartianus, *Hadrian*, translated by Magie, Loeb Classical Library.
Ferdinand Gregorovius, *The Emperor Hadrian* (London, 1898).
Page 301. Translation by Charles Merivale.
B. W. Henderson, *The Life and Principate of the Emperor Hadrian* (London, 1923).

CHAPTER XXXIV

For the monuments, S. B. Platner, *Topography and Monuments of Ancient Rome.*
For the Emperor's life, Henry Dwight Sedgwick, *Marcus Aurelius* (Yale University Press, 1931).
Page 304. *The Thoughts of Marcus Aurelius Antoninus,* translated by George Long (London, 1913), Book I.

CHAPTER XXXV

Page 311 *ff.* See note on Carnuntum, Chapter II.
Page 314, line 4. *Thoughts,* Book I.
Page 314, line 30. *Ibid.,* II, 5.
Page 315, paragraph 1. *Ibid.,* II, 11.
Page 315, paragraph 2. *Ibid.,* II, 12.
Page 315, paragraph 3. *Ibid.,* II, 17.
Page 316. *Ibid.,* XII, 33-36.
Page 317. *Anthology,* II, p. 603, translated by Haines.

INDEX